LATIN MADE SIMPLE

LATIN MADE SIMPLE

BY

RHODA A. HENDRICKS, M.A.

Formerly Head of Latin Department,
St. Timothy's School, Stevenson, Md.

MADE SIMPLE BOOKS
DOUBLEDAY & COMPANY, INC.
GARDEN CITY, NEW YORK

DESIGNED BY CAROL BASEN BAILYN

Library of Congress Catalog Card Number 62-12101

Printed in the United States of America

ABOUT THIS BOOK

Although it is an ancient tongue, one of the "classical" languages, Latin is a vital and living language in every important sense—one of the pillars, part of the foundation, one of the mainstreams of our language, of our culture, indeed of our civilization itself. It is the thread which connects us with our own history; and when such a thread snaps it severs our relationship to our own past.

Fortunately, more and more people are discovering the decisive importance of studying and learning Latin, so that we are at the present time witnessing what amounts to a major revival—which will, from all present signs, continue and grow. But obviously, since Latin is no longer a spoken language—with few special exceptions for ecclesiastical purposes—the interest of the present-day reader and student is primarily in the *reading* of Latin, so that he may read, for pleasure and profit, with reasonable facility and comprehension. It was with this objective in mind that LATIN MADE SIMPLE was conceived, organized and written.

The essentials of the grammatical foundations of Latin are presented in this book with remarkable economy and clarity—and this alone would make it valuable to the reader and student; but of even greater value is the book's steady concentration upon the practical *reading* requirements of the non-specialist, so that it will seem to you as though the author had at all points anticipated your interests, had guessed your needs with uncanny accuracy, had predicted the questions you would ask at the instant those questions were forming in your mind.

For LATIN MADE SIMPLE is for the modern reader and student who wants above all to be able to read in the original—for which there is *never* a really adequate substitute—a religious or secular text; who wants to understand the uses of Latin in the Church; who wants to be able to read the immense treasure-house of literature and other writings in the Latin language; who would like to increase his understanding of the innumerable ways in which Latin has nourished and enriched the English language itself; who wants to be able to cope with the countless ways in which Latin pervades all aspects of contemporary life: the coin in his pocket; the legend on his school diploma; the writing on a medical prescription; the scores of words and phrases he unconsciously uses every day—to cite only a few examples. It is for such a reader and student—in school or no longer in school—that LATIN MADE SIMPLE is intended; and that is to say it is intended for anyone with lively curiosity and active intelligence.

TABLE OF CONTENTS

CHAPTER 1

INFLECTION

In English, the use of a word is generally indicated by its position in the sentence, without any change in spelling. Sometimes, however, a word changes its form or spelling to show a corresponding change in its grammatical use and meaning.

singular:	boy	subject:	I	present:	does
plural:	boys	object:	me	past:	did

This process of change is called *Inflection*. You will notice that the change can take place either at the ending of the word or within the word.

In Latin, *Nouns, Pronouns, Adjectives,* and *Verbs* are inflected. This change in the form or ending of a Noun, Pronoun, or Adjective is called *Declension* and shows *Case, Number,* and *Gender*. As in English, Case indicates that a word is used as Subject, Object, Possessor, etc., and Number means that a word is either singular or plural. Gender can be Masculine, Feminine, or Neuter, but, unlike English, Gender in Latin can be natural (male or female) or grammatical (based not on sex, but on the classification of the word or the spelling of the Nominative Case). The change in a *Verb* is called *Conjugation* and shows *Tense, Mood, Person, Voice,* and *Number*. Tense refers to time (present, past, or future); Mood to the manner in which a sentence is expressed (statement, question, command); Person to the speaker (I, you, he, etc.); Voice to whether the subject is acting or being acted upon (Active or Passive); and Number to one or more than one (Singular or Plural).

Because Latin is a highly inflected language, the ending of a Latin word is of primary importance and must be considered as carefully as the base of the word, which shows only the basic vocabulary meaning. Inflection will be clearly explained throughout this book and ample practice will be given.

PRONUNCIATION

Pronunciation, of course, is not necessary in the reading of Latin, but it is helpful in the comparison of Latin words with those of English and other languages. The consonants are pronounced as in English, except:

c and **ch** are always like k, as in coop.
g is always hard, as in go.
i-consonant is like y, as in you.
s is always s, as in so, not like z.
t is always like t, as in tie, not like sh.
v is always like w, as in woman.
x is like x, as in example.
gu, qu are like gw, qw, as in queen.

The vowels are either long or short. This means that a long vowel takes longer to pronounce than a short vowel does. There are no fixed rules for the length of vowels and the proper pronunciation can be learned best by paying close attention to the phonetic pronunciation given in the practice below and by hearing someone pronounce Latin correctly.

The diphthongs, two vowels pronounced as one, are pronounced:

ae like ai, as in aisle.
au like ou, as in ouch.
ei like ei, as in eight.
oe like oi, as in soil.
ui like we.

Syllables. A Latin word contains as many syllables as it has vowels and diphthongs. When dividing a word into syllables,

1. A single consonant is placed with the following vowel: **pa - ter.**
2. Double consonants are separated: **di - mit - te.**
3. If there are two or more consonants, the first is generally placed with the preceding vowel: **nos - trum.**

Accent. Latin words are accented as follows:

1. On the next to the last syllable, if it is long: **di - mit′ - te.**
2. On the second to last syllable, if the next to last is short: **ad - ve′ - ni - at.**
3. On the first syllable of a two syllable word: **nos′ - ter.**

Practice reading aloud, following the English sound guide, until you can read this passage clearly and without hesitation. Remember that every consonant and vowel is pronounced in Latin.

Pater noster qui es in pah-*tehr* naws-*tehr qwee ehs in*	Our father who art in
caelis, sanctificetur kai-*lees* sahnk-*tih-fih*-kay-*toor*	heaven, hallowed
nomen tuum. Adveniat noh-*mehn* too-*uhm. ahd*-weh-*nee-aht*	be thy name. Thy
regnum tuum. Fiat reg-*nuhm* too-*uhm.* fee-*aht*	kingdom come. Thy will
voluntas tua sicut in *woh*-luhn-*tahs* too-*ah* seek-*uht in*	be done on earth as it is
caelo et in terra. Panem kai-*loh eht in* tehr-*rah.* pah-*nehm*	in heaven. Give us this day
nostrum cotidianum da nohs-*truhm* koh-*tee-dee-ah-nuhm dah*	our daily bread.
nobis hodie. Et dimitte noh-*bees* hoh-*dee-ay. eht dee*-miht-*eh*	And forgive us our debts
nobis debita nostra sicut noh-*bees* deh-*biht-ah* naws-*trah* seek-*uht*	as we forgive our debtors.
et nos dimittimus *eht nohs dee*-miht-*tih-muhs*	And lead us not
debitoribus nostris. Et *deh-bih*-taw-*rih-buhs* naws-*trees. eht*	into temptation,
ne nos inducas in tentationem *nay nohs in*-doo-*kahs in* ten-*tah-tee*-oh-*nehm*	but deliver us
sed libera nos a malo. *sehd* lee-*beh-rah nohs ah* mah-*loh.*	from evil.
Amen. ah-*mehn.*	Amen.

The Lord's Prayer. Matthew VI, 9–13

THE PARTS OF SPEECH

The parts of speech are the same in Latin and English, but Latin has no article (the, a, an). The article must, therefore, be supplied in English.

Noun—the name of a person, place, or thing. e.g., *Caesar, Rome, town*
Pronoun—a word used instead of a noun. e.g., *he*
Adjective—a word that describes a noun or pronoun. e.g., *good*
Verb—a word that shows action or state of being. e.g., *run, is*
Adverb—a word that modifies a verb, adjective, or adverb. e.g., *quickly, very*
Preposition—a word that shows relationship between a noun or pronoun and another word or words. e.g., *in, by, with*
Conjunction—a word that joins words, phrases, clauses, or sentences. e.g., *and*
Interjection—an exclamation showing emotion. e.g, *oh*

CHAPTER 2

WORD DERIVATION

1. Many of our English words have been inherited directly from Latin, with little or no change in spelling.

animal	**labor**	**captivus**	**fortuna**	**multitudo**	**natio**
animal	labor	captive	fortune	multitude	nation

2. Other English words have come to us indirectly through the Romance (Roman) Languages.

LATIN	ITALIAN	FRENCH	SPANISH	PORTUGUESE	ENGLISH
filia	**la figlia**	**la fille**	**la hija**	**a filha**	daughter
vos	**voi**	**vous**	**vosotros**	**vos**	you
bonus	**buono**	**bon**	**bueno**	**bom**	good
terra	**la terra**	**la terre**	**la tierra**	**a terra**	earth

3. A third group of English words comes from Latin in the form of Derivatives.

LATIN	ENGLISH	ENGLISH DERIVATIVE
agricola	farmer	agriculture
stella	star	constellation
terra	earth	terrace
filia	daughter	filial

You will find that you are familiar with more Latin than you realized. Watch for Latin words that have come directly or indirectly into English, for English Derivatives, and for Latin phrases and expressions in everyday use. These will be brought to your attention throughout the book.

SOME GIRLS' NAMES OF LATIN ORIGIN AND THEIR MEANINGS

Rosa, rose	**Regina,** queen	**Flora,** flowers
Victoria, victory	**Gloria,** glory	**Augusta,** majestic
Beatrice, making happiness	**Celestine,** heavenly	**Letitia,** happiness
Barbara, foreign	**Viola, Violet,** violet	**Alma,** cherishing
Amabel, lovable	**Clara,** bright	**Miranda,** worthy of admiration
Amy, beloved	**Laura,** laurel	**Sylvia,** of the forest
Amanda, worthy of love	**Stella, Estelle,** star	**Gratia, Grace,** grace, gratitude

As you study the Reading Grammar in this section, you will see that most of these names end in **-a** because they are feminine and come from the **a-declension.**

READING VOCABULARY

Nouns

stella (**steh**-*lah*), **stellae** (**steh**-*lai*), **f.**, star (stellar, constellation)

puella (*poo*-**eh**-*lah*), **puellae** (*poo*-**eh**-*lai*), **f.**, girl

casa (**kah**-*sah*), **casae** (**kah**-*sai*), **f.**, cottage, house

femina (**fay**-*mih-nah*), **feminae** (**fay**-*mih-nai*), **f.**, woman (feminine)

aqua (**ah**-*kwah*), **aquae** (**ah**-*kwai*), **f.**, water (aquarium)

terra (**tehr**-*rah*), **terrae** (**tehr**-*rai*), **f.**, land, earth (terrace, territory)

agricola (*ah*-**grih**-*koh-lah*), **agricolae** (*ah*-**grih**-*koh-lai*), **m.**, farmer (agriculture)

In giving the vocabulary, the first two forms of a Noun are given, as above, as well as its gender. The first form is the case of the subject. The second form is the case of possession and furnishes the base to which the rest of the case endings are added. Base: **stell-, puell-, cas-, femin-, aqu-, terr-, agricol-.**

Verbs

amo (**ah**-*moh*), **amare** (*ah*-**mah**-*reh*), like, love (amateur)

porto (**por**-*toh*), **portare** (*por*-**tah**-*reh*), carry (portage, deportment)

laudo (**lou**-*doh*), **laudare** *lou*-**dah**-*reh*), praise (laudable)

laboro (*lah*-**bor**-*oh*), **laborare** (*lah*-*bor*-**ah**-*reh*), work (laboratory)

voco (**woh**-*koh*), **vocare** (*woh*-**kah**-*reh*), call (vocation, vocative)

The first form of each Verb given here is the first person singular of the present tense. For example, **amo**, I like, I am liking, I do like. The second form is the present infinitive. For example, **amare**, to like. The infinitive furnishes the base on which the present tenses are formed. Base: **ama-, porta-, lauda-, labora-, voca-.**

Conjunction **et** (eht), and

READING GRAMMAR

A. Nouns.

1. The change in the ending of a Noun to show its use in the sentence is called declension. Note that the endings are added to the second or base form.

2. Nouns that have **-ae** as the ending of the second form are **a-declension.**
3. **a-declension** Nouns have **-a-** in most of the case endings.
4. **a-declension** Nouns are all feminine, unless the word indicates a male.

SINGULAR		USE	PLURAL	
stella	the star	subject	**stellae**	the stars
stellae	of the star	possession	**stellarum**	of the stars
stellae	to, for the star	indirect object	**stellis**	to, for the stars
stellam	the star	direct object	**stellas**	the stars
stella	from, with, by, in the star	prepositional phrases	**stellis**	from, with, by, in the stars

Grammar Practice No. 1

Decline **puella, casa femina, aqua, terra,** and **agricola** in the same way, giving the Latin form and its English meaning, and then check your answers below. Do this until you can give all the forms easily and quickly.

Example: puella, the girl; **puellae,** of the girl; **puellae,** to, for the girl; **puellam,** the girl; etc.

Check on Grammar Practice No. 1

puella, the girl
puellae, of the girl
puellae, to, for the girl
puellam, the girl
puella, from, with, by, in the girl
puellae, the girls
puellarum, of the girls
puellis, to, for the girls
puellas, the girls
puellis, from, with, by, in the girls

casa, the cottage
casae, of the cottage
casae, to, for the cottage
casam, the cottage
casa, from, with, by, in the cottage
casae, the cottages
casarum, of the cottages
casis, to, for the cottages
casas, the cottages
casis, from, with, by, in the cottages

terra, the land
terrae, of the land
terrae, to, for the land
terram, the land
terra, from, with, by, in the land
terrae, the lands
terrarum, of the lands
terris, to, for the lands
terras, the lands
terris, from, with, by, in the lands

femina, the woman
feminae, of the woman
feminae, to, for the woman
feminam, the woman
femina, from, with, by, in the woman
feminae, the women
feminarum, of the women
feminis, to, for the women
feminas, the women
feminis, from, with, by, in the women

aqua, the water
aquae, of the water
aquae, to, for the water
aquam, the water
aqua, from, with, by, in the water
aquae, the waters
aquarum, of the waters
aquis, to, for the waters
aquas, the waters
aquis, from, with, by, in the waters

agricola, the farmer
agricolae, of the farmer
agricolae, to, for the farmer

agricolam, the farmer	**agricolarum,** of the farmers
agricola, from, with, by, in the farmer	**agricolis,** to, for the farmers
agricolae, the farmers	**agricolas,** the farmers
	agricolis, from, with, by, in the farmers

B. Verbs.

1. The change in the ending of a Verb to show tense (time) and person (the subject of the verb) and number (singular or plural) is called conjugation. Note that the endings are added to the second or infinitive form.
2. Verbs that have **-a-** in the infinitive are **a-conjugation.** Note that the endings are added to the second or base form.
3. **a-conjugation** Verbs have **-a-** in most of the forms.
4. A Verb must be in the same person and number as its subject. For example,

agricola laborat, the farmer works (third person singular)
agricolae laborant, the farmers work (third person plural)

C. Present Tense of **a-conjugation** Verbs.

SINGULAR		PLURAL	
amo	I like; am liking; do like	**amamus**	we like; are liking; do like
amas	you like; are liking; do like	**amatis**	you like; are liking; do like
amat	he, she, it likes; is liking; does like	**amant**	they like; are liking; do like

Grammar Practice No. 2

Conjugate the Present Tense of **porto, laudo, laboro,** and **voco** in the same way, giving the Latin form and its English meaning, and then check your answers below. Do this until you can give all the forms easily and quickly. The ability to read Latin depends on the rapid recognition of the meanings of the endings and of the vocabulary and so it is essential that these should be mastered.

Example: porto, I carry, I do carry, I am carrying; **portas,** you carry, you do carry, you are carrying; **portat,** he, she, it carries, he, she, it does carry, he, she, it is carrying; etc.

Check on Grammar Practice No. 2

porto, I carry, do carry, am carrying
portas, you carry, do carry, are carrying
portat, he, she, it carries, does carry, is carrying
portamus, we carry, do carry, are carrying
portatis, you carry, do carry, are carrying
portant, they carry, do carry, are carrying

laudo, I praise, do praise, am praising
laudas, you praise, do praise, are praising
laudat, he, she, it praises, does praise, is praising
laudamus, we praise, do praise, are praising
laudatis, you praise, do praise, are praising
laudant, they praise, do praise, are praising

laboro, I work, do work, am working
laboras, you work, do work, are working
laborat, he, she, it works, does work, is working
laboramus, we work, do work, are working
laboratis, you work, do work, are working
laborant, they work, do work, are working

voco, I call, am calling, do call
vocas, you call, are calling, do call
vocat, he, she, it calls, is calling, does call
vocamus, we call, are calling, do call
vocatis, you call, are calling, do call
vocant, they call, are calling, do call

PRACTICE EXERCISES

No. 1. For each of these singular forms give the corresponding plural.

> Example: **stellam,** the star **stellas,** the stars
> **vocas,** you call **vocatis,** you call

1. **aquam,** the water *aquas*
2. **puellae,** of the girl *puellarum*
3. **terra,** the land *terrae*
4. **agricolae,** for the farmer *agricolis*
5. **stella,** by the star *stellis*
6. **vocat,** he calls *vocant*
7. **laboras,** you work *laboratis*
8. **porto,** I carry *portamus*
9. **laudo,** I praise *laudamus*
10. **amat,** he likes *amant*

No. 2. Supply the English to complete the translation.

> Example: **puellarum,** _____ the girls of the girls

1. **agricolarum,** ___*of*___ the farmers
2. **puellam,** ___*the*___ girl
3. **casae,** ___*the*___ cottages
4. **feminae,** for the ___*girl*___
5. **terris,** by the ___*lands*___
6. **laudat,** ___*He*___ is praising
7. **vocatis,** ___*You*___ call
8. **laborant,** ___*They*___ are working
9. **amamus,** ___*we*___ like
10. **portas,** you ___*do*___ carry

No. 3. What is the English pronoun shown by each of the following?

 1. **-mus** *we* 2. **-t** *he* 3. **-o** *I* 4. **-tis** *you* 5. **-nt** *they* 6. **-s** *you*

No. 4. What use in the sentence would each of these pairs of Noun endings have?

 1. **am, as** *DO* 2. **a, is** *means* 3. **a, ae** *Subj* 4. **ae, is** *IO* 5. **ae, arum** *posses*

No. 5. Change the following to the singular or plural.

> Example: **portat** **portant**

1. **porto** *portamus*
2. **amant** *amat*
3. **portamus** *porto*
4. **laudo** *laudamus*
5. **vocat** *vocant*
6. **laboras** *laboratis*
7. **portant** *portat*
8. **vocatis** *vocas*
9. **amo** *amamus*
10. **laudas** *laudatis*

CHAPTER 3

THE SIGNS OF THE ZODIAC

The Signs of the Zodiac are all Latin words and are easily remembered by associating their meanings with the way in which they are depicted.

Aries, the Ram	**Leo,** the Lion	**Sagittarius,** the Archer
Taurus, the Bull	**Virgo,** the Maiden	**Capricorn,** the Goat
Gemini, the Twins	**Libra,** the Scales	**Aquarius,** the Water Bearer
Cancer, the Crab	**Scorpio,** the Scorpion	**Pisces,** the Fishes

Many of the Planets are named for Roman deities, as:

Jupiter, King of the gods	**Mars,** god of War
Saturn, god of Sowing	**Neptune,** god of the Sea
Mercury, the Messenger god	**Pluto,** god of the Lower World
Venus, goddess of Love	

READING VOCABULARY

Nouns

nauta (**nou**-*tah*), **nautae** (**nou**-*tai*), **m.,** sailor (nautical)
filia (**fee**-*lee-ah*), **filiae** (**fee**-*lee-ai*), **f.,** daughter (filial)

Adjectives

magna (**mahg**-*nah*), large, great
parva (**pahr**-*wah*), small
bona (**boh**-*nah*), good (bonanza)
mala (**mah**-*lah*), bad, evil (malice)
mea (**may**-*ah*), my, mine
tua (**too**-*ah*), your, yours
Romana (*roh*-**mah**-*nah*), Roman (romance)
pulchra (**puhl**-*krah*), pretty, beautiful

Verbs

sum (*suhm*), **esse** (**ehs**-*seh*), be
nato (**nah**-*toh*), **natare** (*nah*-**tah**-*reh*), swim (natatorium)

Adverbs

non (*nohn*), not (non-stop)
bene (**beh**-*neh*), well (benefactor)
male (**mah**-*leh*), badly (malformed)

Sign of a question

-ne (*neh*)

READING GRAMMAR

A. Adjectives.

1. An Adjective describes, or tells something about, a Noun.

filia	**filia pulchra**	**filia bona**
daughter	pretty daughter	good daughter

2. An Adjective must be in the same gender (masculine, feminine, or neuter), number (singular or plural), and have the same use in the sentence, as the Noun it modifies.

SINGULAR		USE	PLURAL	
casa magna	large cottage	subject	**casae magnae**	large cottages
casae magnae	of the large cottage	possession	**casarum magnarum**	of the large cottages
casae magnae	to, for the large cottage	indirect object	**casis magnis**	to, for the large cottages
casam magnam	large cottage	direct object	**casas magnas**	large cottages
casa magna	from, with, by, in the large cottage	prepositional phrase	**casis magnis**	from, with, by, in the large cottages

B. Adverbs.

An Adverb that tells something about the Verb, such as a negative, stands in front of the Verb.

Agricola non natat. The farmer does not swim.

C. Questions.

-ne on the end of the first word of a sentence indicates a question.

Natatne agricola? Does the farmer swim?

D. Present Tense of **sum,** to be.

SINGULAR		PLURAL	
sum	I am	**sumus**	we are
es	you are	**estis**	you are
est	he, she, it is; there is	**sunt**	they are; there are

FAMILIAR PHRASES

Many Latin Phrases are in everyday use and can be recognized and used easily with a little practice.

1. **nota bene,** note well, is used in writing and speaking to draw attention to something that should be noticed especially. It is often abbreviated: **N.B.**
2. **bona fide,** with good faith or honesty. Example: It is a **bona fide** certificate. Thus, a genuine certificate. The opposite is **mala fide,** in bad faith.
3. **adsum,** I am present, is used often in roll call answering.
4. **meum et tuum,** mine and thine, is used frequently in place of the English phrase.
5. **terra firma,** firm land. Example: They were glad to step on **terra firma.**
6. **aqua** occurs frequently in English: **aqua pura,** pure water. **aqua vitae,** water of life, meaning brandy or alcohol. **aqua fortis,** literally, strong water, is nitric acid. **aqueous humor,** a watery fluid between the cornea and lens of the eye.

FAMILIAR QUOTATIONS

Many quotations from Latin authors are in use today, either in their Latin form or in translation. If you become so familiar with these quotations and their meanings that you know them by memory, you will have acquired some of the real flavor of the Latin language and thought.

Roma aeterna, Eternal Rome. Tibullus
Laborare est orare, To labor is to pray. motto of the Benedictine Monks
Errare humanum est, To err is human. Seneca
Dira necessitas, Dire necessity. Horace
Aurea mediocritas, The golden mean. Horace
Rara avis, A rare bird. Horace
Ars longa, vita brevis, Art is long, life is short. Seneca
Fortuna caeca est, Fortune is blind. Cicero

PRACTICE EXERCISES

No. 6. Supply the correct ending for each adjective.

Example: aquam mal______, bad water **aquam malam**

1. **casam parv**______, small cottage
2. **me**______ **filiarum,** of my daughters
3. **pulchr**______ **stellas,** pretty stars
4. **tu**______ **terra,** your land
5. **filiae mal**______, to the bad girl
6. **casis Roman**______, for Roman cottages
7. **puellas parv**______, small girls
8. **aquam bon**______, good water
9. **feminae parv**______, to the small woman
10. **casarum pulchr**______, of small cottages

No. 7. What is the English for each of the following?

1. **estis** 2. **est** 3. **sunt** 4. **sum** 5. **es** 6. **sumus**

No. 8. Make questions of the following and then translate the questions.

Example: natat natatne? Does he (she, it) swim?

1. **natant**	6. **sunt**	11. **laudat**
2. **portas**	7. **natamus**	12. **vocant**
3. **amamus**	8. **portat**	13. **est**
4. **laborat**	9. **estis**	14. **natas**
5. **vocatis**	10. **laudas**	15. **amant**

No. 9. Give three translations for each of the following.

1. **amas**	3. **vocas**	5. **amant**	7. **natat**	9. **laboras**
2. **laudamus**	4. **laboro**	6. **vocatis**	8. **portamus**	10. **laudat**

CHAPTER 4

ROMAN NUMERALS

The basic Roman numerals, and the corresponding Arabic numerals, are:

I	1	**X**	10	**C**	100	**M**	1000
V	5	**L**	50	**D**	500		

These Roman numerals are used in various combinations to form any desired numeral:

1. A smaller numeral placed in front subtracts from the larger. For example, **IV**, 4; **IX**, 9; **XC**, 90; **CM**, 900.

2. A smaller numeral placed after adds to the larger. For example, VI, 6; XI, 11; CX, 110; MC, 1100.
3. Repeated numerals double, triple, and so on. For example, XX, 20; XXX, 30; CC, 200; CCC, 300.
4. When a line is drawn over a numeral, it multiplies that numeral by 1000. For example, V̄, 5000; X̄, 10,000; C̄, 100,000; D̄, 500,000.

A GUIDE TO ROMAN NUMERALS

I	1	XV	15	LXI	61	CDI	401
II	2	XVI	16	LXX	70	D	500
III	3	XVII	17	LXXI	71	DI	501
IV or IIII	4	XVIII	18	LXXX or XXC	80	DC	600
V	5	XIX	19	LXXXI or XXCI	81	DCI	601
VI	6	XX	20	XC	90	DCC	700
VII	7	XXI	21	XCI	91	DCCI	701
VIII	8	XXX	30	C	100	DCCC or CCM	800
IX or VIIII	9	XXXI	31	CI	101	DCCCI or CCMI	801
X	10	XL or XXXX	40	CC	200	CM	900
XI	11	XLI	41	CCI	201	CMI	901
XII	12	L	50	CCC	300	M	1000
XIII	13	LI	51	CCCI	301	MI	1001
XIV	14	LX	60	CD	400	MM	2000
						MMI	2001

Roman Numeral Practice No. 1

Give the corresponding Arabic numerals for the following.

XIII	MC	XLIII	DII	CXX
CCC	XXV	DCX	CDXX	X̄CCC
IX	CM	XXXVI	XCV	LXXIV

Check on Roman Numeral Practice No. 1

13	1100	43	502	120
300	25	610	420	10,300
9	900	36	95	74

Roman Numeral Practice No. 2

Give the corresponding Roman numeral for the following.

59	42	65	2222	818
304	5040	1066	26	271
85	1492	753	960	101

Check on Roman Numeral Practice No. 2

LIX	MCDXCII	XXVI
CCCIV	LXV	CMLX
LXXXV or XXCV	MLXVI	DCCCXVIII or CCMXVIII
XLII	DCCLIII	CCLXXI
V̄XL	MMCCXXII	CI

READING VOCABULARY

Nouns

insula (**een**-*soo-lah*), **insulae** (**een**-*soo-lai*), **f.**, island (insular, insulate)
patria (**pah**-*tree-ah*), **patriae** (**pah**-*tree-ai*), **f.**, native country (patriot)
paeninsula (*pai*-**neen**-*soo-lah*), **paeninsulae** (*pai*-**neen**-*soo-lai*), **f.**, peninsula (peninsular)
copia (**koh**-*pee-ah*), **copiae** (**koh**-*pee-ai*), **f.**, supply, abundance (copious, cornucopia). In the plural, **copiae** means forces, troops
silva (**sihl**-*wah*), **silvae** (**sihl**-*wai*), **f.**, forest, woods (sylvan)
Germania (*gehr*-**mah**-*nee-ah*), **Germaniae** (*gehr*-**mah**-*nee-ai*), **f.**, Germany
Britannia (*brih*-**tah**-*nee-ah*), **Britanniae** (*brih*-**tah**-*nee-ai*), **f.**, Britain
Italia (*ih*-**tah**-*lee-ah*), **Italiae** (*ih*-**tah**-*lee-ai*), **f.**, Italy (Italian)
Iulia (**yoo**-*lee-ah*), **Iuliae** (**yoo**-*lee-ai*), **f.**, Julia

Adjectives

multa (**muhl**-*tah*), much. In the plural, **multae** means many (multicolored)
clara (**klah**-*rah*), clear, famous, bright (clarity)
antiqua (*ahn*-**tee**-*kwah*), ancient, old (antique)

Verbs

pugno (**puhg**-*noh*), **pugnare** (*puhg*-**nah**-*reh*), fight (pugnacious)
oppugno (*ohp*-**puhg**-*noh*), **oppugnare** (*ohp-puhg*-**nah**-*reh*), attack (oppugnance)
iuvo (**yoo**-*woh*), **iuvare** (*yoo*-**wah**-*reh*), help, aid

Adverbs

cur (*kuhr*), why

Conjunction

quod (*kwohd*), because

READING GRAMMAR

A. The Nominative Case shows:

1. the Subject of the Verb.

Nauta pugnat. The sailor fights.
Nautae pugnant. The sailors fight.

nauta is the Subject of **pugnat; nautae** is the Subject of **pugnant;** both are in the Nominative Case.

2. the Predicate Noun. **Britannia est insula.** Britain is an island. **insula** is a Noun in the Predicate and tells something about the subject **(Britannia).**
3. the Predicate Adjective. **Britannia est pulchra.** Britain is pretty. **pulchra** is an Adjective in the Predicate and describes the Subject **(Britannia).**

The **a-declension** Nouns and Adjectives end in **-a** in the Nominative Singular and **-ae** in the Nominative Plural.

B. The Genitive Case shows Possession and tells something about the Noun next to it, almost the way an Adjective does.

terra agricolae, the land of the farmer—the farmer's land
terra agricolarum, the land of the farmers—the farmers' land

agricolae (of the farmer) and **agricolarum** (of the farmers) tell something about **terra.** Compare this to the use of an Adjective: **terra pulchra,** the pretty land—**pulchra** (pretty) tells something about **terra.** The **a-declension** Nouns and Adjectives end in **-ae** in the Genitive Singular and **-arum** in the Genitive Plural.

PRACTICE EXERCISES

No. 10. Give the English for each of the following.

Example: filiae nautarum, the daughters of the sailors

1. casa puellae *house of the girl*
2. copia aquae *plenty of water*
3. terra agricolarum *land of the farmers*
4. casae feminarum *houses of the girls*
5. patria nautae *land of the sailor*
6. insula nautae *island of the sailor*
7. filia agricolae *daughter of the farmer*
8. casae nautarum *house of the sailors*
9. copia stellarum *supply of stars*
10. patria feminae *the country of the girl*

No. 11. Pick out and translate the Subjects.

Example: Femina laborat. Femina, the woman

1. Feminae laborant.
2. Puella portat.
3. Agricolae amant.
4. Copiae pugnant.
5. Nauta oppugnat.
6. Agricola amat.
7. Filiae laudant.
8. Patria est.
9. Insulae sunt.
10. Filia laborat.

No. 12. Pick out and translate the Predicate Adjectives.

Example: Insula est pulchra. pulchra, pretty

1. Insula est magna.
2. Silvae sunt pulchrae.
3. Filiae sunt bonae.
4. Casa est mea.
5. Copiae sunt Romanae.
6. Terra est mala.
7. Paeninsula est tua.
8. Casae sunt parvae.
9. Silva est pulchra.
10. Femina est bona.

No. 13. Pick out and translate the Predicate Nouns.

Example: Sunt agricolae. agricolae, farmers

1. Est agricola.
2. Sunt nautae.
3. Germania est patria mea.
4. Estne insula?
5. Sunt casae.
6. Sum nauta.
7. Estis feminae.
8. Es puella.
9. Sumus agricolae.
10. Non est silva.

CHAPTER 5

READING

Italia

1. Italia est paeninsula in Europa.
2. Paeninsula longa est et non lata.
3. Incolae multae sunt agricolae et nautae.
4. Italia est clara et antiqua.
5. Magna est fama Italiae.
6. In Italia sunt viae multae et pulchrae et longae.
7. Sicilia et Sardinia et Corsica sunt magnae et pulchrae insulae.
8. Incolae patriam amant et bene laborant.

Italy

1. Italy is a peninsula in Europe.
2. The peninsula is long and not wide.
3. Many inhabitants are farmers and sailors.
4. Italy is famous and old.
5. The fame of Italy is great.
6. In Italy there are many beautiful and long roads.
7. Sicily and Sardinia and Corsica are large and pretty islands.
8. The inhabitants love their country and work hard.

READING VOCABULARY

Nouns

fabula (fah-*buh-lah*), **fabulae** (fah-*buh-lai*), **f.**, story (fable, fabulous)
via (wee-*ah*), **viae** (wee-*ai*), **f.**, road, way, street (via, viaduct)
incola (ihn-*koh-lah*), **incolae** (ihn-*koh-lai*), **m.** or **f.**, inhabitant
fama (fah-*mah*), **famae** (fah-*mai*), **f.**, rumor, renown, report (fame)
Europa (*yoo*-roh-*pah*), **Europae** (*yoo*-roh-*pai*), **f.**, Europe

Adjectives

longa (lawn-*gah*), long (longitude)
lata (lah-*tah*), wide (latitude)

Verbs

do (*doh*), **dare** (dah-*reh*), give (dative)
ambulo (ahm-*buh-loh*), **ambulare** (*ahm-buh-lah-reh*), walk (ambulance, perambulator)
narro (nah-*roh*), **narrare** (*nah*-rah-*reh*), tell, relate (narrate)
monstro (mawn-*stroh*), **monstrare** (*mawn*-strah-*reh*), point out, show (monstrance)
habito (hah-*bih-toh*), **habitare** (*hah-bih*-tah-*reh*), dwell, live (habitat)
navigo (nah-*wih-goh*), **navigare** (*nah-wih*-gah-*reh*), sail, cruise (navigate)

Prepositions

ad (*ahd*), to, toward (administer)
a (*ah*) or **ab** (*ahb*), from, away from (abdicate)
e (*ay*) or **ex** (*ehks*), from, out from (emit, exceed)
cum (*kuhm*), with
in (*ihn*), in, on, into, onto (inhabit, induce)

READING GRAMMAR

A. The Dative Case shows the Indirect Object of the Verb.
1. The Indirect Object shows to whom or what something is given, said, or directed.

Puellae aquam do.	I give the water *to the girl.*
Puellis aquam do.	I give the water *to the girls.*

Puella (to the girl) and **Puellis** (to the girls) are the Indirect Objects of **do** (I give). Both are in the Dative Case.

2. The **a-declension** Nouns and Adjectives end in **-ae** (*ai*) in the Dative Singular and **-is** (*ees*) in the Dative Plural.

B. The Accusative Case shows the Direct Object of the Verb.
1. The Direct Object shows the person or thing that receives the action of the Verb.

Fabulam narro.	I tell *a story.*
Fabulas narro.	I tell *stories.*

Fabulam (story) and **Fabulas** (stories) are the Direct Objects of **narro** (I tell). Both are in the Accusative Case.

2. The **a-declension** Nouns and Adjectives end in **-am** (*ahm*) in the Accusative Singular and **-as** (*ahss*) in the Accusative Plural.

C. Prepositional Phrases in Latin are in either the Accusative or Ablative Case.

1. Accusative Prepositional Phrases are used with these Prepositions:

ad, to, toward	**Ad casam ambulo.**	I walk *toward the cottage.*
	Ad casas ambulo.	I walk *toward the cottages.*
in, into	**In casam ambulo.**	I walk *into the cottage.*
	In casas ambulo.	I walk *into the cottages.*

2. Ablative Prepositional Phrases are used with these Prepositions:

cum, with	**Cum puella ambulo.**	I walk *with the girl.*
	Cum puellis ambulo.	I walk *with the girls.*

Cum is used only with Nouns or Pronouns indicating people.

in, in, on	**In casa sum.**	I am *in the cottage.*
	In casis sunt.	They are *in the cottages.*
	In terra sum.	I am *on land.*
	In viis sunt.	They are *on the streets.*
e or **ex**, from, out from	**ex via**	*out of the street*
	ex viis	*out of the streets*
a or **ab**, from, away from	**a silva**	*away from* the forest
	a silvis	*away from* the forests

a or **e** is not used before a vowel or **h**.

WORD DERIVATION

Derivatives are words that come from the same origin or source. Thus, many English words have the same basic meaning as their Latin sources, even though there may have been some changes in spelling and general meaning during the course of time. For example, **terra**, *earth, land.* From this Latin word are derived: 1) *terrestrial,* having to do with the earth or land; 2) *territory,* a tract of land or earth; 3) *terrace,* a flat raised area of earth or land. Therefore, these three English words are derived from the Latin word **terra** and contain the same basic meaning.

Remember that similarity of sound and appearance alone are not enough, but must be combined with similarity of meaning to make a derivative. Continue to notice the English derivatives given in the Reading Vocabularies and see if you can add to them.

PRACTICE EXERCISES

No. 14. Give the English for the following.

Example: in vias, into the roads

1. **ad viam**	6. **ab terra**	11. **in silvas**	16. **ad insulam**
2. **in casa**	7. **a casis**	12. **cum puella**	17. **ex terra**
3. **cum femina**	8. **e silvis**	13. **in aqua**	18. **cum agricola**
4. **in silvam**	9. **in insulas**	14. **ad aquam**	19. **in patria**
5. **ex casis**	10. **ad vias**	15. **ab puellis**	20. **cum puellis**

No. 15. Pick out and translate the Direct Objects in the following.

Example: Puellam amat. **Puellam,** the girl

1. **Puellis aquam do.**
2. **Puellae fabulam narro.**
3. **Puellae aquam do.**
4. **Nautam monstro.**
5. **Agricolas iuvat.**
6. **Nautis fabulam narrat.**
7. **Nautae viam monstras.**
8. **Terram amant.**
9. **Nautae terram amant.**
10. **Insulas amo.**

No. 16. Pick out and translate the Indirect Objects in the following.

Example: Nautis aquam do. **Nautis,** to the sailors

1. **Feminae silvas monstramus.**
2. **Nautae aquam dat.**
3. **Nautis fabulas narrant.**
4. **Puellae viam monstrat.**
5. **Puellis fabulam narrat.**
6. **Feminis casas monstratis.**
7. **Agricolis terram dant.**
8. **Feminae casam das.**
9. **Puellis silvas monstrat.**
10. **Agricolae fabulas narratis.**

No. 17. Give three English meanings for each of the following, except 13 and 14, which have one English meaning each.

1. **ambulatis**	6. **das**	11. **laudatis**	16. **natas**
2. **narrat**	7. **dat**	12. **amant**	17. **pugnat**
3. **ambulant**	8. **vocant**	13. **estis**	18. **pugnamus**
4. **habito**	9. **laboras**	14. **sumus**	19. **oppugno**
5. **navigamus**	10. **portamus**	15. **natant**	20. **oppugnant**

FIRST REVIEW SECTION (CHAPTERS 1–5)

VOCABULARY REVIEW

NOUNS

1. **agricola**	9. **fama**	17. **nauta**
2. **aqua**	10. **femina**	18. **paeninsula**
3. **Britannia**	11. **filia**	19. **patria**
4. **casa**	12. **Germania**	20. **puella**
5. **copia**	13. **incola**	21. **silva**
6. **copiae**	14. **insula**	22. **stella**
7. **Europa**	15. **Italia**	23. **terra**
8. **fabula**	16. **Iulia**	24. **via**

1. farmer	9. rumor, renown, report	17. sailor
2. water	10. woman	18. peninsula
3. Britain	11. daughter	19. native country
4. cottage	12. Germany	20. girl
5. supply, abundance	13. inhabitant	21. forest, woods
6. troops	14. island	22. star
7. Europe	15. Italy	23. land, earth
8. story	16. Julia	24. road, way, street

ADJECTIVES

1. **antiqua**	6. **magna**	11. **parva**
2. **bona**	7. **mala**	12. **pulchra**
3. **clara**	8. **mea**	13. **Romana**
4. **lata**	9. **multa**	14. **tua**
5. **longa**	10. **multae**	

1. ancient, old	6. large, great	11. small
2. good	7. bad, evil	12. pretty, beautiful
3. clear, bright, famous	8. my, mine	13. Roman
4. wide	9. much	14. your, yours
5. long	10. many	

VERBS

1. **ambulo**	6. **laboro**	11. **navigo**
2. **amo**	7. **laudo**	12. **oppugno**
3. **do**	8. **monstro**	13. **porto**
4. **habito**	9. **narro**	14. **pugno**
5. **iuvo**	10. **nato**	15. **sum**
		16. **voco**

1. walk	6. work	11. sail, cruise
2. love, like	7. praise	12. attack
3. give	8. point out, show	13. carry
4. dwell, live	9. tell, relate	14. fight
5. help, aid	10. swim	15. be
		16. call

ADVERBS

1. **bene**	2. **cur**	3. **male**	4. **non**
1. well	2. why	3. badly	4. not

PREPOSITIONS

1. a, ab	**3. cum**	**5. in**	**1. from, away from**	**3. with**	**5. in, on; into**
2. ad	**4. e, ex**		**2. to, toward**	**4. from, out from**	

CONJUNCTIONS

1. et	**2. quod**	**1. and**	**2. because**

PRACTICE EXERCISES

No. 18. Give the correct form of these Adjectives with their Nouns.

Example: aquam (pulchra), aquam pulchram

1. Europam (antiqua)	**5. insularum (multa)**	**8. famam (mala)**
2. aquae (pulchra)	**6. terra (Romana)**	**9. puellarum (pulchra)**
3. silvis (parva)	**7. filias (bona)**	**10. incolis (multa)**
4. stellas (clara)		

No. 19. Give the Genitive and Gender of these Nouns.

Example: casa, casae, f.

1. casa	**6. insula**	**11. terra**	**16. patria**
2. femina	**7. puella**	**12. Britannia**	**17. incola**
3. stella	**8. copia**	**13. fama**	**18. Europa**
4. aqua	**9. filia**	**14. Italia**	**19. agricola**
5. fabula	**10. nauta**	**15. silva**	**20. via**

No. 20. Give the Infinitive for each of these Verbs.

Example: amo, amare

1. amo	**4. sum**	**7. monstro**	**10. porto**	**13. nato**
2. laudo	**5. voco**	**8. do**	**11. narro**	**14. pugno**
3. navigo	**6. oppugno**	**9. habito**	**12. laboro**	**15. ambulo**

No. 21.

1. Make a list of the Latin cases and give the use of each.
2. Give the complete declension of these phrases, with the English meaning of each form.

insula lata, the wide island
insulae latae, of the wide island

via longa, long road
viae longae, of the long road

3. Give the complete Present Tense of these Verbs, with the English meaning of each form.

laboro, I work; I am working; I do work
laudo, I praise; I am praising; I do praise
sum, I am

The author of this hymn is unknown, but it was composed in the seventeenth century and translated by Frederick Oakley in the nineteenth century.

Adeste, Fideles

Adeste, fideles, laeti triumphantes,
Venite, venite in Bethlehem;
Natum videte regem Angelorum;
Venite adoremus Dominum.

Oh Come All Ye Faithful

Oh come, all ye faithful, joyful and triumphant,
Oh come ye, oh come ye to Bethlehem;
Come and behold him, born the King of Angels;
Oh come, let us adore him, Christ the Lord.

Adeste, Fideles	Oh Come All Ye Faithful
Deum de Deo, Lumen de Lumine,	God of God, Light of Light,
Gestant puellae viscera;	Lo! he abhors not the Virgin's womb;
Deum verum, genitum non factum;	Very God, begotten, not created;
Venite adoremus Dominum.	Oh come, let us adore him, Christ the Lord.
Cantet nunc hymnos, Chorus Angelorum;	Sing, choirs of angels, sing in exultation,
Cantet nunc aula caelestium,	Sing, all ye citizens of heaven above:
Gloria in excelsis Deo!	"Glory to God in the highest!"
Venite adoremus Dominum.	Oh come, let us adore him, Christ the Lord.
Ergo Qui natus die hodierna,	Yea, Lord, we greet thee, born this happy morning,
Iesu, tibi sit gloria;	Jesu, to thee be glory given,
Patris aeterni verbum caro factum;	Word of the Father, now in flesh appearing;
Venite adoremus Dominum.	Oh come, let us adore him, Christ the Lord.

CHAPTER 6

READING

Proserpina	Proserpina
1. **Dea agricolarum est Ceres.**	1. The goddess of the farmers is Ceres.
2. **Filia est Proserpina et Ceres filiam pulchram amat.**	2. Her daughter is Proserpina and Ceres loves her beautiful daughter.
3. **Ceres et Proserpina terram et silvas amant et agricolas iuvant.**	3. Ceres and Proserpina love the land and woods and help the farmers.
4. **Proserpina est clara et incolae terrarum multarum Proserpinam bene amant et laudant.**	4. Proserpina is famous and the inhabitants of many lands love Proserpina well and praise her.
5. **Pluto Proserpinam ad terram infernam[1] portat quod puellam amat.**	5. Pluto carries Proserpina to the lower world because he loves the girl.
6. **Dea Ceres filiam vocat quod misera est et agricolae non laborant et terra non bona est.**	6. The goddess, Ceres, calls her daughter because she is unhappy and the farmers do not work and the land is not good.
7. **Pluto agricolis Proserpinam dat et terra est pulchra et bona quod bene laborant.**	7. Pluto gives Proserpina to the farmers and the earth is pretty and good because they work hard.
8. **Aestate[2] Proserpina est hic cum agricolis et hieme[3] est ibi in terra inferna et non cum agricolis.**	8. In summer Proserpina is here with the farmers and in winter she is there in the lower world and not with the farmers.

NOTES: 1. **inferna**, lower. 2. **aestate**, in summer. 3. **hieme**, in winter.

READING VOCABULARY

Nouns

provincia, provinciae, f., province (provincial)
gloria, gloriae, f., glory (glorious)
praeda, praedae, f., booty, plunder (predatory)
victoria, victoriae, f., victory (victorious)
Graecia, Graeciae, f., Greece
Hispania, Hispaniae, f., Spain
fossa, fossae, f., ditch (foss)

Adjective

alta, high, deep (alto, altitude)

Verbs

supero, superare, surpass, overcome, conquer (superable)
aedifico, aedificare, build (edify)
sto, stare, stand (station)
exspecto, exspectare, to await, expect, wait for (expectant)

Adverbs

saepe, often
ubi, where, when (ubiquitous)
ibi, there, in that place
hic, here, in this place

Prepositions

ante, before, in front of With the Accusative Case (antedate, antecedent)
post, behind, in back of With the Accusative Case (postdate, postpone)

READING GRAMMAR

A. Latin Sentence Construction.

Because the meaning of an English sentence is shown by the position of the words, any change in the position of the words changes the meaning of the sentence. For example, The farmer calls the girl. -or- The girl calls the farmer.

Since the inflection or form of the endings of Latin words shows their use in the sentence, a change in the position of the words in a Latin sentence does not change the actual meaning of the sentence. For example, **Agricola puellam vocat.** -or- **Puellam agricola vocat.** Both sentences have the same meaning.

B. Latin Word Order.

1. There is a normal order of words in a Latin sentence.

a. The Subject or question word stands first.

Puella fabulas narrat.	The girl (subject) tells stories.
Narratne puella fabulas?	Does (question) the girl tell stories?

b. Adjectives and Genitives stand next to their nouns.

filia pulchra -or- **pulchra filia**	pretty daughter
filia agricolae -or- **agricolae filia**	the farmer's daughter

c. Adverbs precede the word they modify.

non narrat	she does not tell
non multae puellae	not many girls
non saepe	not often

d. An Indirect Object usually precedes the Direct Object.

Puella agricolae fabulas narrat.	The girl tells stories to the farmer.

e. Verbs stand at the end of their clauses. The Verb "to be", however, usually has the same position as in English.

Puella fabulas narrat.	The girl tells stories.
Puella est pulchra.	The girl is pretty.

2. Any change in the normal word order of a Latin sentence is usually for emphasis or a special effect.

Puellam femina amat quod bona est.	The woman likes the girl because she is good.

C. The word "there".
Be careful to distinguish between the two uses of the word "there".
1. With the third person of the Verb "to be", *there is* or *there are.*

Est femina in casa.	There is a woman in the cottage.
Sunt feminae in casa.	There are women in the cottage.

2. The Adverb **ibi,** *there* or *in that place.*

Ibi pugnant.	They are fighting there.
Ibi sunt feminae.	There are the women.

FAMILIAR QUOTATIONS

Many of the words in these quotations belong to the **a-declension** or to the **a-conjugation.**

Sed non culpa mea est. But the blame is not mine. Ovid.
Licentia poetica. Poetic license. Seneca
Summa summarum. The total of totals. Plautus
Periculum in mora. Peril in delay. Livy
Si qua via est. If there is any way. Virgil
Tanta potentia formae est. So great is the power of beauty. Ovid
Sollicitae tu causa, pecunia, vitae. You, money, are the cause of an anxious life. Propertius

PRACTICE EXERCISES

No. 22. Give the English meanings for these forms.

1. **sumus**	4. **est**	7. **sunt**	10. **navigant**	13. **aedificamus**
2. **superant**	5. **exspectatis**	8. **natamus**	11. **datis**	14. **ambulant**
3. **stat**	6. **aedificat**	9. **superat**	12. **vocas**	15. **statis**

No. 23. Translate these Prepositional Phrases.

1. **in Italia**	5. **in provincia**	9. **post casas**	13. **ad insulam**
2. **ad Britanniam**	6. **cum copiis**	10. **cum puella**	14. **in casas**
3. **cum feminis**	7. **in paeninsula**	11. **in silvis**	15. **ante fossam**
4. **ad Italiam**	8. **ante casas**	12. **ad viam**	

No. 24. Give the English translations for the following.

1. **incolae**
2. **Cur laborant?**
3. **Patriam tuam iuvas.**
4. **Praedam portat.**
5. **Bene pugnat.**
6. **Sunt pulchrae.**
7. **multarum victoriarum**
8. **patria clara**
9. **fabulam longam**
10. **ex casa**
11. **ab via**
12. **Ubi est?**
13. **Hic sum.**
14. **ante insulam**
15. **post victoriam**
16. **cum copiis**
17. **ex provinciis**
18. **Sunt copiae hic.**
19. **ad vias**
20. **Ibi est provincia.**
21. **Ibi sunt feminae.**
22. **Est gloria.**
23. **Sunt multae puellae.**
24. **Ubi sunt?**
25. **Hic sunt.**

CHAPTER 7

SOME BOYS' NAMES OF LATIN ORIGIN AND THEIR MEANINGS

Rex, king, ruler
Sylvester, of the woods
Victor, conqueror
Claude, lame
Augustus, majestic, august
Lucius, light
Constant, firm, true
Valentine, healthy, strong
Felix, happy, lucky
Patrick, patrician
Dominic, of the Lord
Septimus, the seventh child
Octavius, the eighth child
Martin, of Mars
Aurelius, golden
Dexter, on the right, fortunate
Vincent, conquering
Benedict, blessed
Pius, devoted, faithful
Rufus, red
Clement, kind, mild
Leo, Leon, lion
Clarence, Clare, bright
Paul, small

READING VOCABULARY

Nouns

amicus, amici, m., friend (amicable)
inimicus, inimici, m., (personal) enemy (inimical)
puer, pueri, m., boy (puerile)
vir, viri, m., man (virile)
ager, agri, m., field (agriculture)
bellum, belli, n., war (bellicose)
oppidum, oppidi, n., town (oppidan)
arma, armorum, n. pl., arms, weapons (armory)
castra, castrorum, n. pl., camp (castle)
periculum, periculi, n., danger (peril)
socius, socii or soci, m., ally, comrade (social)
gladius, gladii or gladi, m., sword (gladiatorial)
nuntius, nuntii or nunti, m., messenger, message (nuncio)
proelium, proelii or proeli, n., battle
auxilium, auxilii or auxili, n., help, aid (auxiliary)

Adjective

angusta, narrow (anguish)

Verbs

aro, arare, plow (arable)
occupo, occupare, seize, take possession of (occupy)
armo, armare, arm (army)
neco, necare, kill
nuntio, nuntiare, announce, report (pronounce)

Prepositions

per, through With the Accusative Case (persevere, permeate)
de, about, concerning, down from With the Ablative Case (descend)

Adverb

etiam, even, also

Conjunction

sed, but

READING GRAMMAR

A. 1. Nouns that have **-i** as the ending of the second or Genitive form are **o-declension.**
2. **o-declension** Nouns that end in **-us** or **-er** or **-ir** in the Nominative Case, or first form, are masculine.
3. **o-declension** Nouns that end in **-um** in the Nominative Case, or first form, are neuter.

B. **o-declension** Nouns fall into two main groups—the masculine and the neuter.
1. masculine **o-declension** Nouns.

SINGULAR		USE	PLURAL	
amicus	the friend	subject	**amici**	the friends
amici	of the friend	possession	**amicorum**	of the friends
amico	to, for the friend	indirect object	**amicis**	to, for the friends
amicum	the friend	direct object	**amicos**	the friends
amico	from, with, by, in the friend	prepositional phrases	**amicis**	from, with, by, in the friends

Other masculine **o-declension** Nouns are spelled with an **-i-** in the stem. Compare **socius** with **amicus:**

SINGULAR		PLURAL	
socius	the ally	**socii**	the allies
socii or soci	of the ally	**sociorum**	of the allies
socio	to, for the ally	**sociis**	to, for the allies
socium	the ally	**socios**	the allies
socio	from, with, by, in the ally	**sociis**	from, with, by, in the allies

Some masculine **o-declension** Nouns end in **-er.** Of these, some keep the **-e-** in all forms and others drop the **-e-** after the Nominative. Notice these Nouns and compare them with **amicus** and **socius** above:

SINGULAR		PLURAL	
puer	the boy	**pueri**	the boys
pueri	of the boy	**puerorum**	of the boys
puero	to, for the boy	**pueris**	to, for the boys
puerum	the boy	**pueros**	the boys
puero	from, with, by, in the boy	**pueris**	from, with, by, in the boys

SINGULAR		PLURAL	
ager	the field	**agri**	the fields
agri	of the field	**agrorum**	of the fields
agro	to, for the field	**agris**	to, for the fields
agrum	the field	**agros**	the fields
agro	from, with, by, in the field	**agris**	from, with, by, in the fields

2. neuter **o-declension** Nouns.

SINGULAR		PLURAL	
bellum	the war	**bella**	the wars
belli	of the war	**bellorum**	of the wars
bello	to, for the war	**bellis**	to, for the wars
bellum	the war	**bella**	the wars
bello	from, with, by, in the war	**bellis**	from, with, by, in the wars

Some neuter **o-declension** Nouns are spelled with an **-i-** in the stem. Compare **proelium** with **bellum:**

SINGULAR		PLURAL	
proelium	the battle	**proelia**	the battles
proelii or **proeli**	of the battle	**proeliorum**	of the battles
proelio	to, for the battle	**proeliis**	to, for the battles
proelium	the battle	**proelia**	the battles
proelio	from, with, by, in the battle	**proeliis**	from, with, by, in the battles

PREFIXES

In both Latin and English, prefixes are used to modify the basic meaning of a word. These prefixes are usually Latin Prepositions. An understanding of the meaning of the prefix makes the meaning of the Latin or English compound word clearer. Prefixes occur most frequently in Verb forms. These are some of the most common Latin Prepositions and their meanings as prefixes:

a, ab, abs, away	**absum,** be away, be absent
ad, to, toward	**advoco,** call to
ante, before, in front	**antecedo,** go before
post, after, behind	**postpono,** put after, put behind
de, down, from, away	**depono,** put down, put away

PRACTICE EXERCISES

No. 25. Give the English for these forms.

1. **agro**	4. **pueri**	7. **castra**	10. **nuntio**	13. **oppidi**
2. **bellis**	5. **socium**	8. **gladios**	11. **pericula**	14. **virum**
3. **proeliorum**	6. **amicos**	9. **auxilium**	12. **armorum**	15. **inimicos**

No. 26. Change each of these forms to the plural, and give the English.

1. **amicus**	4. **belli**	7. **periculum**	10. **auxilio**	13. **periculo**
2. **pueri**	5. **oppidum**	8. **gladi**	11. **nuntio**	14. **ager**
3. **agro**	6. **vir**	9. **nuntium**	12. **viro**	15. **bellum**

No. 27. Fill in the blanks with the correct English.

1. **castrorum,** __________ the camp
2. **socius,** __________ ally
3. **gladium,** __________ sword
4. **de bello,** __________ the war
5. **per periculum,** __________ the danger
6. **oppidi,** __________ the town
7. **viri,** __________ the man
8. **inimici,** __________ enemies
9. **agros,** __________ fields
10. **pueri,** __________ the boy

No. 28. Give the English translation for the following.

1. **ex agro**
2. **Armantne?**
3. **angusta via**
4. **amicos**
5. **cum puero**
6. **Ibi arat.**
7. **post castra**
8. **amicorum**
9. **cum viro**
10. **Bellum pugnant.**
11. **Oppida monstrant.**
12. **Viro arma dant.**
13. **Fabulas de bello narramus.**
14. **Pericula amat.**
15. **Castra sunt in agro.**
16. **Per agros ambulatis.**
17. **Sunt oppida.**
18. **Auxilium das.**
19. **Gladii necant.**
20. **In castris habitant.**

CHAPTER 8

THE HISTORICAL PRESENT

Latin sometimes uses the Present Tense in narrative where English would use the Past Tense. This use in Latin is called the Historical Present.

READING

Servi	Slaves
1. **Romani servos multos in bello occupant.**	1. The Romans seized many slaves in war.
2. **Ex oppidis Graeciae ad Italiam servos portant.**	2. They carried the slaves to Italy from the towns of Greece.
3. **Servi erant boni, sed in Italia saepe non erant laeti.**	3. The slaves were good, but in Italy they were often not happy.
4. **Servi erant praeda belli et multi servos bene curant, sed multi servos male curant.**	4. Slaves were the booty of war and many people cared for their slaves well, but many cared for them badly.

5. **Servi in agris et in casis et in viis laborant.**
6. **Saepe aegri erant, sed multi servos aegros bene curant.**
7. **Romani servis multa dant et curam bonam dant.**
8. **Servi dominos bonos et dominas bonas amant.**
9. **Multi servi erant clari et filios dominorum bene iuvant.**
10. **Multi domini servos liberant et multi servi liberi erant viri clari.**

5. The slaves worked in the fields and in the houses and on the roads.
6. They were often sick, but many people took good care of the sick slaves.
7. The Romans gave many things to the slaves and gave them good care.
8. The slaves liked good masters and good mistresses.
9. Many slaves were famous and aided the sons of their masters very much.
10. Many masters freed their slaves and many free slaves were famous men.

READING VOCABULARY

Nouns

filius, filii or **fili, m.,** son (filial)
cura, curae, f., care (curate)
equus, equi, m., horse (equestrian)
frumentum, frumenti, n., grain (frumentaceous)
servus, servi, m., slave, servant (servitude)
dominus, domini, m., master (dominion)
domina, dominae, f., mistress

Adjectives

miser, misera, miserum, wretched, unhappy (miser)
laetus, laeta, laetum, happy
liber, libera, liberum, free (liberal)
aeger, aegra, aegrum, sick, ill

Verbs

libero, liberare, free, set free (liberate)
curo, curare, care for, cure (curator)
erat, he, she, it was; there was
erant, they were; there were

Adverb

hodie, today

READING GRAMMAR

A. **a-declension** and **o-declension** Adjectives.
You have already had **a-declension** Adjectives. These Adjectives also belong to the **o-declension. a-declension** and **o-declension** Adjectives have the same endings as the Nouns of these declensions.

a-declension—fem.	**o-declension**—masc.		
bona	**bonus**	**miser**	**pulcher**
bonae	**boni**	**miseri**	**pulchri**
bonae, etc.	**bono,** etc.	**misero,** etc.	**pulchro,** etc.

o-declension—neuter

bonum	**miserum**	**pulchrum**
boni	**miseri**	**pulchri**
bono, etc.	**misero,** etc.	**pulchro,** etc.

B. Agreement of Adjectives.

Adjectives must agree with the Nouns they modify in Gender, Number, and Case. Note that they do not necessarily agree in declension or spelling.

cura bona, good care (fem.)
nauta bonus, good sailor (masc.)
equus bonus, good horse (masc.)
puer bonus, good boy (masc.)
servus miser, wretched slave (masc.)
equus pulcher, pretty horse (masc.)
frumentum bonum, good grain (neut.)
bellum miserum, wretched war (neut.)
oppidum pulchrum, pretty town (neut.)

C. Omission of the Noun with the Adjective.

The masculine and neuter Nominative and Accusative plural of Adjectives are commonly used to mean men (or persons) or things. Because the gender makes it clear, the Noun may be omitted.

boni, good people (subject)
bonos, good people (direct object)
bona, good things or goods (subject, direct object)
multi, many people (subject)
multos, many people (direct object)

Sometimes the Noun is omitted with other cases in the plural.

multorum, of many people (possession)
multis, to, for many people (indirect object)

FAMILIAR PHRASES

ante bellum, before the war.
post bellum, after the war. These two phrases usually apply to the Civil War.
ad nauseam, to the point of nausea, or disgust. She talked about it **ad nauseam.**
summum bonum, the greatest good, and source of all other benefits. It was the **summum bonum** for all.
ut supra, as above.
ut infra, as below. These phrases are used to refer to something mentioned in writing, either above or below. **ut supra,** see above. **ut infra,** see below.

PRACTICE EXERCISES

No. 29. Give the English for the following.

1. **Amicus meus ibi est.**
2. **ad casas tuas**
3. **ex fossis altis**
4. **in via longa**
5. **cum viris claris**
6. **ante castra Romana**
7. **post agros meos**
8. **de aqua bona**
9. **per silvam magnam**
10. **mali amici**

No. 30. Complete the correct ending of the Adjectives.

1. **virorum mult_____**
2. **filiae me_________**
3. **frumento bon______**
4. **equis tu_________**
5. **me_________ filiis**
6. **pueros aegr_______**
7. **puellae miser_____**
8. **soci liber_________**
9. **feminam miser_____**
10. **agris pulchr_______**

No. 31. Match the Latin Adjective in Column II with the English Adjective in Column I.

Column I	Column II	Column I	Column II
1. many **viros**	1. **pulchrum**	6. good **fili**	6. **boni**
2. sick **pueri**	2. **multorum**	7. bad **famam**	7. **laetus**
3. pretty **oppidum**	3. **multos**	8. wretched **equis**	8. **malam**
4. many **servorum**	4. **laetam**	9. Roman **terrae**	9. **miseris**
5. happy **puellam**	5. **aegri**	10. happy **agricola**	10. **Romanae**

No. 32. Complete the Verbs with the correct endings.

1. **cura**____ (we)	5. **porta**____ (he)	8. **nuntia**____ (she)
2. **libera**____ (you s.)	6. **ar**____ (I)	9. **occupa**____ (we)
3. **labora**____ (you pl.)	7. **neca**____ (they)	10. **sta**____ (you pl.)
4. **lauda**____ (they)		

No. 33. Give the English for the following.

1. **Sunt liberi.**	6. **de dominis bonis**	11. **in terris liberis**
2. **dominarum laetarum**	7. **Cur estis laeti?**	12. **Est pulchra.**
3. **in aquam altam**	8. **Sunt multi.**	13. **Suntne pulchrae?**
4. **de curis magnis**	9. **Sumus aegri.**	14. **Est miser.**
5. **in agris latis**	10. **cum amicis bonis**	15. **multa**

CHAPTER 9

READING

Dei Antiqui	The Ancient Gods
1. **Romani deos multos et deas multas adorant et fabulas antiquas de deis suis narrant.**	1. The Romans worshiped many gods and many goddesses and told old stories about their gods.
2. **Iuppiter in caelo habitat et erat bonus et magnus.**	2. Jupiter lived in the sky and was good and great.
3. **Mercurius erat nuntius deorum et trans terram et aquam viris et deis famas portat.**	3. Mercury was the messenger of the gods and carried reports to men and gods across land and water.
4. **Nautae Neptunum adorant quod deus oceani erat.**	4. The sailors worshiped Neptune because he was the god of the ocean.
5. **In aqua habitat et amicus nautarum erat.**	5. He lived in the water and was the sailors' friend.
6. **Mars viros in proeliis et in bellis curat.**	6. Mars took care of men in battles and in wars.
7. **Vulcanus erat deus et deis arma dat.**	7. Vulcan was a god and he gave weapons to the gods.
8. **In patria nostra et in vestra deas et deos non adoramus, sed in Italia antiqua deae et dei erant amici virorum et feminarum.**	8. In our native country and in yours we do not worship goddesses and gods, but in ancient Italy goddesses and gods were the friends of the men and women.
9. **Hodie in Italia deos multos non adorant.**	9. Today in Italy they do not worship many gods.

Deae Antiquae	The Ancient Goddesses
1. **Multas fabulas de deabus Romanis narrant.**	1. They tell many stories about the Roman goddesses.
2. **Feminae Romanae deas in templis et in casis suis saepe adorant.**	2. Roman women often worshiped the goddesses in the temples and in their homes.
3. **Iuno regina dearum erat.**	3. Juno was the queen of the goddesses.
4. **Clara et bona erat et deas regnat.**	4. She was famous and good and she ruled the goddesses.
5. **Vesta curam casarum habet.**	5. Vesta had the care of houses.
6. **Diana puellas curat et nautae non timent quod nautis in oceano fortunam bonam et auxilium dat.**	6. Diana cared for girls and sailors were not afraid because she gave good fortune and help to sailors on the ocean.
7. **Dea lunae etiam erat et silvas bene amat.**	7. She was also the goddess of the moon and liked the forests very much.
8. **Venus pulchra erat et erant feminae multae in templo.**	8. Venus was beautiful and there were many women in her temple.
9. **Agricolae bene arant quod Ceres agricolas iuvat et frumentum curat.**	9. Farmers plowed well because Ceres helped farmers and cared for the grain.
10. **Etiam hodie magna est fama dearum Romanarum.**	10. Even today the fame of the Roman goddesses is great.

READING VOCABULARY

Nouns

deus, dei, m., god (deity)
dea, deae, f., goddess
oceanus, oceani, m., ocean (oceanic)
caelum, caeli, n., sky, heaven (celestial)
regina, reginae, f., queen
sapientia, sapientiae, f., wisdom (sapience)
templum, templi, n., temple (templar)
luna, lunae, f., moon (lunar)
fortuna, fortunae, f., fortune, fate, luck (fortunate)

Adjectives

suus, sua, suum, his, her, its, their (own)
noster, nostra, nostrum, our, ours (nostrum)
vester, vestra, vestrum, your, yours

Verbs

adoro, adorare, worship, adore (adorable)
habeo, habere, have, hold (habit)
timeo, timere, fear, be afraid of (timid)
video, videre, see (vision, video)
regno, regnare, rule (regnant)

Preposition

trans, across With the Accusative Case (trans-Atlantic)

READING GRAMMAR

A. Note the spelling of **deabus** in the Reading above. The Dative and Ablative Plural of **dea** is **deabus,** to distinguish it from **deis.**

B. Possessive Adjectives are used when the Subject of the Verb is the possessor. Thus, the word "own" may always be added for clarity.

SINGULAR	1st person	**meus, mea, meum,** my (own), mine
	2nd person	**tuus, tua, tuum,** your (own), yours
	3rd person	**suus, sua, suum,** his (own), her (own), its (own)
PLURAL	1st person	**noster, nostra, nostrum,** our (own), ours
	2nd person	**vester, vestra, vestrum,** your (own), yours
	3rd person	**suus, sua, suum,** their (own), theirs

C. **e-conjugation** Verbs have an **-e-** in the Present Infinitive.

hab-e-re, to have **tim-e-re,** to fear **vid-e-re,** to see

e-conjugation Verbs form the Present Tense in the same way as the **a-conjugation** Verbs, but there is an **-e-** in each form.

SINGULAR	**habeo**	I have, do have, am having	PLURAL	**habemus**	we have
	habes	you have		**habetis**	you have
	habet	he, she, it has		**habent**	they have

LATIN ON TOMBSTONES AND MONUMENTS

Latin often appears on tombstones and monuments. The following are some of the abbreviations and phrases frequently used.

c., standing for **circa** or **circum**, meaning about, used with dates.
in aeternum, forever
in perpetuum, forever
ae.; aet.; aetat., standing for **aetatis**, of age
anno aetatis suae, in the year of his (her) age.
ob., standing for **obiit**, meaning he (she) died

hic iacet, here lies
R.I.P., standing for **requiescat in pace**, meaning may he (she) rest in peace.
in memoriam, in memory, to the memory of
A.D., standing for **Anno Domini**, meaning In the year of (our) Lord.

PRACTICE EXERCISES

No. 34. Fill in the correct Possessive Adjective.

1. *our* **reginam**
2. *your (sing.)* **deas**
3. *his own* **fortuna**
4. *my own* **deis**
5. *their own* **templa**
6. *your (pl.)* **reginae**
7. *our own* **patriam**
8. *its own* **oceani**
9. *their own* **filiarum**
10. *my* **sapientiam**

No. 35. Give the English for the following.

1. **timeo**
2. **videt**
3. **timetis**
4. **adorat**
5. **regnant**
6. **vides**
7. **timent**
8. **habemus**
9. **regnamus**
10. **habent**
11. **timet**
12. **videtis**
13. **habeo**
14. **regnas**
15. **adoratis**

No. 36. Give the English for the following.

1. **antiquos deos**
2. **deae Romanae**
3. **meorum amicorum**
4. **vestri nautae**
5. **tuam praedam**
6. **filias nostras**
7. **suus dominus**
8. **suum filium**
9. **sua sapientia**
10. **gloriam nostram**

No. 37. Translate the following sentences into English.

1. **Gloria vestra non est magna.**
2. **Cur inimicum tuum necas?**
3. **Nuntiusne multa narrat?**
4. **Viri trans agros suos ambulant.**
5. **Feminae in casis suis sunt.**
6. **Filiae tuae hodie sunt aegrae.**
7. **Multi trans oceanum navigant.**
8. **Sunt deae nostrae.**
9. **Sunt dei nostri.**
10. **Femina suas filias curat.**
11. **Ante casas sto.**
12. **Non multa habet.**
13. **De luna narramus.**
14. **Fortuna vestra est bona.**
15. **Servi dominos timent.**
16. **Cur non timetis?**
17. **Templa pulchra videmus.**
18. **Castra ibi habet.**
19. **Pueros post fossam videmus.**
20. **Sapientiam magnam habetis.**

SECOND REVIEW SECTION (CHAPTERS 6–9)

VOCABULARY REVIEW

NOUNS

1. ager	**14. filius**	**27. periculum**	1. field	14. son	27. danger
2. amicus	**15. fortuna**	**28. praeda**	2. friend	15. fortune, fate, luck	28. booty, plunder
3. arma	**16. fossa**	**29. proelium**	3. arms, weapons	16. ditch	29. battle
4. auxilium	**17. frumentum**	**30. provincia**	4. aid, help	17. grain	30. province
5. bellum	**18. gladius**	**31. puer**	5. war	18. sword	31. boy
6. caelum	**19. gloria**	**32. regina**	6. sky, heaven	19. glory	32. queen
7. castra	**20. Graecia**	**33. sapientia**	7. camp	20. Greece	33. wisdom
8. cura	**21. Hispania**	**34. servus**	8. care	21. Spain	34. slave, servant
9. dea	**22. inimicus**	**35. socius**	9. goddess	22. (personal) enemy	35. comrade, ally
10. deus	**23. luna**	**36. templum**	10. god	23. moon	36. temple
11. domina	**24. nuntius**	**37. victoria**	11. mistress	24. messenger, message	37. victory
12. dominus	**25. oceanus**	**38. vir**	12. master	25. ocean	38. man
13. equus	**26. oppidum**		13. horse	26. town	

ADJECTIVES

1. aeger	**4. laetus**	**7. noster**	1. sick, ill	4. happy	7. our, ours
2. altus	**5. liber**	**8. suus**	2. high, deep	5. free	8. his, her, its, their
3. angustus	**6. miser**	**9. vester**	3. narrow	6. wretched, unhappy	9. your, yours

VERBS

1. adoro	**9. neco**	1. worship, adore	9. kill
2. aedifico	**10. nuntio**	2. build	10. announce, report
3. armo	**11. occupo**	3. arm	11. seize, take possession of
4. aro	**12. regno**	4. plow	12. rule
5. curo	**13. sto**	5. care for, cure	13. stand
6. exspecto	**14. supero**	6. await, expect, wait for	14. surpass, overcome
7. habeo	**15. timeo**	7. have, hold	15. fear, be afraid of
8. libero	**16. video**	8. free, set free	16. see

ADVERBS

1. etiam	**3. hodie**	**5. saepe**	1. even, also	3. today	5. often
2. hic	**4. ibi**	**6. ubi**	2. here, in this place	4. there, in that place	6. where, when

PREPOSITIONS

1. ante	**3. per**	**5. trans**	1. before, in front of	3. through	5. across
2. de	**4. post**		2. about, concerning, down from	4. behind, in back of	

CONJUNCTION

1. sed	1. but

PRACTICE EXERCISES

No. 38. Give the Infinitive of each of these Verbs.

1. **aedifico**	4. **supero**	7. **regno**	10. **curo**	13. **timeo**
2. **nuntio**	5. **video**	8. **aro**	11. **neco**	14. **habeo**
3. **exspecto**	6. **libero**	9. **sto**	12. **adoro**	15. **occupo**

No. 39. Give the Genitive and Gender of these Nouns.

1. **dea**	5. **oceanus**	9. **inimicus**	13. **castra**	17. **gladius**
2. **proelium**	6. **socius**	10. **regina**	14. **periculum**	18. **cura**
3. **provincia**	7. **fortuna**	11. **puer**	15. **victoria**	19. **praeda**
4. **bellum**	8. **amicus**	12. **ager**	16. **vir**	20. **equus**

No. 40.

1. Rearrange these sentences in the correct Latin order:

   a. **Frumentum cur datis non viris?**
   b. **Curam dat insularum bonamne incolis?**

2. Give the Present Tense with English meanings of **sto** and **timeo.**

No. 41. Put into English:

1. **agricolas nostros**	6. **suos filios**	11. **multi**
2. **filiarum laetarum**	7. **miseros**	12. **parvus puer**
3. **caelum altum**	8. **vias angustas**	13. **agrorum latorum**
4. **patriae liberae**	9. **tuus nuntius**	14. **cura bona**
5. **vester servus**	10. **fortuna mea**	15. **gladi longi**

GAIUS VALERIUS CATULLUS

Catullus was born about 84 B.C. at Verona, in northeastern Italy, but spent most of his life in Rome. He was a master of lyric poetry, especially love poems, and made use of many of the best features of Greek verse. Catullus died in 54 B.C.

Da mi basia mille, deinde centum,
dein mille altera, dein secunda centum,
deinde usque altera mille, deinde centum.
Dein, cum milia multa fecerimus,
conturbabimus illa, ne sciamus,
aut ne quis malus invidere possit,
cum tantum sciat esse basiorum.

Catullus V

Give me a thousand kisses, then a hundred,
then another thousand, then a second hundred,
then up to a thousand more, then a hundred.
At the last, when we have given many thousands,
we shall mix their count, lest we know,
or lest any wicked person might envy us,
when he learns our kisses are so many.

Catullus 5

Odi et amo. Quare id faciam, fortasse requiris.
Nescio, sed fieri sentio et excrucior.

Catullus LXXXV

I hate and I love. Why I do this, perhaps you ask.
I do not know, but I feel it happen and I am tortured.

Catullus 85

Toward the end of the fourth century, the Bible was translated into Latin by Saint Jerome and others, and this Latin version is called the Vulgate, or commonly accepted, Bible.

In principio erat Verbum et Verbum erat apud Deum, et Deus erat Verbum. Hoc erat in principio apud Deum. Omnia, per ipsum facta sunt, et sine ipso factum est nihil, quod factum est; in ipso vita erat, et vita erat lux hominum; et lux in tenebris lucet, et tenebrae eam non comprehenderunt. Fuit homo missus a Deo, cui nomen erat Ioannes. Hic venit in testimonium, ut testimonium perhiberet de lumine, ut omnes crederent per illum. Non erat ille lux, sed ut testimonium perhiberet de lumine. Erat lux vera, quae illuminat omnem hominem venientem in hunc mundum: in mundo erat, et mundus per ipsum factus est et mundus eum non cognovit.	In the beginning was the Word, and the Word was with God, and the Word was God. The same was in the beginning with God. All things were made by him; and without him was not any thing made that was made; in him was life, and the life was the light of men. And the light shineth in darkness; and the darkness comprehended it not. There was a man sent from God, whose name was John. The same came for a witness, to bear witness of the Light, that all men through him might believe. He was not that Light, but was sent to bear witness of that Light. That was the true Light, which lighteth every man that cometh into the world. He was in the world, and the world was made by him, and the world knew him not.
Evangelium Secundum Ioannem, I, i–x	St. John, 1, 1–10

CHAPTER 10

READING

Populus Romanus	The Roman People
1. **Populus Romanus certe clarus erat.**	1. The Roman people were indeed famous.
2. **Nonne populum Romanum amas? Ita.**	2. You like the Roman people, don't you? Yes.
3. **Populos terrarum multarum superant et viri Romani in provinciis Romanis habitant.**	3. They conquered the peoples of many lands and the Roman men lived in the Roman provinces.
4. **Multae copiae in provinciis manent et incolas bene regnant.**	4. Many troops stayed in the provinces and ruled the inhabitants well.
5. **Vias bonas et aedificia magna et templa pulchra ibi aedificant.**	5. They built good roads and large buildings and beautiful temples there.
6. **Incolis fortunam bonam portant.**	6. They brought good fortune to the inhabitants.
7. **Incolae provinciarum saepe erant socii et populus Romanus erat dominus bonus.**	7. The inhabitants of the provinces often were allies and the Roman people were good masters.
8. **Socii populo Romano auxilium vero dant.**	8. The allies truly gave aid to the Roman people.

Alba Longa

1. **Alba Longa erat oppidum in Italia antiqua.**
2. **In Latio erat et agros latos et bonos habet.**
3. **Vergilius de Alba Longa in fabula sua narrat.**
4. **Quod populus Graeciae Troiam superat, multi viri erant clari.**
5. **Aeneas est vero clarus.**
6. **In Troia non manet, sed ad Latium navigat.**
7. **Latinus in Latio regnat.**
8. **Aeneas Latinum oppugnare parat et castra ibi aedificat.**
9. **Castra erant Alba Longa.**
10. **Aeneas Latinum superat et Latium occupat.**
11. **Populus Lati erat Latinus et lingua erat Latina.**

Alba Longa

1. Alba Longa was a town in ancient Italy.
2. It was in Latium and had wide and good fields.
3. Vergil told about Alba Longa in his story.
4. Because the people of Greece conquered Troy, many men were famous.
5. Aeneas is truly famous.
6. He did not stay in Troy, but sailed to Latium.
7. Latinus ruled in Latium.
8. Aeneas prepared to attack Latinus and built a camp there.
9. The camp was Alba Longa.
10. Aeneas conquered Latinus and seized Latium.
11. The people of Latium were Latin and the language was Latin.

READING VOCABULARY

Nouns

populus, populi, m., people (popular)
aedificium, aedificii or aedifici, n., building (edifice)
lingua, linguae, f., language (linguist)
Latinus, Latini, m., Latinus
Troia, Troiae, f., Troy
Latium, Latii or Lati, n., Latium

Adjective

latinus, latina, latinum, Latin

Verbs

paro, parare, prepare, get ready (preparation)
maneo, manere, remain, stay (manor, mansion)
debeo, debere, owe, ought (debit)
propero, properare, hurry, hasten

Adverbs

nonne, expects the answer "yes"
num, expects the answer "no"
ita, yes; thus, so
minime, by no means, not at all (minimum)
vero, truly, in truth (verity)
certe, certainly, surely, indeed (certes, certo)

When **populus** is a collective Noun (represents a group), it is in the singular and its Verb is also singular. In the plural, it means peoples.

populus est, the people are **populi terrae sunt,** the peoples of the earth are

READING GRAMMAR

A. Questions and Answers.

1. Questions. Latin had no question mark and so a question had to be shown by a word in the sentence.

   a. A question word like **cur**, why?, asks a direct question.

   Cur manes, Why do you stay?

   b. A simple question is indicated by **-ne** on the end of the first word.

   Suntne boni, Are they good?

   c. **Nonne** at the beginning of a sentence asks a question expecting the answer "yes".

   Nonne sunt boni, They are good, aren't they?

   d. **Num** at the beginning of a sentence asks a question expecting the answer "no".

   Num sunt boni, They are not good, are they?

2. Answers to questions may be stated in various ways.

   a. By a statement, either positive or negative.

   Sunt boni, They are good.
   Non sunt boni, They are not good.

   b. By a positive or affirmative word.

   Ita, Yes. **Vero,** Yes, truly. **Certe,** Certainly.

   c. By a negative word.

   Non, No. **Minime,** By no means or Not at all.

B. Completing Infinitives.

Some Verbs, such as **paro** (prepare), **debeo** (ought), or **propero** (hasten), are not complete unless another Verb is used with them to complete their meaning. The completing Verb is always an Infinitive.

Manere debeo, I ought to stay. **Manere parat,** He prepares to stay.
Navigare properas, You hasten to sail.

FAMILIAR PHRASES

persona grata, an acceptable (or welcome) person.
persona non grata, an unacceptable (or unwelcome) person.
verbatim ac litteratim, word for word and letter for letter.
pro bono publico, for the public good.
ad infinitum, to infinity; with no limit.
sine dubio, without doubt.
vice versa, changed and turned; turned about.
addenda et corrigenda, things added and corrected; a supplement, especially to a book.

PRACTICE EXERCISES

No. 42. Give the English for these questions and answers.

1. **Nonne amicos habetis? Certe.**
2. **Aedificantne casas? Ita. Casas aedificant.**
3. **Nonne vero times? Vero timeo.**
4. **Num populus pugnat? Populus non pugnat.**
5. **Num viae sunt longae? Viae minime sunt longae.**
6. **Cur ad oppidum ambulant?**
7. **Manetne vir in aedificio? Vir in aedificio manet.**
8. **Estne provinca libera? Provincia vero est libera.**
9. **Num in oceano navigat? In oceano non navigat.**
10. **Estne regina tua magna? Regina mea certe magna est.**

No. 43. Complete these Verbs by filling in the correct vowel.

1. **vid______tis**	6. **iuv______t**	11. **par______nt**
2. **oppugn______t**	7. **hab______o**	12. **deb______mus**
3. **hab______s**	8. **man______nt**	13. **proper______t**
4. **ador______s**	9. **tim______t**	14. **aedific______s**
5. **vid______o**	10. **st______tis**	15. **ambul______tis**

No. 44. Fill in the correct completing Infinitive.

1. (To walk) **debeo.**
2. (To fight) **parat.**
3. (To kill) **non debent.**
4. (To conquer) **paratis.**
5. (To call) **debemus.**
6. (To swim) **non parant.**
7. (To help) **properatis.**
8. (To work) **non debetis.**
9. (To attack) **parat.**
10. (To stay) **debes.**

No. 45. Translate these sentences into English.

1. **Cur frumentum ibi parat?**
2. **Nonne linguam latinam amatis?**
3. **Ubi aedificia vestra stant?**
4. **Pueris gladios dare non debetis.**
5. **Dei arma sua etiam habent.**
6. **De bello longo Troiae fabulam narrant.**
7. **Aeneas cum viris suis ad Italiam navigat.**
8. **Deus populum Graeciae iuvat.**
9. **Cur Romani socios suos timent?**
10. **In caelo lunam claram videt.**

CHAPTER 11

READING

Romulus et Remus	Romulus and Remus
1. **Quod Romulus et Remus filii erant dei armorum et belli, populus Romanus proelia amabat.**	1. Because Romulus and Remus were the sons of the god of weapons and of war, the Roman people liked battles.
2. **Erant etiam filii Rheae Silviae.**	2. They were also the sons of Rhea Silvia.
3. **Amulius erat avunculus Rheae Silviae et Albam Longam regnabat, sed pueros non amabat.**	3. Amulius was the uncle of Rhea Silvia and ruled Alba Longa, but he did not love the boys.
4. **Pueros amare debebat.**	4. He ought to have loved the boys.
5. **Amulius filios Rheae Silviae necare parabat, sed servus in aqua in arca pueros locabat et vitas puerorum servabat.**	5. Amulius prepared to kill the sons of Rhea Silvia, but a slave placed the boys in the water in a chest and saved the lives of the boys.
6. **Mars filios suos ad ripam Tiberis portabat.**	6. Mars carried his sons to the bank of the Tiber.
7. **Lupa pueros ibi curabat et agricola bonus ad casam suam Romulum et Remum portabat.**	7. A wolf took care of the boys there and a good farmer carried Romulus and Remus to his cottage.

Sabini	The Sabines
1. **Romulus et Remus cum amicis suis Romam aedificabant, sed oppidum erat parvum et viri erant miseri quod sine feminis tum ibi erant.**	1. Romulus and Remus were building Rome with their friends, but the town was small and the men were unhappy because then they were there without women.
2. **Romulus ad ludos magnos Sabinos vocat et Sabini ad ludos feminas et filias suas portant.**	2. Romulus calls the Sabines to great games and the Sabines bring their women and daughters to the games.
3. **Viri Romani ad casas suas puellas portant et Sabini pugnare properant.**	3. The Roman men carry the girls to their cottages and the Sabines hasten to fight.
4. **In Foro Romano tum pugnabant, sed feminae erant miserae quod Sabini multos necabant.**	4. They fought then in the Roman Forum, but the women were unhappy because the Sabines were killing many people.
5. **Sabini vitas virorum suorum servabant, sed Romani praemium victoriae habebant.**	5. The Sabines saved the lives of their men, but the Romans had the reward of victory.
6. **Feminae et filiae Sabinorum cum Romanis nunc habitabant.**	6. The women and daughters of the Sabines now lived with the Romans.

READING VOCABULARY

Nouns

avunculus, avunculi, m., uncle (avuncular)
arca, arcae, f., chest, box (ark)
vita, vitae, f., life (vital)
ripa, ripae, f., bank (of a river) (riparious)
lupa, lupae, f., wolf (lupine)
praemium, praemii or **praemi, n.,** reward (premium)
ludus, ludi, m., game (ludicrous)
forum, fori, n., forum, market place (forensic)
Roma, Romae, f., Rome
Sabini, Sabinorum, m., the Sabines
Romanus, Romani, m., a Roman

Verbs

servo, servare, save, preserve (preservation)
loco, locare, place, put

Adverbs

nunc, now
tum, then

Preposition

sine, without With the Ablative Case (sinecure)

READING GRAMMAR

A. 1. The Imperfect Tense is used to show action going on in the past over a period of time. The **-ba-** in the Latin Verb may be translated "was", "used to", or "did".

2. Imperfect Tense of **a-conjugation** Verbs.

SINGULAR		PLURAL	
amabam	I was loving; I loved	**amabamus**	we were loving; we loved
amabas	you were loving; you loved	**amabatis**	you were loving; you loved
amabat	he, she, it was loving; he, she, it loved	**amabant**	they were loving; they loved

3. Imperfect Tense of **e-conjugation** Verbs.

SINGULAR		PLURAL	
habebam	I was having; I had	**habebamus**	we were having; we had
habebas	you were having; you had	**habebatis**	you were having; you had
habebat	he, she, it was having; he, she, it had	**habebant**	they were having; they had

4. The Imperfect Tense of **sum** is irregular, but may be recognized easily by the Stem, **era-**.

SINGULAR		PLURAL	
eram	I was	**eramus**	we were
eras	you were	**eratis**	you were
erat	he, she, it was	**erant**	they were

B. **Cum** is used as both a Conjunction and a Preposition.

1. **Cum,** as a Conjunction, means "when" or "while" and introduces a clause showing time.

Cum puerum videbat, ambulabat. When he saw the boy, he was walking.
Cum ambulabat, puerum videbat. While he was walking, he saw the boy.

2. **Cum,** as a Preposition, means "with" and is used with the Ablative Case.

Cum puero ambulabat. He was walking with the boy.
Cum pueris ambulabat. He was walking with the boys.

STATE MOTTOES

Ditat Deus, God enriches. Arizona
Regnant populi, The people rule. Arkansas
Esto perpetua, May it be everlasting. Idaho
Ad astra per aspera, To the stars through hardships. Kansas
Dirigo, I direct. Maine
Virtute et armis, By courage and weapons. Mississippi
Excelsior, Loftier. New York
Imperium in imperio, An empire in an empire. Ohio
Montani semper liberi, Mountaineers are always free. West Virginia
Cedant arma togae, Let weapons yield to the toga. Wyoming

PRACTICE EXERCISES

No. 46. Fill in the blanks with the correct forms of the Imperfect Tense.

1. **deb_____mus**	6. **vid_____s**	11. **hab_____tis**	16. **hab_____s**
2. **par_____m**	7. **cur_____m**	12. **st_____t**	17. **port_____tis**
3. **proper_____nt**	8. **ador_____mus**	13. **laud_____m**	18. **iuv_____t**
4. **man_____nt**	9. **loc_____s**	14. **man_____s**	19. **voc_____t**
5. **tim_____t**	10. **d_____tis**	15. **vid_____mus**	20. **tim_____mus**

No. 47. Give the English for the following.

1. **monstrabat**	5. **debebas**	9. **properabam**	13. **superabatis**	17. **locabam**
2. **voco**	6. **timetis**	10. **videbant**	14. **narrant**	18. **oppugnabas**
3. **paramus**	7. **erat**	11. **laudabatis**	15. **manemus**	19. **habebatis**
4. **regnabatis**	8. **pugnatis**	12. **portatis**	16. **servabat**	20. **eratis**

No. 48. Translate these phrases and clauses.

1. **cum stabat**	6. **cum superat**	11. **cum puella**
2. **cum filia**	7. **cum lupa**	12. **cum erant**
3. **cum laboramus**	8. **cum videtis**	13. **cum avunculo meo**
4. **cum exspecto**	9. **cum erat**	14. **cum Romanis**
5. **cum amicis**	10. **cum pugnabatis**	15. **cum feminis multis**

No. 49. Translate the following into English.

1. **Num viros in castris habet?**
2. **Ibi esse hodie parabamus.**
3. **Amicus tuus in oppido nostro famam bonam habet.**
4. **Cum puellis manere parabam.**
5. **Nonne in silvis multas lupas saepe necat?**
6. **Romani gladios Sabinorum timere non debent.**
7. **Cum oppidum aedificant, templa et aedificia ibi locant.**
8. **Cur servis suis praemia dant?**
9. **Agricola cum amico suo in agro erat.**
10. **Nonne sine aqua estis?**

CHAPTER 12

READING

Graecia

1. **Gloria Graeciae et fama incolarum suarum sunt clarae.**
2. **Graecia est paeninsula et agri et silvae populo bonam fortunam et vitam laetam dabant.**
3. **Nautae trans oceanum ad terras multas navigabant et multa ad fora oppidorum Graeciae portabant.**
4. **Graecia est propinqua Italiae, sed non est finitima.**
5. **Proelia et bella non erant grata incolis, sed cum populis finitimis pugnare saepe parabant.**
6. **Populus multis amicus erat et bellum populo non idoneum erat.**
7. **Italia erat inimica Graeciae et terram occupabat.**
8. **Tum populus Graeciae erat socius populi Italiae, sed populus Romanus linguam et templa et aedificia Graeciae laudabat.**

Greece

1. The glory of Greece and the fame of her inhabitants are well-known.
2. Greece is a peninsula and the fields and forests gave good fortune and a happy life to the people.
3. The sailors sailed across the ocean to many lands and brought many things to the market places of the towns of Greece.
4. Greece is near to Italy, but it is not neighboring.
5. Battles and wars were not pleasing to the inhabitants, but they often got ready to fight with the neighboring peoples.
6. The people were friendly to many and war was not suitable to the people.
7. Italy was unfriendly to Greece and seized the land.
8. Then the people of Greece were allies of the people of Italy, but the Roman people praised the language and temples and buildings of Greece.

Barbari

1. **Romani multos finitimos barbaros habebant.**
2. **Barbari ob praedam bella et proelia saepe incitabant.**
3. **Nonne nuntii de periculo monebant?**
4. **Cum nuntium portabant, socii auxilium portare atque copias suas armare debebant.**
5. **Romani non timebant, sed in terris barbaris pugnabant.**
6. **Oppida multa ibi oppugnabant et superabant.**
7. **Populus Germanus non erat amicus Romanis.**
8. **Erat barbarus et patriae Romanorum finitimus.**

The Barbarians

1. The Romans had many uncivilized neighbors.
2. The barbarians often stirred up wars and battles on account of booty.
3. The messengers warned about the danger, didn't they?
4. When they brought the message, the allies had to bring aid and arm their troops.
5. The Romans were not afraid, but they fought in barbarian lands.
6. They used to attack many towns there and conquer them.
7. The German people were not friendly to the Romans.
8. They were uncivilized and neighboring to the native country of the Romans.

Barbari	The Barbarians
9. **Victoriae copiarum Romanarum erant clarae et magnae.**	9. The victories of the Roman troops were famous and great.
10. **Copiis praemia dabant, cum nuntii famas bonas de gloria in provinciis narrabant.**	10. They gave the troops rewards, when the messengers related good reports about their glory in the provinces.

READING VOCABULARY

Nouns

barbarus, barbari, m., barbarian (barbarous)
finitimus, finitimi, m., neighbor

Adjectives

propinquus, propinqua, propinquum, near (propinquity)
finitimus, finitima, finitimum, neighboring
idoneus, idonea, idoneum, fit, suitable
amicus, amica, amicum, friendly (amicable)
gratus, grata, gratum, pleasing (grateful)
inimicus, inimica, inimicum, unfriendly (inimical)
barbarus, barbara, barbarum, savage, uncivilized, barbarian (barbarous)

Verbs

moneo, monere, warn, advise (monition, monitor)
incito, incitare, arouse, stir up, incite (incitement)

Adverb

cras, tomorrow (procrastinate)

Preposition

ob, on account of, because of With the Accusative Case

Conjunction

atque or **ac,** and also, also **ac** is used only before consonants.

READING GRAMMAR

A. Some Adjectives are followed by the Dative Case. They are translated with the Preposition *to* or *for* in English. Some of these Adjectives are **propinquus** (near), **idoneus** (fit), **amicus** (friendly), **inimicus** (unfriendly), **gratus** (pleasing), and **finitimus** (neighboring).

Est propinquus agro.	He is near to the field.
Est idoneum bello.	It is fit for war.
Est amicus puero.	He is friendly to the boy.
Est inimicus populo.	He is unfriendly to the people.
Est gratus viris.	He is pleasing to the men.
Est finitimum oppido.	It is neighboring to the town.

B. 1. The Future Tense shows action going on in the future and is translated "shall" or "will". All but the first and last forms have **-bi-** to show the future tense. In the first form, **-bo,** and in the last form, **-bu-** show the future tense.

2. Future Tense of **a-conjugation** Verbs.

SINGULAR		PLURAL	
amabo	I shall love; like	**amabimus**	we shall love; like
amabis	you will love; like	**amabitis**	you will love; like
amabit	he, she, it will love; like	**amabunt**	they will love; like

3. Future Tense of **e-conjugation** Verbs.

SINGULAR		PLURAL	
habebo	I shall have; hold	**habebimus**	we shall have; hold
habebis	you will have; hold	**habebitis**	you will have; hold
habebit	he, she, it will have; hold	**habebunt**	they will have; hold

4. The Future Tense of **sum** is irregular, but is recognized by the Stem, **eri-.**

SINGULAR		PLURAL	
ero	I shall be	**erimus**	we shall be
eris	you will be	**eritis**	you will be
erit	he, she, it will be	**erunt**	they will be

LEGAL TERMS

Latin is used extensively in legal phrases and terminology. Some of the more common Latin legal terms are given below.

ius civile, civil law, referring to the laws of legal systems modeled after the Roman law.

ius gentium, the law of nations, referring to International Law.

lex scripta, written law. Written laws are those passed and put into effect by a legislative body or corporation.

lex non scripta, unwritten law. Unwritten law develops out of common practice, custom, and usage. It is sometimes called common law.

sub iudice, before the judge, referring to a case under consideration by the judge, or court, but not yet decided.

corpus iuris, the body of law, comprised of all the laws of a sovereign power or legislative body collectively.

subpoena, under penalty or punishment. A **subpoena** is a writ naming a person and ordering him to appear in court, under penalty for failure to do so.

corpus delicti, the body of the crime or offense. The **corpus delicti** refers to the circumstances necessary to a crime. In murder, the **corpus delicti** is the fact of a criminal agent or of the death of the victim. It does not refer to the victim's body.

onus probandi, the burden of proof. The burden of proving its case rests with the side that makes the affirmation in a suit.

prima facie, on or at first appearance. **Prima facie** evidence is evidence that, at first presentation, is adequate enough to establish a fact.

PRACTICE EXERCISES

No. 50. Give the English for these Verb forms.

1. oppugnat
2. liberabant
3. videbo
4. manebit
5. erant
6. sunt
7. debent
8. amare
9. habebitis
10. pugnabas
11. dabant
12. erit
13. incitabunt
14. monebit
15. portare
16. timebit
17. pugnabis
18. superabimus
19. parabamus
20. erunt
21. narrabunt
22. incitabat
23. monebatis
24. sumus
25. oppugnabamus
26. incitabit
27. natabant
28. locabatis
29. servabis
30. iuvabitis

No. 51. Give the English for these phrases.

1. de caelo claro
2. finitimus patriae meae
3. propinquum insulis
4. cum amico nostro
5. ad aedificia alta
6. in fossis latis
7. gratus socio suo
8. ante agros
9. amicus servis
10. post bellum
11. inimici reginae
12. de victoria tua
13. per proelia multa
14. idoneus viro
15. sine praeda

No. 52. Give the tense of the following Verbs.

1. sum
2. monebunt
3. manebat
4. debet
5. erat
6. dabat
7. narrabit
8. oppugnant
9. pugnabis
10. erit
11. iuvabis
12. natabas
13. amabunt
14. timebat
15. incitabis
16. liberabam
17. debebit
18. narrabant
19. pugnabamus
20. erunt

No. 53. Translate the following into English.

1. Ad vias angustas ambulabit.
2. Ante templa stabant.
3. Ex oceano natabatis.
4. In aqua pugnabunt.
5. Feminis grata est.
6. Patriam liberam habere debebunt.
7. Puellae natabunt.
8. Finitimos suos amabat.
9. Avunculos tuos servabis.
10. Reginam laudabunt.
11. Ubi esse debetis?
12. Puerum vocabas.
13. Erit inimicus nuntio.
14. Non est provinciae propinquum.
15. Gladios tuos non timebimus.
16. Servi vestri iuvant.
17. Vir ibi manebit.
18. Fossam altam parabamus.
19. Dominus fabulam narrabit.
20. Agrum arabimus.

CHAPTER 13

READING

Gallia

1. **Patria Gallorum erat Germaniae et Hispaniae finitima.**
2. **Galli proelia et bella non amabant, sed bellum non timebant.**
3. **Romani contra Gallos saepe pugnabant et Galli pro patria sua tum bene pugnabant.**
4. **Romani in Gallia legatos habebant quod Galli Romanis amici non erant.**
5. **Legati bellum cum Gallis pugnare saepe parabant.**
6. **Caesar ob victorias suas in Gallia gloriam magnam habebat.**
7. **Oppida in Gallia erant clara.**
8. **Ibi erant oppida multa et pulchra ac silvae multae et agri boni.**
9. **Ob periculum belli Romani in multis terris finitimis legatos habebant.**
10. **Romani pro patria etiam sine praemiis magnis et praeda pugnabant.**
11. **Erant in Gallia multi agri lati atque agricolis idonea erat.**
12. **Cum in Gallia habitabant, Romani linguam Latinam tenebant.**

Gaul

1. The native country of the Gauls was neighboring to Germany and Spain.
2. The Gauls did not like battles and wars, but they did not fear war.
3. The Romans often fought against the Gauls and the Gauls then fought hard for their native country.
4. The Romans had lieutenants in Gaul because the Gauls were not friendly to the Romans.
5. The lieutenants often got ready to fight with the Gauls.
6. Caesar had great glory because of his victories in Gaul.
7. The towns in Gaul were famous.
8. There were many and beautiful towns there, and also many forests and good fields.
9. On account of the danger of war the Romans had legates in many neighboring lands.
10. The Romans fought for their country even without large rewards and booty.
11. There were many wide fields in Gaul and it was suitable for farmers.
12. When they were living in Gaul, the Romans kept the Latin language.

READING VOCABULARY

Nouns

memoria, memoriae, f., memory (memorize)
legatus, legati, m., lieutenant, legate (legation)
Gallia, Galliae, f., Gaul (the country) (Gallic)
Gallus, Galli, m., a Gaul (person)
Germanus, Germani, m., a German (person) (Germanic)

Verbs

teneo, tenere, hold, keep, have (tenable)
memoria tenere, to remember (literally, to keep by memory)

Prepositions

contra, against With the Accusative Case (contradict)
pro, for, in behalf of, on behalf of (procurator)

READING GRAMMAR

A. A Noun in apposition (that is, the same position or use in the sentence) with another Noun must be in the same case, and the same number.

Puella, filia legati, ibi est. The girl, the daughter of the lieutenant, is there.

In this sentence, **filia** is in apposition with **puella. Filia** is, therefore, also in the Nominative Case and also singular number.

B. The Vocative Case is the case of address and is used for the person or thing addressed directly. It is spelled the same as the Nominative Case, with these exceptions:

o-declension Nouns in the singular end in **-e** instead of **-us.** Thus,

puella, girl	**puellae,** girls
amice, friend	**amici,** friends
puer, boy	**pueri,** boys
bellum, war	**bella,** wars

The vocative singular of **filius** and proper Nouns ends in **-i.** Thus,

fili, son **filii,** sons **Mercuri,** Mercury

The vocative singular of **meus** is **mi.** Thus,

mea puella, my girl	**meae puellae,** my girls
mi puer, my boys	**mei pueri,** my boys

C. The Imperative of a Verb is used for a direct command. It is used with the second person singular and plural understood (you or ye not expressed).

1. **a-conjugation** Verbs form the Imperative:

SINGULAR	PLURAL
ama love; like	**amate** love; like

2. **e-conjugation** Verbs form the Imperative:

SINGULAR	PLURAL
habe have; hold	**habete** have; hold

FAMILIAR QUOTATIONS

Virginibus puerisque, For boys and girls. Horace

Non scholae sed vitae discimus, We learn not for school but for life. Seneca

Parvum parva decent, Small things become the small. Horace

Eheu fugaces anni, Alas the fleeting years. Horace

Vera amicitia est inter bonos, There is true friendship only among good men. Cicero

Ave atque vale, Hail and farewell. Catullus

Da dextram misero, Give your right hand to the wretched. Virgil

PRACTICE EXERCISES

No. 54. Translate these Imperatives.

1. **ambula**	5. **laudate**	9. **timete**	13. **tene**	17. **sta**
2. **amate**	6. **navigate**	10. **vide**	14. **regna**	18. **iuvate**
3. **natate**	7. **date**	11. **state**	15. **tenete**	19. **monete**
4. **pugna**	8. **habita**	12. **habete**	16. **superate**	20. **mane**

No. 55. Translate these Appositives.

1. **vir, agricola**
2. **viri, nautae**
3. **patria, Britannia**
4. **puer, amicus**
5. **regina, puella**
6. **Galli, socii nostri**
7. **nuntius, puer**
8. **Gallos, inimicos**
9. **dominum, amicum**
10. **filiorum, puerorum**

No. 56. Translate these Vocatives.

1. **amici**
2. **bella**
3. **deae**
4. **deus**
5. **domine**
6. **domina**
7. **fili**
8. **gloria**
9. **nuntii**
10. **mi serve**
11. **bone vir**
12. **bona lingua**
13. **multi amici**
14. **bone agricola**
15. **amice noster**

No. 57. Translate these sentences into English.

1. **Puer aeger, filius tuus, in oppido manebit.**
2. **In proelio, amice, socios habere debes.**
3. **Contra bellum, popule Romane, viros tuos incita.**
4. **Incolas Galliae, nuntii, monete.**
5. **Sabinos, finitimos nostros, ad ludos vocabo.**
6. **Templa, puellae, aedificia pulchra, videte.**
7. **Roma, oppidum in Italia, clara erit.**
8. **Galliam, fili mi, memoria tene.**
9. **Habebimusne, amici, forum magnum?**
10. **Avunculos meos, nuntios, exspectabo.**

THIRD REVIEW SECTION (CHAPTERS 10–13)

VOCABULARY REVIEW

NOUNS

1. aedificium	1. building
2. arca	2. chest, box
3. avunculus	3. uncle
4. barbarus	4. barbarian
5. finitimus	5. neighbor
6. forum	6. forum, market place
7. Gallia	7. Gaul
8. Gallus	8. a Gaul
9. Germanus	9. a German
10. Latinus	10. Latinus
11. Latium	11. Latium
12. legatus	12. lieutenant, legate
13. lingua	13. language
14. ludus	14. game
15. lupa	15. wolf
16. memoria	16. memory
17. populus	17. people
18. praemium	18. reward
19. ripa	19. river bank
20. Roma	20. Rome
21. Romanus	21. a Roman
22. Sabini	22. the Sabines
23. Troia	23. Troy
24. vita	24. life

ADJECTIVES

1. amicus	1. friendly
2. barbarus	2. savage, uncivilized, barbarian
3. finitimus	3. neighboring
4. gratus	4. pleasing
5. idoneus	5. fit, suitable
6. inimicus	6. unfriendly
7. latinus	7. Latin
8. propinquus	8. near

VERBS

1. debeo	1. owe, ought
2. incito	2. arouse, stir up, incite
3. loco	3. place, put
4. maneo	4. remain, stay
5. moneo	5. warn, advise
6. paro	6. prepare, get ready
7. propero	7. hurry, hasten
8. servo	8. save, preserve
9. teneo	9. hold, keep, have
10. memoria tenere	10. remember

ADVERBS

1. certe	1. certainly, indeed, surely
2. cras	2. tomorrow
3. ita	3. thus, so; yes
4. minime	4. not at all, by no means
5. nonne	5. expects the answer "yes"
6. num	6. expects the answer "no"
7. nunc	7. now
8. tum	8. then
9. vero	9. truly, in truth

PREPOSITIONS

1. contra	1. against
2. ob	2. on account of, because of
3. pro	3. for, in behalf of
4. sine	4. without

CONJUNCTION

1. atque, ac	1. and also, also

PRACTICE EXERCISES

No. 58. Tell whether these questions are simple questions, expect the answer yes, or expect the answer no.

1. **Estne aeger?**
2. **Ubi est puer?**
3. **Cur times?**
4. **Nonne memoria tenent?**
5. **Num manebat?**
6. **Nonne amici sunt?**
7. **Num manetis?**
8. **Properatne?**
9. **Cur debent?**
10. **Ubi arcam locat?**

No. 59. Change these Verbs to the Imperfect Tense.

1. **debeo**
2. **locas**
3. **incitat**
4. **properant**
5. **paratis**
6. **tenemus**
7. **servas**
8. **teneo**
9. **manemus**
10. **monet**

No. 60. Change these Verbs to the Future Tense.

1. **videbam**
2. **stabant**
3. **timebas**
4. **regnabat**
5. **necabatis**
6. **habebamus**
7. **aedificabam**
8. **superabas**
9. **curabamus**
10. **nuntiabant**

No. 61. Give the Singular and Plural Imperatives of these Infinitives.

1. **servare**
2. **monere**
3. **incitare**
4. **manere**
5. **navigare**
6. **parare**
7. **tenere**
8. **properare**
9. **necare**
10. **pugnare**

No. 62. Give the Singular and Plural Vocative of these Nouns.

1. **populus**
2. **memoria**
3. **legatus**
4. **amicus**
5. **femina**
6. **bellum**
7. **avunculus**
8. **vir**
9. **puer**
10. **puella**
11. **filius**
12. **agricola**

GAIUS IULIUS CAESAR

Caesar was born in Rome, of a noble family, in 100 B.C. He was educated as an orator and lawyer, but soon turned to politics and became consul in 59 B.C. For the next seven years he was proconsul in Gaul, where he was successful in subduing and conquering the Gallic tribes. The **Commentaries on the Gallic War** are a military history of this period. Caesar's refusal to surrender the command of his army led to Civil War, his long dictatorship, and political turmoil, resulting in his assassination in 44 B.C.

Natio est omnis Gallorum admodum dedita religionibus . . . Deum maxime Mercurium colunt. Huius sunt plurima simulacra; hunc omnium inventorem artium ferunt, hunc viarum atque itinerum ducem, hunc ad quaestus	The entire nation of the Gauls is quite devoted to religious rites . . . They worship the god Mercury especially. There are very many statues of him; they say he is the inventor of all the arts, they believe he is the guide on roads

pecuniae mercaturasque habere vim maximam arbitrantur. Post hunc Apollinem et Martem et Iovem et Minervam. De his eandum fere, quam reliquae gentes, habent opinionem: Apollinem morbos depellere, Minervam operum atque artificiorum initia tradere, Iovem imperium caelestium tenere, Martem bella regere.

Commentarii de Bello Gallico, VI, xvi, xvii

and journeys, and that he has the greatest power over money transactions and merchants. After him come Apollo and Mars and Jupiter and Minerva. About these, they have almost the same idea as other races: Apollo dispels diseases, Minerva hands down the skills of handcrafts and arts, Jupiter holds the power over the gods, and Mars rules over wars.

Commentaries on the Gallic War, 6, 16, 17

THE BIBLE

In principio creavit Deus caelum et terram. Terra autem erat inanis et vacua, et tenebrae erant super faciem abyssi, et spiritus Dei ferebatur super aquas.

Dixitque Deus: Fiat lux. Et facta est lux. Et vidit Deus lucem quod esset bona et divisit lucem a tenebris. Appellavitque lucem diem et tenebras noctem. Factumque est vespere et mane, dies unus.

Dixit quoque Deus: Fiat firmamentum in medio aquarum et dividit aquas ab aquis. Et fecit Deus firmamentum, divisitque aquas, quae erant sub firmamento, ab his quae erant super firmamentum. Et factum est ita. Vocavitque Deus firmamentum caelum. Et factum est vespere et mane, dies secundus.

Dixit vero Deus: Congregentur aquae, quae sub caelo sunt, in locum unum, et appareat arida. Et factum est ita. Et vocavit Deus aridam terram congregationesque aquarum appellavit maria. Et vidit Deus quod esset bonum. Et ait: Germinet terra herbam virentem et facientem semen et lignum pomiferum faciens fructum iuxta genus suum, cuius semen in semetipso sit super terram. Et factum est ita. Et protulit terra herbam virentem et facientem semen iuxta genus suum lignumque faciens fructum et habens unumquodque sementem secundum speciem suam. Et vidit Deus quod esset bonum. Et factum est vespere et mane, dies tertius.

Liber Genesis I, i–xiii

In the beginning God created the heaven and the earth. And the earth was without form, and void; and darkness was upon the face of the deep. And the Spirit of God moved upon the face of the waters.

And God said: Let there be light. And there was light. And God saw the light, that it was good; and God divided the light from the darkness. And God called the light Day, and the darkness he called Night. And the evening and the morning were the first day.

And God said: Let there be a firmament in the midst of the waters, and let it divide the waters from the waters. And God made the firmament, and divided the waters which were under the firmament from the waters which were above the firmament. And it was so. And God called the firmament Heaven. And the evening and the morning were the second day.

And God said: Let the waters under the heaven be gathered together unto one place, and let the dry land appear. And it was so. And God called the dry land Earth; and the gathering together of the waters called he Seas. And God saw that it was good. And God said: Let the earth bring forth grass, the herb yielding seed, and the fruit tree yielding fruit after his kind, whose seed is in itself, upon the earth. And it was so. And the earth brought forth grass, and herb yielding seed after his kind, and the tree yielding fruit, whose seed was in itself, after his kind. And God saw that it was good. And the evening and the morning were the third day.

Genesis I, 1–13

CHAPTER 14

READING

Germani	The Germans
1. **Germania Galliae finitima erat et Italiae propinqua.**	1. Germany was neighboring to Gaul and near Italy.
2. **Incolae Germaniae, terrae magnae, non in oppidis magnis et pulchris, sed in silvis aut in casis parvis habitabant, quod barbari erant.**	2. The inhabitants of Germany, a big country, did not live in large and beautiful towns, but in the forests or in small cottages, because they were uncivilized.
3. **Inter Germanos erant multi sagittarii boni et in silvis lupae multae sagittis Germanorum necabantur.**	3. Among the Germans there were many good archers and in the forests many wolves used to be killed by the arrows of the Germans.
4. **Multae terrae et patriae a Vandiliis oppugnabantur atque superabantur.**	4. Many lands and native countries used to be attacked by the Vandals and conquered.
5. **Germani populis Galliae et Italiae non erant amici.**	5. The Germans were not friendly to the peoples of Gaul and Italy.
6. **Vandilii robusti Italiam oppugnabant et populus certe terrebatur quod pro vita sua timebat.**	6. The strong Vandals attacked Italy and the people were indeed frightened because they feared for their lives.
7. **Ubi Vandilii populum superabant, multi vero erant miseri.**	7. When the Vandals conquered the people, many were truly wretched.

READING VOCABULARY

Nouns

pecunia, pecuniae, f., money (pecuniary)
donum, doni, n., gift, present (donation)
sagitta, sagittae, f., arrow (sagittal)
sagittarius, sagittarii or **sagittari, m.,** archer (Sagittarius)
littera, litterae, f., letter (of the alphabet) In the plural, a letter or epistle (literal, literature)

Adjective

robustus, robusta, robustum, strong, robust

Adverb

mox, soon, presently

Verbs

moveo, movere, move (movable)
castra movere, to break camp
doleo, dolere, grieve, be sorry (dolorous)
terreo, terrere, frighten, scare, terrify (terrorize)

Prepositions

a or **ab,** by; away from, from With the Ablative Case (absent)
inter, between, among With the Accusative Case (interlinear)

Conjunction

aut, or

READING GRAMMAR

A. The Passive Voice of a Verb shows the subject as the receiver of the action.

Puer amatur., The boy is loved.

The Passive Voice of the Present, Imperfect, and Future Tenses is formed in the same way as the Active Voice, except that the personal endings are passive instead of active.

1. Present Passive Tense

a-conjugation		e-conjugation	
amor	I am loved; being loved	**habeor**	I am held; being held
amaris	you are loved; being loved	**haberis**	you are held; being held
amatur	he, she, it is loved; being loved	**habetur**	he, she, it is held; being held
amamur	we are loved; being loved	**habemur**	we are held; being held
amamini	you are loved; being loved	**habemini**	you are held; being held
amantur	they are loved; being loved	**habentur**	they are held; being held

2. Imperfect Passive Tense

a-conjugation		e-conjugation	
amabar	I was loved; being loved	**habebar**	I was held; being held
amabaris	you were loved; etc.	**habebaris**	you were held; etc.
amabatur	he, she, it was loved; etc.	**habebatur**	he, she, it was held; etc.
amabamur	we were loved; etc.	**habebamur**	we were held; etc.
amabamini	you were loved; etc.	**habebamini**	you were held; etc.
amabantur	they were loved; etc.	**habebantur**	they were held; etc.

3. Future Passive Tense

a-conjugation		e-conjugation	
amabor	I shall be loved	**habebor**	I shall be held
amaberis	you will be loved	**habeberis**	you will be held
amabitur	he, she, it will be loved	**habebitur**	he, she, it will be held
amabimur	we shall be loved	**habebimur**	we shall be held
amabimini	you will be loved	**habebimini**	you will be held
amabuntur	they will be loved	**habebuntur**	they will be held

The only irregularities are in the Future Tense: **amaberis, habeberis.**
The Passive Voice of **video** often means "seem".

B. The doer of the action expressed by a Passive Verb is in the Ablative Case with the Preposition **a** or **ab.** It is always a person.

Puer ab agricola amatur. The boy is loved by the farmer.

C. The thing by which the action of either an Active or a Passive Verb is done is in the Ablative Case, without any Preposition.

Puer sagitta necatur. The boy is killed by an arrow.
Puer sagitta lupam necat. The boy kills the wolf with an arrow.

FAMILIAR PHRASES

vi et armis, by force and arms.
pax vobiscum, peace be with you.
tempus fugit, time flies.
agenda, things that have to be done.
sic passim, thus everywhere.
multum in parvo, much in little.
senatus populusque Romanus, the Senate and the Roman people. Abbr. S.P.Q.R.
res gestae, things done; acts or deeds.
alter idem, another self, referring to a close friend.
apparatus criticus, critical apparatus or material; reference material used in the critical study of a piece of literature.

PRACTICE EXERCISES

No. 63. Give the English for the following.

1. **timeberis**	6. **stabo**	11. **necabat**	16. **monstrabar**
2. **laudabam**	7. **armabatur**	12. **aedificabuntur**	17. **ambulabant**
3. **curor**	8. **aras**	13. **superabo**	18. **dabitur**
4. **laudantur**	9. **occupabitur**	14. **navigabit**	19. **iuvamini**
5. **narrabuntur**	10. **stabitis**	15. **habitabam**	20. **vocabor**

No. 64. Change these Verbs to the Passive Voice.

1. **exspectabam**	6. **habet**	11. **laudabunt**	16. **monebas**
2. **tenent**	7. **videbatis**	12. **locatis**	17. **servas**
3. **monebit**	8. **portabit**	13. **properabunt**	18. **debebat**
4. **videbat**	9. **movebitis**	14. **timemus**	19. **vident**
5. **amabit**	10. **parant**	15. **incito**	20. **monebant**

No. 65. Give the English for these phrases, in the Ablative Case.

1. **cum legato**	6. **a nuntio**	11. **equis**	16. **sapientia**
2. **gladio**	7. **cum avunculis**	12. **sagittis**	17. **a populo**
3. **a pueris**	8. **bellis**	13. **a sagittario**	18. **cum inimicis**
4. **fossis**	9. **ab dominis**	14. **a dea**	19. **aqua**
5. **ab amicis**	10. **cum socio**	15. **cum servo**	20. **ab viro**

No. 66. Translate the following into English.

1. **Pecunia viro atque puellae dabitur quod puer aeger est.**
2. **Memoria tenebar cum ad oppidum finitimum movebam.**
3. **Dolere videntur sed donum portabitur.**
4. **Ob pericula viri litteras timebant.**
5. **Pro Britannia, patria vestra, bene pugnate.**
6. **Multi ad templa deorum ambulabant.**
7. **Ubi ludus ab amico vestro dabitur?**
8. **In casa ubi puellas videtis habitabamus.**
9. **Num vir gladio oppugnabitur?**
10. **Nonne populus castra movere parabat?**

CHAPTER 15

READING

Cincinnatus

1. **Roma pacem saepe non habebat, sed in periculo erat et contra finitimos suos pugnabat.**
2. **Roma copias bonas atque arma habebat, sed oppugnabatur et populus caput habere debebat quod terrebatur.**
3. **Nuntii ad Cincinnatum properant et ubi Cincinnatum, agricolam Romanum, in agro vident, de bello et magno periculo narrant.**
4. **Cincinnatus agros suos bene amabat et bellum gratum non erat, sed Romam bene amabat et ab nuntiis movebatur.**
5. **Populo Romano magnum auxilium portabat quod dictator erat et Romam servabat.**
6. **Copiae Romanae a periculo patriam suam liberabant et Cincinnatus a Romanis semper memoria tenebatur.**

Cincinnatus

1. Often Rome did not have peace, but was in danger and fought against her neighbors.
2. Rome had good troops and weapons, but she was being attacked and the people needed to have a leader because they were frightened.
3. Messengers hurry to Cincinnatus and when they see Cincinnatus, a Roman farmer, in the field they tell about the war and great danger.
4. Cincinnatus loved his fields well and war was not pleasing, but he loved Rome very much and was moved by the messengers.
5. He brought great help to the Roman people because he was dictator and he saved Rome.
6. The Roman troops freed their country from danger and Cincinnatus was always remembered by the Romans.

Horatius

1. **Magnae copiae hostium Romam oppugnabant.**
2. **Pars urbis Romae erat in periculo quod hostes pontem ibi occupare parabant.**
3. **Homines Romae ab Horatio, milite bono, contra hostes incitabantur, sed pontem non tenebant.**
4. **Tum Horatius in ponte sine auxilio stat. Pro vita sua non timet.**
5. **Gladio suo multos milites hostium mox necat et hostes ab ponte tenet. Magna erat caedes.**
6. **Post Horatium milites Romani laborabant et mox pons non stabat.**
7. **Romani victoriam habent et Roma servatur quod aqua inter Romam et hostes stat.**
8. **Horatius trans aquam ad ripam ubi erant socii natat.**
9. **Horatius inter Romanos laudabatur et multi agri Horatio dabantur.**

Horatius

1. Large forces of the enemy were attacking Rome.
2. Part of the city of Rome was in danger because the enemy was preparing to seize the bridge there.
3. The men of Rome were being stirred up against the enemy by Horatius, a good soldier, but they did not hold the bridge.
4. Then Horatius stood on the bridge without aid. He did not fear for his life.
5. Soon he killed many of the enemy's soldiers with his sword and held the enemy away from the bridge. The slaughter was great.
6. In back of Horatius the Roman soldiers were working and soon the bridge was not standing.
7. The Romans had the victory and Rome was saved because the water stood between Rome and the enemy.
8. Horatius swam across the water to the river bank where his comrades were.
9. Horatius was praised among the Romans and many fields were given to Horatius.

READING VOCABULARY

Nouns

miles, militis, m., soldier (military)
pax, pacis, f., peace (pacific)
caput, capitis, n., head (capital)
dictator, dictatoris, m., dictator (dictatorial)
homo, hominis, m., man (homicide)
Cincinnatus, Cincinnati, m., Cincinnatus
hostis, hostis, m., enemy **(hostium)** (hostile)
pars, partis, f., part **(partium)** (partake, particle)
mare, maris, n., sea **(marium)** (marine)
urbs, urbis, f., city **(urbium)** (suburb)
caedes, caedis, f., slaughter, murder **(caedium)**
pons, pontis, m., bridge **(pontium)** (pontoon)
Horatius, Horati, m., Horatius

Adverb

semper, always, ever (sempiternal)

Hostis in the singular means an individual enemy in war; in the plural, it is a collective noun, the enemy, and its Verb must also be plural.

READING GRAMMAR

A. **i-declension** Nouns.

1. More Nouns belong to the **i-declension** than to any other declension.
2. **i-declension** Nouns are masculine, feminine, and neuter. The masculine and feminine have the same endings.
3. **i-declension** Nouns have a wide variety of spellings. The Genitive Case always ends in **-is.**

B. **i-declension** Nouns are divided into two groups—those that have **-ium** for the Genitive Plural ending and those that have **-um.** From now on those Nouns that have **-ium** in the Genitive Plural will be indicated in the Vocabulary. These Nouns may have **-i** as an alternate ending in the Ablative Singular.

1. **i-declension** Nouns with **-ium** in the Genitive Plural.

Masculine or Feminine

SINGULAR		USE	PLURAL	
urbs	the city	subject	**urbes**	the cities
urbis	of the city	possession	**urbium**	of the cities
urbi	to, for the city	indirect object	**urbibus**	to, for the cities
urbem	the city	direct object	**urbes**	the cities
urbe, urbi	from, with, by, in the city	prepositional phrases	**urbibus**	from, with, by, in the cities

Neuter

SINGULAR		USE	PLURAL	
mare	the sea	subject	**maria**	the seas
maris	of the sea	possession	**marium**	of the seas
mari	to, for the sea	indirect object	**maribus**	to, for the seas
mare	the sea	direct object	**maria**	the seas
mare, mari	from, with, by, in the sea	prepositional phrases	**maribus**	from, with, by, in the seas

Notice that the Neuter Plural Nominative and Accusative end in **-ia.**

2. **i-declension** Nouns with **-um** in the Genitive Plural.

Masculine and Feminine

SINGULAR		USE	PLURAL	
homo	the man	subject	**homines**	the men
hominis	of the man	possession	**hominum**	of the men
homini	to, for the man	indirect object	**hominibus**	to, for the men
hominem	the man	direct object	**homines**	the men
homine	from, with, by, in the man	prepositional phrases	**hominibus**	from, with, by, in the men

Neuter

SINGULAR		USE	PLURAL	
caput	the head	subject	**capita**	the heads
capitis	of the head	possession	**capitum**	of the heads
capiti	to, for the head	indirect object	**capitibus**	to, for the heads
caput	the head	direct object	**capita**	the heads
capite	from, with, by, in the head	prepositional phrases	**capitibus**	from, with, by, in the heads

SUFFIXES

Suffixes are applied to the stems of Nouns and Adjectives to give a certain meaning to both Latin and English words or to form one part of speech from another. These are some of the more common suffixes that are added to Latin words to give them a special meaning:

-tor (masc.), **-trix** (fem.) denote the doer or agent. English, -er, -or.

victor, conqueror
genitor, father
genetrix, mother

-or denotes an action or state. English, -or.

terror, fear, terror

-tio denotes an action. English, -tion.

natio, nation

-ia, -tia, -tudo, -tas denote quality or state.

-ia becomes -y in English.

miseria, misery
iniuria, injury
victoria, victory

-tia becomes -ce, -ship, -ness in English.

potentia, force
amicitia, friendship
laetitia, happiness.

-tudo becomes -tude in English.

longitudo, longitude
latitudo, latitude
altitudo, altitude
magnitudo, magnitude

-tas becomes -ty in English.

gravitas, gravity
dignitas, dignity

PRACTICE EXERCISES

No. 67. Give the English for the following phrases.

1. **pacis longae**
2. **pro milite**
3. **milites clari**
4. **pax Romana**
5. **capita vestra**
6. **dictatoribus suis**
7. **caput tuum**
8. **ab hominibus laetis**
9. **pars idonea**
10. **in urbe antiqua**
11. **maris nostri**
12. **milites robustos**
13. **homines boni**
14. **pacem longam**
15. **in capitibus suis**
16. **contra dictatores**
17. **cum hominibus**
18. **sine militibus tuis**
19. **de pace grata**
20. **homo amicus**

No. 68. Fill in the blanks with the correct English.

1. **militum,** ________ the soldiers	6. **maria,** ________ seas
2. **pacis,** ________ peace	7. **cum milite,** ________ the soldier
3. **caput,** ________ head	8. **pontium,** ________ the bridges
4. **partem,** ________ part	9. **hostes,** ________ enemy
5. **in urbibus,** ________ the cities	10. **de caede,** ________ slaughter

No. 69. Change each of the following to the plural, and give the English.

1. **pax**	5. **hosti**	9. **homo**	13. **hominem**	17. **maris**
2. **milite**	6. **urbis**	10. **caput**	14. **pacis**	18. **pontis**
3. **capiti**	7. **caedem**	11. **militis**	15. **dictatorem**	19. **hostem**
4. **partem**	8. **pons**	12. **partis**	16. **ponti**	20. **urbe**

No. 70. Translate the following into English.

1. **Cincinnatus ex agro suo vocabatur et auxilium dabat.**
2. **Homines in terra regnant sed dei caelum atque terram regnant.**
3. **Praemia homini magno ab populo Romano dabuntur.**
4. **Lingua Latina semper servabitur.**
5. **Cras non arabit sed patriam nostram mox servabit.**
6. **Ad ripam natabat quod pons non stabat.**
7. **Gladio pro patria tua, Horati, bene pugna.**
8. **Milites, filii mei, gladiis armabuntur.**
9. **Ob pericula tuam aquam servare debes.**
10. **Nauta mare amat sed agricola agros suos amat.**

CHAPTER 16

READING

Daedalus et Icarus	Daedalus and Icarus
1. **Daedalus hominem necat et cum filio suo, Icaro, ex Graecia ad Cretam, insulam in mari, properat.**	1. Daedalus killed a man and with his son, Icarus, hurried from Greece to Crete, an island in the sea.
2. **Parva in insula diu manebant et tum pater filiusque ad Graeciam volare parant.**	2. They stayed for a long time on the small island and then the father and son prepared to fly toward Greece.
3. **Bene laborant et alas parant.**	3. They work hard and get wings ready.
4. **Pater puerum monet: "Per caelum, sed non ad solem volabimus."**	4. The father warns the boy: "We shall fly through the sky, but not toward the sun."
5. **Sol erat clarus et Icarus ob alas suas erat laetus.**	5. The sun was bright and Icarus was happy because of his wings.
6. **Consilium patris sui non diu memoria tenebat.**	6. He did not remember the advice of his father for long.
7. **Cum patre suo non manebat, sed summo in caelo ante solem volebat.**	7. He did not stay with his father, but flew very high in the sky in front of the sun.

Daedalus et Icarus

8. **Cera in alis pueri non manebat.**
9. **Pater filium suum medio in mari mox videt.**
10. **Icarus non servatur et Daedalus vero dolebat quod puer consilio patris non bene monebatur.**

Daedalus and Icarus

8. The wax did not stay on the boy's wings.
9. The father soon sees his son in the middle of the sea.
10. Icarus was not saved and Daedalus was truly grieved because the boy was not well warned by his father's advice.

READING VOCABULARY

Nouns

Daedalus, Daedali, m., Daedalus
Icarus, Icari, m., Icarus
Creta, Cretae, f., Crete
labor, laboris, m., work, toil, labor (laboratory)
magnitudo, magnitudinis, f., size, great size (magnitude)
celeritas, celeritatis, f., speed, swiftness (celerity, accelerator)
virtus, virtutis, f., courage, valor (virtue)
natio, nationis, f., nation (national)
consilium, consilii or **consili, n.,** plan, advice (council)
pater, patris, m., father (paternal)
cera, cerae, f., wax (ceramics)
ala, alae, f., wing (alar)
sol, solis, m., sun (solar)

Adjectives

medius, media, medium, middle, middle of (medium)
summus, summa, summum, greatest, highest, top of (summit, sum)

Verb

volo, volare, fly (volatile)

Adverb

diu, long, for a long time

Conjunctions

-que, and
et...et, both...and

Preposition

circum, around, about (circumnavigate)

READING GRAMMAR

A. As you notice in the reading, the Preposition **in** (in, on) may stand after the Adjective and before the Noun.

parva in insula, on a small island **medio in caelo,** in the middle of the sky

B. The Conjunction **-que** (and) never stands alone, but is added to the second of two similarly used words or phrases. **-que** is the same as **et** in front of a word.

vir feminaque, the man and the woman **pueris puellisque,** to the boys and girls

C. The "of" in "in the middle of" or "top of" is part of the Adjective and therefore does not affect the case of the Noun. The Noun has whatever case it would have anyway and the Adjective simply agrees with the Noun.

in caelo, in the sky **medio in caelo,** in the middle of the sky
in terra, on the land **in summa terra,** on the top of the land

D. These rules are helpful in remembering the gender of some **i-declension** Nouns.
1. Nouns in -**or** are usually masculine. **labor**
2. Nouns in -**io** are usually feminine. **natio**
3. Nouns in -**tudo**, -**tus**, or -**tas** are feminine. **magnitudo, virtus, celeritas**

CHEMICAL ELEMENTS

The following are some of the Chemical Elements, with their Latin derivations.

Calcium Ca from **calx, calcis**, lime.
Carbon C from **carbo**, coal.
Copper Cu from **cuprum**, derived from the island Cyprus, anciently renowned for its copper mines.
Gold Au from **aurum**, gold.
Iron Fe from **ferrum**, iron.
Lead Pb from **plumbum**, lead.
Radium Ra from **radius**, ray, because of the alpha, beta, and gamma rays.
Silicon Si from **silex, silicis**, flint.
Silver Ag from **argentum**, silver.
Tellurium Te from **tellus, telluris**, earth.

PRACTICE EXERCISES

No. 71. Give the English for the following.

1. **dei et deae**
2. **deus deaque**
3. **tenemus et damus**
4. **tenebat dabatque**
5. **hominem et feminas**
6. **hominum feminarumque**
7. **ad solem et lunam**
8. **ad solem lunamque**
9. **ex mare et terra**
10. **ex terra mareque**

No. 72. Translate these phrases.

1. **in mediis viis**
2. **multis in oppidis**
3. **bello in magno**
4. **in summis aedificiis**
5. **parte in bona**
6. **in oceanis latis**
7. **multis in terris**
8. **medio in caelo**
9. **summo in mare**
10. **medio in oceano**

No. 73. Translate these phrases.

1. **ad mare**
2. **ex urbibus**
3. **cum patribus suis**
4. **ante forum**
5. **post templum**
6. **de arca**
7. **sine consilio**
8. **trans oceanum**
9. **per maria**
10. **ob alas**
11. **pro regina tua**
12. **contra populum**
13. **inter hostes**
14. **ab viris**
15. **ab oppidis**
16. **ante castra**
17. **per pericula**
18. **ad dominum**
19. **trans agrum**
20. **de pace**

No. 74. Give the English for these Verbs.

1. **erit**
2. **terrebitur**
3. **volabat**
4. **natabit**
5. **dolent**
6. **portamur**
7. **tenebatur**
8. **amabimur**
9. **movebo**
10. **laudabantur**
11. **pugnabat**
12. **locabis**
13. **vocabor**
14. **monebamur**
15. **laborabunt**
16. **incitantur**
17. **debebit**
18. **parant**
19. **curabantur**
20. **liberaberis**

No. 75. Translate these Vocatives and Appositives.

1. **Homo, avunculus meus**
2. **Amici boni**
3. **Fili bone**
4. **Nationum, Italiae Germaniaeque**
5. **Ob pecuniam, praemium**
6. **Feminarum, reginarum**
7. **Vir clare**
8. **Puer, servus**
9. **Puellis, filiis meis**
10. **Pater noster**

CHAPTER 17

READING

Proserpina

1. Ceres, dea frumenti, filiam, Proserpinam, habebat.
2. Pluto, deus Inferorum, Proserpinam in agro videt et ad Inferos Proserpinam portat.
3. Quod filiam suam non videbat, Ceres, mater, dolebat.
4. Quod Ceres misera erat, frumentum in agris agricolarum non erat.
5. Tum Iuppiter vitam populi in terra servat quod Mercurium vocat et Mercurius pro Iove ad Plutonem nuntium portat.
6. Iuppiter movebatur et agricolis auxilium dabat.
7. Tum Proserpina cum Iove non semper manebat, sed in terra partem anni habebat.
8. Cum Proserpina in terra erat, Ceres laeta erat et agricolis copiam magnam frumenti dabat, sed cum Proserpina sub terra erat Ceres misera erat et frumentum non erat.

Proserpina

1. Ceres, the goddess of grain, had a daughter, Proserpina.
2. Pluto, god of Those Below, saw Proserpina in a field and carried Proserpina to Those Below.
3. Because she did not see her daughter, Ceres, the mother, grieved.
4. Because Ceres was unhappy, there was not grain in the farmers' fields.
5. Then Jupiter saved the lives of the people on earth because he called Mercury and Mercury carried a message for Jupiter to Pluto.
6. Jupiter was moved and gave help to the farmers.
7. Then Proserpina did not always stay with Jupiter, but had part of the year on earth.
8. When Proserpina was on the earth, Ceres was happy and gave a great plenty of grain to the farmers, but when Proserpina was under the earth Ceres was unhappy and there was not grain.

Colosseum

1. Romani in urbe sua aedificia multa habebant.
2. Colosseum bene amabant quod ludos ibi spectabant.
3. Colosseum erat magnum amphitheatrum et etiam nunc stat.
4. Milites Romani bello servos captivosque obtinebant.
5. Captivi, gladiatores, gladiis suis contra homines aut contra animalia ibi pugnabant.
6. Multi captivi virtutem magnam habebant et liberabantur quod bene pugnabant.

The Colosseum

1. The Romans had many buildings in their city.
2. They liked the Colosseum very much because they watched the games there.
3. The Colosseum was a large amphitheater and is standing even now.
4. The Roman soldiers secured slaves and captives in war.
5. The captives, as gladiators, fought there with their swords against men or against animals.
6. Many captives had great courage and were freed because they fought well.

READING VOCABULARY

Verbs

specto, spectare, spectavi, spectatus, look at, watch (spectacle)

obtineo, obtinere, obtinui, obtentus, secure, obtain (obtainable)

Preposition

sub, under, below, at the foot of (subordinate)

1. With the Accusative Case after Verbs showing motion.
2. With the Ablative Case after Verbs showing rest.

Nouns

annus, anni, m., year (annual)
mater, matris, f., mother (maternal)
Inferi, Inferorum, m. pl., Those Below, the shades of Hades
Ceres, Cereris, f., Ceres (cereal)
Proserpina, Proserpinae, f., Proserpina
Mercurius, Mercuri, m., Mercury (mercurial)
Iuppiter, Iovis, m., Jupiter (jovial)
Pluto, Plutonis, m., Pluto (plutonium)
animal, animalis, n., animal **(animalium)**
captivus, captivi, m., captive (captivity)
amphitheatrum, amphitheatri, n., amphitheater (amphitheatrical)
gladiator, gladiatoris, m., gladiator (gladiatorial)
Colosseum, Colossei, n., the Colosseum (colossal)

READING GRAMMAR

You have already had two of the Principal Parts of Verbs:

1. **amo, habeo** First Person Singular Present Active Tense.
2. **amare, habere** Present Active Infinitive.

A. The first two Principal Parts are used to form the tenses you have had so far:
1. Present Tense, Active and Passive
2. Imperfect Tense, Active and Passive
3. Future Tense, Active and Passive

B. The second Principal Part shows the conjugation to which the Verb belongs:
1. **amare, a-conjugation**
2. **habere, e-conjugation**

C. The third Principal Part is the First Person Singular Perfect Active Tense.

1. **amavi, a-conjugation** I have loved
I have liked
2. **habui, e-conjugation** I have had
I have held

D. The fourth Principal Part is the Perfect Passive Participle.

1. **amatus, a-conjugation** having been loved
having been liked
2. **habitus, e-conjugation** having been had
having been held

Most of the **a-conjugation** Verbs form their Principal parts like **amo:**

amo, amare, amavi, amatus

Those that do not are:

do, dare, dedi, datus	give
iuvo, iuvare, iuvi, iutus	help, aid
sto, stare, steti, status	stand

Many of the **e-conjugation** Verbs form their Principal Parts like **habeo.**

habeo, habere, habui, habitus

Of those you have met so far, these do not:

maneo, manere, mansi, mansus	remain, stay
moveo, movere, movi, motus	move
video, videre, vidi, visus	see

The Principal Parts of **sum** are: **sum, esse, fui, futurus**

futurus is the Future Active Participle—about to be

PREFIXES

These Latin Prepositions are commonly used as prefixes.

e, ex, out. **exspecto,** look out for, wait for, expect.
per, through; thoroughly, very. **perduco,** lead through. **pervenio,** arrive (come thoroughly).
inter, between. **interpono,** put between.
in, in, on; into; not. **invenio,** discover (come on). **infirmus,** weak (not firm, not strong).
trans, across. **transmitto,** send across.

PRACTICE EXERCISES

No. 76. Give the Present Active Infinitive of these Verbs and the English translation.

1. voco	**5. sum**	**9. curo**	**13. terreo**	**17. servo**
2. debeo	**6. moneo**	**10. doleo**	**14. adoro**	**18. laudo**
3. ambulo	**7. timeo**	**11. nuntio**	**15. moveo**	**19. do**
4. sto	**8. narro**	**12. volo**	**16. paro**	**20. video**

No. 77. Give the third Principal Part, the First Person Singular Perfect Active Tense, and the translation.

1. paro	**5. libero**	**9. habito**	**13. do**	**17. timeo**
2. incito	**6. loco**	**10. moneo**	**14. teneo**	**18. nato**
3. aro	**7. terreo**	**11. propero**	**15. servo**	**19. moveo**
4. debeo	**8. aedifico**	**12. habeo**	**16. monstro**	**20. maneo**

No. 78. Give the fourth Principal Part, the Perfect Passive Participle, and the translation.

1. amo	**5. moneo**	**9. occupo**	**13. servo**	**17. moveo**
2. habeo	**6. exspecto**	**10. porto**	**14. iuvo**	**18. specto**
3. libero	**7. narro**	**11. do**	**15. video**	**19. obtineo**
4. neco	**8. terreo**	**12. moneo**	**16. adoro**	**20. loco**

No. 79. Translate the following into English.

1. **Et mater tua et pater vester de virtute consilium dabant.**
2. **Medio in oppido erant aedificia multa.**
3. **Fama de natione mea ab nuntiis portabitur.**
4. **Puella puerque sub aqua natant.**
5. **Circum urbem ambulare et multa videre debemus.**
6. **Nonne multa mala memoria tenes?**
7. **Sol summa in aqua esse videbatur.**
8. **Nationes Europae non semper pugnabunt.**
9. **Nautae in maribus oceanisque navigant.**
10. **Milites Romani virtutem magnam habent.**

FOURTH REVIEW SECTION (CHAPTERS 14–17)

VOCABULARY REVIEW

NOUNS

1. ala	16. dictator	31. miles	1. wing	16. dictator	31. soldier
2. amphitheatrum	17. donum	32. natio	2. amphitheater	17. gift	32. nation
3. animal	18. gladiator	33. pars	3. animal	18. gladiator	33. part
4. annus	19. homo	34. pater	4. year	19. man	34. father
5. caedes	20. Horatius	35. pax	5. slaughter	20. Horatius	35. peace
6. captivus	21. hostis	36. pecunia	6. captive	21. enemy	36. money
7. caput	22. Icarus	37. Pluto	7. head	22. Icarus	37. Pluto
8. celeritas	23. Inferi	38. pons	8. speed, swiftness	23. Those Below	38. bridge
9. cera	24. Iuppiter	39. Proserpina	9. wax	24. Jupiter	39. Proserpina
10. Ceres	25. labor	40. sagitta	10. Ceres	25. work, toil, labor	40. arrow
11. Cincinnatus	26. littera	41. sagittarius	11. Cincinnatus	26. letter	41. archer
12. Colosseum	27. magnitudo	42. sol	12. the Colosseum	27. size, great size	42. sun
13. consilium	28. mare	43. stella	13. plan, advice	28. sea	43. star
14. Creta	29. mater	44. urbs	14. Crete	29. mother	44. city
15. Daedalus	30. Mercurius	45. virtus	15. Daedalus	30. Mercury	45. courage, valor

ADJECTIVES

1. medius	1. middle, middle of
2. robustus	2. strong, robust
3. summus	3. greatest, highest, top of

VERBS

1. doleo	1. grieve
2. moveo	2. move
3. obtineo	3. secure, obtain
4. specto	4. look at, watch
5. terreo	5. frighten, terrify, scare
6. volo	6. fly

ADVERBS

1. diu	1. long, for a long time
2. mox	2. soon, presently
3. semper	3. always

PREPOSITIONS

1. a, ab	1. by; away from, from
2. circum	2. around, about
3. inter	3. among, between
4. sub	4. under

CONJUNCTIONS

1. aut	1. or
2. et . . . et	2. both . . . and
3. -que	3. and

PRACTICE EXERCISES

No. 80. Complete these Infinitives by filling in the correct vowel.

1. dol______re
2. terr______re
3. mov______re
4. voc______re
5. obtin______re
6. d______re
7. spect______re
8. vol______re
9. laud______re
10. man______re
11. deb______re
12. tim______re
13. hab______re
14. vid______re
15. nec______re
16. par______re
17. occup______re
18. st______re
19. iuv______re
20. mon______re

No. 81. Fill in the missing principal part.

1. specto, spectare, ________, spectatus
2. curo, ________, curavi, curatus
3. ________, monere, monui, monitus
4. do, dare, ________, datus
5. moveo, movere, movi, ________
6. paro, parare, ________, paratus
7. servo, servare, servavi, ________
8. terreo, terrere, terrui, ________
9. ________, habitare, habitavi, habitatus
10. laudo, ________, laudavi, laudatus

No. 82. Translate these phrases.

1. animalium hominumque
2. ab patre
3. a matribus
4. mare stellamque
5. patres matresque
6. celeritatis magnitudinisque
7. a Mercurio
8. ab militibus
9. a Plutone
10. bellum paxque

No. 83. Translate these Verb forms.

1. laudabatur
2. dolebunt
3. monebamur
4. necantur
5. vocamini
6. obtinebimus
7. videris
8. iuvabatis
9. habebo
10. moveberis
11. occupantur
12. timebantur
13. parabitur
14. dabis
15. servaris
16. parabamur
17. debebitur
18. curabaris
19. spectabamur
20. terrebunt

EUTROPIUS

Very little is known about Eutropius except that he held official positions in Rome and the provinces, and may have been a secretary to the Emperor Constantine. Of his works, the only one extant is the **Breviarium**, a brief history of Rome from the founding of the city in 753 B.C. to 364 A.D.

Hic quoque ingens bellum civile commovit cogente uxore Cleopatra, regina Aegypti, dum cupiditate muliebri optat etiam in urbe regnare. Victus est ab Augusto navali pugna clara et inlustri apud Actium, qui locus in Epiro est, ex qua fugit in Aegyptum et desperatis rebus, cum omnes ad Augustum transirent, ipse se interemit. Cleopatra sibi aspidem admisit et veneno eius exstincta est. Aegyptus per Octavianum Augustum imperio Romano adiecta est praepositusque ei C. Cornelius Gallus. Hunc primum Aegyptus Romanum iudicem habuit.

Breviarii, Liber VII, vii

He (Antony) also stirred up a great Civil War, with his wife Cleopatra, queen of Egypt, urging it, since she hoped, with a womanly desire, to rule also in the City (Rome). He was defeated by Augustus in a famous and glorious naval battle near Actium, which is a place in Epirus, from which he escaped to Egypt and, because his future was without hope, since everyone was going over to the side of Augustus, he killed himself. Cleopatra let a snake bite her and died from its poison. Egypt was added to the Roman Empire by Octavius Augustus and Gaius Cornelius Gallus was put in command of it. Egypt had him as its first Roman judge.

Breviarium, Book 7, 7

Psalmus David, cum fugeret a facie Absalom filii sui

Domine, quid multiplicati sunt qui tribulant me?
Multi insurgunt adversum me;
multi dicunt animae meae:
Non est salus ipsi in Deo eius.
Tu autem, Domine, susceptor meus es,
gloria mea et exaltans caput meum.
Voce mea ad Dominum clamavi,
et exaudivit me de monte sancto suo.
Ergo dormivi et soporatus sum
et exsurrexi, quia Dominus suscepit me.
Non timebo milia populi circumdantis me.

Exsurge, Domine, salvum me fac, Deus meus;
quoniam tu percussisti omnes adversantes mihi sine causa,
dentes peccatorum contrivisti.
Domini est salus, et super populum tuum benedictio tua.

Liber Psalmorum iii

A Psalm of David, when he fled from Absalom his son

Lord, how are they increased that trouble me!

Many are they that rise up against me;
many there be which say of my soul:
There is no help for him in God.
But thou, O Lord, art a shield for me;
my glory, and the lifter up of mine head.
I cried unto the Lord with my voice,
and he heard me out of his holy hill.
I laid me down and slept;
I awaked; for the Lord sustained me.
I will not be afraid of ten thousands of people, that have set themselves against me round about.

Arise, O Lord; save me, O my God;
for thou hast smitten all mine enemies upon the cheek bone;
thou hast broken the teeth of the ungodly.
Salvation belongeth unto the Lord; thy blessing is upon thy people.

Psalm 3

CHAPTER 18

READING

Libri Sibyllini	The Sibylline Books
1. **Inter antiquos erat fabula de libris Sibyllinis.**	1. Among the ancients there was a story about the Sibylline books.
2. **Tarquinius Superbus urbem Romam regnabat.**	2. Tarquin the Proud was ruling the city of Rome.
3. **Femina ad Tarquinium libros novem portavit et pro libris pecuniam rogavit.**	3. A woman brought nine books to Tarquin and asked for money for the books.
4. **Tarquinius feminae pecuniam non dedit.**	4. Tarquin did not give the money to the woman.
5. **Femina in igni libros tres tum locavit.**	5. The woman then put three books in the fire.
6. **Pro sex libris pretium librorum novem rogabat.**	6. For the six books she asked the price of the nine books.
7. **Tarquinius feminae pecuniam non dedit.**	7. Tarquin did not give the money to the woman.
8. **Postquam femina in igni libros sex locaverat Tarquinius feminae pro libris pecuniam dedit quod audacia feminae movebatur.**	8. After the woman had placed six books in the fire, Tarquin gave the money to the woman for the books because he was moved by the woman's boldness.
9. **Libri erant libri Sibyllini.**	9. The books were the Sibylline books.
10. **Cum populus Romanus periculo incitabatur aut cum Roma oppugnabatur ad libros properabant.**	10. When the Roman people were aroused by danger or when Rome was being attacked they hurried to the books.
11. **Libri Romanis auxilium multum semper dabant.**	11. The books always gave much help to the Romans.
12. **Erantne libri deorum?**	12. Were they the books of the gods?

READING VOCABULARY

Nouns

liber, libri, m., book (library)
ignis, ignis, m., fire (ignium) (ignite)
pretium, pretii or preti, n., price (precious)
audacia, audaciae, f., boldness, bravery, daring (audacity)
Tarquinius, Tarquini, m., Tarquin

Adjectives

Sibyllinus, Sibyllina, Sibyllinum, Sibylline
superbus, superba, superbum, proud (superb)
sex, six (sextet)
novem, nine (November)

Verb

rogo, rogare, rogavi, rogatus, ask, ask for (interrogate)

Conjunction

postquam, after, when

READING GRAMMAR

The three perfect tenses (perfect, pluperfect, and future perfect) are based on the third principal part in the Active.

A. The Perfect tense shows action completed in the past—*I have loved*—and the third principal part is the first person singular of the Perfect tense.

a-conjugation	I have loved; I loved	**e-conjugation**	I have had; I had
amavi	I have loved	**habui**	I have had
amavisti	you have loved	**habuisti**	you have had
amavit	he, she, it has loved	**habuit**	he, she, it has had
amavimus	we have loved	**habuimus**	we have had
amavistis	you have loved	**habuistis**	you have had
amaverunt	they have loved	**habuerunt**	they have had

B. The Pluperfect tense shows action completed at a definite point of time in the past—*I had loved*—.

a-conjugation	I had loved	**e-conjugation**	I had had
amaveram	I had loved	**habueram**	I had had
amaveras	you had loved	**habueras**	you had had
amaverat	he, she, it had loved	**habuerat**	he, she, it had had
amaveramus	we had loved	**habueramus**	we had had
amaveratis	you had loved	**habueratis**	you had had
amaverant	they had loved	**habuerant**	they had had

C. The Future Perfect tense shows action to be completed before a definite point of time in the future—*I shall have loved*—.

a-conjugation	I shall have loved	**e-conjugation**	I shall have had
amavero	I shall have loved	**habuero**	I shall have had
amaveris	you will have loved	**habueris**	you will have had
amaverit	he, she, it will have loved	**habuerit**	he, she, it will have had
amaverimus	we shall have loved	**habuerimus**	we shall have had
amaveritis	you will have loved	**habueritis**	you will have had
amaverint	they will have loved	**habuerint**	they will have had

D. The Verb **sum** is regular in the Perfect tenses.

PERFECT TENSE		PLUPERFECT TENSE		FUTURE PERFECT TENSE	
fui	I have been	**fueram**	I had been	**fuero**	I shall have been
fuisti	you have been	**fueras**	you had been	**fueris**	you will have been
fuit	he, she, it has been	**fuerat**	he, she, it had been	**fuerit**	he, she, it will have been
fuimus	we have been	**fueramus**	we had been	**fuerimus**	we shall have been
fuistis	you have been	**fueratis**	you had been	**fueritis**	you will have been
fuerunt	they have been	**fuerant**	they had been	**fuerint**	they will have been

FAMILIAR ABBREVIATIONS

fl. or **flor., floruit,** he (she) flourished. Used with the date at which an artist produced his work.

I.H.S., In hoc signo, In this sign. or **Iesus Hominum Salvator,** Jesus Saviour of Men.

I.N.R.I., Iesus Nazarenus, Rex Iudaeorum, Jesus of Nazareth, King of the Jews.

pinx., pinxit, he (she) painted it.

sculp., sculpsit, he (she) carved it.

op. cit., opere citato, in the work cited. Used in footnotes instead of repeating the title of the book referred to.

ibid. or **ib., ibidem,** in the same place. Used in footnotes, if the reference is the same as one made just previously.

PRACTICE EXERCISES

No. 84. Complete these principal parts.

1. **ambulo, ambulare, __________, ambulatus**
2. **laudo, laudare, __________, laudatus**
3. **moneo, monere, __________, monitus**
4. **debeo, debere, __________, debitus**
5. **porto, portare, __________, portatus**
6. **servo, servare, __________, servatus**
7. **voco, vocare, __________, vocatus**
8. **moveo, movere, __________, motus**
9. **do, dare, __________, datus**
10. **rogo, rogare, __________, rogatus**

No. 85. Translate these Perfect tenses.

1. **rogavit**	6. **necavisti**	11. **doluisti**	16. **monstravit**
2. **spectaverunt**	7. **narravistis**	12. **habuistis**	17. **narraverunt**
3. **monuimus**	8. **habitavi**	13. **debuimus**	18. **occupavistis**
4. **iuvi**	9. **vidi**	14. **laboraverunt**	19. **paravimus**
5. **fuisti**	10. **timuerunt**	15. **superavisti**	20. **volavit**

No. 86. Translate these Pluperfect tenses.

1. **ambulaveram**	6. **videratis**	11. **paraverat**	16. **dolueramus**
2. **adoraverant**	7. **paraveras**	12. **locaverant**	17. **rogaverat**
3. **araverat**	8. **dederas**	13. **incitaveras**	18. **spectaverant**
4. **moverant**	9. **tenueratis**	14. **curaveratis**	19. **viderat**
5. **manseramus**	10. **steteram**	15. **nataveram**	20. **vocaveratis**

No. 87. Translate these Future Perfect tenses.

1. **amaveris**	6. **terruerit**	11. **vocaverimus**	16. **narraverimus**
2. **curaverit**	7. **moverit**	12. **servavero**	17. **habueritis**
3. **laudavero**	8. **dederint**	13. **portaverit**	18. **debuerit**
4. **locaverimus**	9. **steteris**	14. **paraverint**	19. **adoraverint**
5. **habuerint**	10. **tenuerit**	15. **nuntiaveris**	20. **ambulaveris**

CHAPTER 19

READING

Reges Romae

1. **Urbs Roma septem reges habuit. Romulus urbem parvam in monte Palatino aedificavit.**
2. **Urbi nomen Romam dedit. Romulus ob sapientiam suam urbem bene regnabat.**
3. **Populo consilium bonum dedit.**
4. **Quod in urbe non erant mulieres Romani finitimos suos ad ludos vocaverunt.**
5. **Tum feminas puellasque pugna obtinuerunt.**
6. **Et Sabini et socii sui contra Romanos bella multa pugnaverunt, sed copiae Romanae hostes superaverunt.**
7. **Postea Numa Pompilius erat rex Romanorum.**
8. **Pacem amavit et populo erat gratus quod Romanis leges multas bonasque dedit.**
9. **Aedificia templaque etiam aedificavit.**
10. **Tum Romani ab Anco Marcio regnabantur.**
11. **Multos bello superavit et murum circum montem Caelium aedificavit.**
12. **Postea Roma a Prisco Tarquinio regnabatur.**
13. **Circum Maximum, ubi Romani ludos habebant, aedificavit.**
14. **Contra Sabinos bellum pugnavit et agris finitimis et monte Capitolio fines urbis auxit.**
15. **Proximus rex, Servius Tullius, Sabinos superavit.**
16. **Colles Romae ad septem auxit. Circum colles murum et circum murum fossas aedificavit.**
17. **Multi in urbe habitaverunt et multi erant agricolae in agris et post colles et post flumen.**

The Kings of Rome

1. The city of Rome had seven kings. Romulus built a small city on the Palatine mount.
2. To the city he gave the name Rome. Romulus ruled the city well because of his wisdom.
3. He gave good advice to the people.
4. Because there were not women in the city, the Romans called their neighbors to games.
5. Then they got women and girls by a fight.
6. Both the Sabines and their allies fought many wars against the Romans, but the Roman forces conquered the enemy.
7. Afterwards, Numa Pompilius was king of the Romans.
8. He liked peace and he was pleasing to the people because he gave many and good laws to the Romans.
9. He also built buildings and temples.
10. Then the Romans were ruled by Ancus Marcius.
11. He defeated many people in war and he built a wall around the Caelian mount.
12. Afterwards, Rome was ruled by Tarquinius Priscus.
13. He built the Circus Maximus, where the Romans held their games.
14. He fought a war against the Sabines and increased the territory of the city by neighboring fields and the Capitoline mount.
15. The next king, Servius Tullius, overcame the Sabines.
16. He increased the hills of Rome to seven. Around the hills he built a wall and around the wall ditches.
17. Many people lived in the city and many were farmers in the fields both in back of the hills and in back of the river.

Reges Romae	The Kings of Rome
18. **Tarquinius Superbus erat ultimus rex Romae, sed bene diuque regnavit.**	18. Tarquin the Proud was the last king of Rome, but he ruled well and for a long time.
19. **Copiae Tarquini Superbi bella multa pugnaverunt et nationes proximas Romae superaverunt.**	19. The troops of Tarquin the Proud fought many wars and defeated the nations next to Rome.

READING VOCABULARY

Nouns

collis, collis, m., hill **(collium)**
flumen, fluminis, n., river, stream (flume)
finis, finis, m., end, border **(finium)**
In the plural, territory, boundaries. (finish)
rex, regis, m., king (regal)
nomen, nominis, n., name (nominative)
mulier, mulieris, f., woman
pugna, pugnae, f., fight
mons, montis, m., mountain, mount **(montium)** (monticule)
lex, legis, f., law (legal)
murus, muri, m., wall (mural)

Adjectives

proximus, proxima, proximum, next, nearest (approximate)
ultimus, ultima, ultimum, last, farthest (ultimate)
septem, seven (September)

Verb

augeo, augere, auxi, auctus, increase, enlarge (augment)

Adverb

postea, afterwards

READING GRAMMAR

A. The Perfect Passive Participle is an Adjective and therefore must agree with the word it modifies in *gender, number,* and *case.* When it is used with the Verb **sum** to form the Perfect Passive tenses, it is always in the Nominative Case, but must agree with the subject in gender and number.

mulier amata est, the woman has been loved
mulieres amatae sunt, the women have been loved
vir amatus est, the man has been loved
viri amati sunt, the men have been loved
nomen vocatum est, the name has been called
nomina vocata sunt, the names have been called

B. The Perfect Passive tense is formed by the fourth principal part with **sum.**

amatus sum, *I have been loved*
a-conjugation

amatus, a, um sum	I have been loved
amatus, a, um es	you have been loved
amatus, a, um est	he, she, it has been loved
amati, ae, a sumus	we have been loved
amati, ae, a estis	you have been loved
amati, ae, a sunt	they have been loved

habitus sum, *I have been held*
e-conjugation

habitus, a, um sum	I have been held
habitus, a, um es	you have been held
habitus, a, um est	he, she, it has been held
habiti, ae, a sumus	we have been held
habiti, ae, a estis	you have been held
habiti, ae, a sunt	they have been held

C. The Pluperfect Passive tense is formed by the fourth principal part and **eram**.

amatus eram, *I had been loved* **habitus eram,** *I had been held*

a-conjugation **e-conjugation**

amatus, a, um eram	I had been loved	**habitus, a, um eram**	I had been held
amatus, a, um eras	you had been loved	**habitus, a, um eras**	you had been held
amatus, a, um erat	he, she, it had been loved	**habitus, a, um erat**	he, she, it had been held
amati, ae, a eramus	we had been loved	**habiti, ae, a eramus**	we had been held
amati, ae, a eratis	you had been loved	**habiti, ae, a eratis**	you had been held
amati, ae, a erant	they had been loved	**habiti, ae, a erant**	they had been held

D. The Future Perfect Passive tense is formed by the fourth principal part and **ero**.

amatus ero, *I shall have been loved* **habitus ero,** *I shall have been held*

a-conjugation **e-conjugation**

amatus, a, um ero	I shall have been loved	**habitus, a, um ero**	I shall have been held
amatus, a, um eris	you will have been loved	**habitus, a, um eris**	you will have been held
amatus, a, um erit	he, she, it will have been loved	**habitus, a, um erit**	he, she, it will have been held
amati, ae, a erimus	we shall have been loved	**habiti, ae, a erimus**	we shall have been held
amati, ae, a eritis	you will have been loved	**habiti, ae, a eritis**	you will have been held
amati, ae, a erunt	they will have been loved	**habiti, ae, a erunt**	they will have been held

FAMILIAR PHRASES

carpe diem, seize the opportunity.
cave canem, beware the dog.
ex libris, from the library of. Used often on bookplates.
ex officio, because of an office (held previously).
in toto, in the whole; completely.
per capita, by heads; per person or individual.

post mortem, after death.
exeunt omnes, all go out. Used as a stage direction.
ultimatum, the last thing; the farthest thing. Used for the final terms offered by one party to another.

PRACTICE EXERCISES

No. 88. Give the English for these Perfect tenses.

1. fuerunt	6. laudatae sunt	11. vocati sumus	16. timuisti
2. ambulavit	7. monitus sum	12. natavi	17. paratus est
3. portatus est	8. debuimus	13. servatae estis	18. locata sunt
4. amati sunt	9. stetistis	14. nuntiatum est	19. laudaverunt
5. curata es	10. narratum est	15. moti sunt	20. movistis

No. 89. Give the English for these Pluperfect tenses.

1. dederant	6. pugnaverat	11. parati erant	16. monuerat
2. moverat	7. laudata eram	12. occupaveras	17. habueratis
3. territus erat	8. curati erant	13. liberati eratis	18. tenueras
4. manseratis	9. amata eras	14. necatus erat	19. iuti eramus
5. tenueras	10. incitati eratis	15. servati eramus	20. adoraverant

No. 90. Give the English for these Future Perfect tenses.

1. **monuero**
2. **fuerit**
3. **portatum erit**
4. **moniti erunt**
5. **habuerint**
6. **terrueris**
7. **moverimus**
8. **visi eritis**
9. **timuerit**
10. **mota erit**
11. **dederimus**
12. **steterint**
13. **fuerimus**
14. **necati eritis**
15. **laudatae erimus**
16. **armatus eris**
17. **curati erunt**
18. **locatum erit**
19. **fuerint**
20. **servata erit**

No. 91. Translate these Verb forms.

1. **habitum erat**
2. **videro**
3. **oppugnata erunt**
4. **laudata eris**
5. **portata eras**
6. **debitum erit**
7. **debuerant**
8. **exspectavisti**
9. **vidistis**
10. **monstratum est**
11. **moniti sunt**
12. **rogatae sumus**
13. **spectaverunt**
14. **moti sumus**
15. **paraveramus**
16. **monitus est**
17. **steterat**
18. **dati erant**
19. **narraverunt**
20. **tenuero**

CHAPTER 20

READING

Labores Herculis	The Labors of Hercules
1. **Pythia ab Apolline docebatur et populo consilium dei dedit.**	1. Pythia was taught by Apollo and gave the advice of the god to the people.
2. **Hercules a femina amorem suum Apollinis demonstrare iussus est.**	2. Hercules was ordered by the woman to show his love for Apollo.
3. **Hercules ad urbem regis, Eurysthei, properavit. Ibi Eurystheus Herculi labores duodecim dedit.**	3. Hercules hurried to the city of the king, Eurystheus. There Eurystheus gave Hercules twelve labors.
4. **Sunt multae fabulae de laboribus Herculis.**	4. There are many stories about the labors of Hercules.
5. **Duodecim annos laborabat quod erat servus regis, sed Hercules de laboribus suis minime dolebat.**	5. He labored for twelve years because he was the servant of the king, but Hercules grieved very little about his labors.
6. **Corpus robustum habebat et regem laboremque non timebat.**	6. He had a strong body and did not fear the king and the work.
7. **A rege diu tenebatur, sed post duodecim annos liberatus est quod regem bene iuverat.**	7. He was held for a long time by the king, but after twelve years he was freed because he had helped the king well.
8. **Deo Apollini amorem suum demonstraverat.**	8. He had shown the god, Apollo, his love.

Poma Aurea Hesperidum	The Golden Apples of the Hesperides
1. **Hercules pro rege, Eurystheo, bene laboravit, sed etiam tum non erat liber et domi non mansit.**	1. Hercules worked well for the king, Eurystheus, but even then he was not free and did not stay at home.

Poma Aurea Hesperidum

2. **Rex Herculem poma aurea ex horto Hesperidum obtinere iussit.**
3. **Hesperides erant filiae pulchrae Atlantis et in loco ultimo in fini terrae ruri habitabant.**
4. **Pro Iunone poma aurea ibi curabant.**
5. **Multi praemio pomorum moti erant, sed Hesperides poma semper bene servabant.**
6. **Erat murus magnus altusque circum hortum ubi erant poma, atque ante hortum erat serpens.**
7. **Serpens capita multa habuit.**
8. **Hercules multa milia passuum ambulavit. Post annum ad hortum venit.**
9. **Erat in fini ultimo terrae et proximus Oceano.**
10. **Hercules Atlantem, virum robustum et amicum, ibi vidit.**
11. **Auxilium rogavit.**

The Golden Apples of the Hesperides

2. The king ordered Hercules to get the golden apples from the garden of the Hesperides.
3. The Hesperides were the beautiful daughters of Atlas and lived in the country in the farthest place on the end of the earth.
4. They took care of the golden apples there for Juno.
5. Many people had been moved by the reward of the apples, but the Hesperides always preserved the apples well.
6. There was a large and high wall around the garden where the apples were, and in front of the garden was a serpent.
7. The serpent had many heads.
8. Hercules walked many miles. After a year he came to the garden.
9. It was on the farthest end of the earth and next to the Ocean.
10. Hercules saw Atlas there, a strong and friendly man.
11. He asked for help.

READING VOCABULARY

Nouns

corpus, corporis, n., body (corporal)
hora, horae, f., hour (horology)
amor, amoris, m., love (amorous)
Apollo, Apollinis, m., Apollo
Eurystheus, Eurysthei, m., Eurystheus
mille passus, a mile **milia passuum,** miles
Hesperides, Hesperidum, f., the Hesperides
Atlas, Atlantis, m., Atlas
Iuno, Iunonis, f., Juno
Pythia, Pythiae, f., Pythia
Hercules, Herculis, m., Hercules
locus, loci, m., place, position. Sometimes neuter in the plural. (location, local)
serpens, serpentis, f., snake, serpent (serpentium) (serpentine)
hortus, horti, m., garden (horticulture)

Adjectives

duodecim, twelve (duodecimal)
aureus, aurea, aureum, golden, of gold (aureate)

Verbs

doceo, docere, docui, doctus, teach, show (docile, docent)
iubeo, iubere, iussi, iussus, order, command (jussive)
demonstro, demonstrare, demonstravi, demonstratus, point out, show (demonstrate)

Adverbs

domi, at home (domicile)
ruri, in the country (rural)
quam diu, how long

Preposition

in, into, onto With the Accusative Case (in-, inhale)

READING GRAMMAR

A. Both the Accusative and Ablative Cases are used to show time.

1. The Accusative Case shows *how long* something goes on.

multos annos, for many years
duodecim horas, for twelve hours

2. The Ablative Case shows *when* something happens.

anno, in (during) a year
hora, in (during) an hour

B. Both the Accusative and Ablative Cases are used to show place.

1. The Accusative Case shows *to* or *into* what place motion is directed, or *how far.*

ad urbem, to the city
in oppidum, into the town
multa milia passuum, many miles, for many miles

2. The Ablative Case shows *where* the place is, or *from where* the motion is directed.

in oppido, in the town
ab oppido, away from the town
de muro, down from the wall
in mare, on the sea
ex urbe, out of the city

C. With the names of cities, towns, and small islands, and with the words **ruri** (in the country) and **domi** (at home), no Preposition is used.

Romam, to Rome **Roma,** from Rome

ACADEMIC DEGREES AND TERMS

The following are some of the Academic Degrees and terms used.

cum laude, with praise. Given with a diploma that has been earned with a grade of work higher than ordinary.
magna cum laude, with great praise.
summa cum laude, with highest praise.
Alumnus, pl. **Alumni,** male graduate or graduates.
Alumna, pl. **Alumnae,** female graduate or graduates.
Alma Mater, Foster Mother. Refers to one's school or college.
A.M. or **M.A., Artium Magister,** Master of Arts.
B.A. or **A.B., Baccalaureus Artium,** Bachelor of Arts.
B.Sc., Baccalaureus Scientiae, Bachelor of Science.
D.D., Divinitatis Doctor, Doctor of Divinity.
D.Litt. or **Litt.D., Doctor Litterarum,** Doctor of Literature or Letters.
M.D., Medicinae Doctor, Doctor of Medicine.
Ph.D., Philosophia Doctor, Doctor of Philosophy.
LL.D., Legum Doctor, Doctor of Laws.
D.M.D., Dentariae Medicinae Doctor, Doctor of Dental Medicine.

PRACTICE EXERCISES

No. 92. Give the English for these expressions of time.

1. **multos annos**
2. **proximo anno**
3. **multas horas**
4. **proxima hora**
5. **septem horas**
6. **medio anno**
7. **sex horis**
8. **annos longos**
9. **hora**
10. **duodecim horas**

No. 93. Give the English for these expressions of place.

1. **ad urbes**
2. **ex oppidis**
3. **Roma**
4. **Romam**
5. **in castra**
6. **ante forum**
7. **post hortum**
8. **in agro**
9. **in agros**
10. **de collibus**
11. **ex casa**
12. **ruri**
13. **domi**
14. **ab flumine**
15. **sub maribus**
16. **sub muris**
17. **in fossam**
18. **ab templo**
19. **e viis**
20. **de sole**

No. 94. Translate these Verbs.

1. **videbo**
2. **pugnaverat**
3. **stabatis**
4. **laborabimus**
5. **fuerat**
6. **obtinebunt**
7. **natabamus**
8. **erit**
9. **videmus**
10. **spectatum est**
11. **movebitur**
12. **aedificata erant**
13. **fuisti**
14. **oppugnabamur**
15. **manserunt**

No. 95. Translate these sentences.

1. **Proximo anno Romam movebimus.**
2. **Sex horas in urbe manserunt.**
3. **Medio in colle oppugnati erant.**
4. **Multas horas in Italia manebam.**
5. **Ibi erit horam.**
6. **Nonne multos annos laborabunt?**
7. **Ad oppidum multas horas longas ambulabat.**
8. **Ab rege non liberatus est.**
9. **Suntne in horto cum pueris?**
10. **Septem milia passuum ab urbe movi.**

CHAPTER 21

READING

Poma Aurea Hesperidum (concl'd.)	The Golden Apples of the Hesperides (concl'd.)
1. **Postquam Hercules auxilium petiverat, causam itineris sui ad finem terrae Atlantem docuit.**	1. After Hercules had sought help, he showed Atlas the cause of his journey to the end of the earth.
2. **Atlas erat pater Hesperidum et Herculi de loco ubi erant poma aurea narravit, sed Atlas caelum in umeris suis tenebat.**	2. Atlas was the father of the Hesperides and he told Hercules about the place where the golden apples were, but Atlas was holding the sky on his shoulders.
3. **Atlas Herculi caelum dedit et Herculem in umeris caelum tenere iussit.**	3. Atlas gave the sky to Hercules and he ordered Hercules to hold the sky on his shoulders.
4. **Atlas ad hortum Hesperidum properavit.**	4. Atlas hurried to the garden of the Hesperides.
5. **Diu Hercules in umeris suis caelum tenebat. Diu Atlantem non viderat.**	5. For a long time Hercules held the sky on his shoulders. He had not seen Atlas for a long time.

Poma Aurea Hesperidum (concl'd.)

6. **Hercules famam de Atlante non habuerat. Et timebat et dolebat.**
7. **Pretium pomorum erat certe magnum.**
8. **Post multas noctes Atlantem vidit et laetus erat.**
9. **Mox poma aurea habuit. Tum Atlas caelum in umeris suis locavit et Hercules erat liber.**
10. **Ad Graeciam cum pomis properavit.**

The Golden Apples of the Hesperides (concl'd.)

6. Hercules had not had a report about Atlas. He was both afraid and grieving.
7. The price of the apples was certainly great.
8. After many nights he saw Atlas and he was happy.
9. Soon he had the golden apples. Then Atlas placed the sky on his own shoulders and Hercules was free.
10. He hurried to Greece with the apples.

Atalanta

1. **Atalanta erat puella Graeciae et vero pulchra.**
2. **Multi viri contra eam cucurrerant, sed magnam celeritatem habebat et non superata erat.**
3. **Venus consilium habebat. Puella erat praemium victoriae et pedibus eos currere iussit.**
4. **Hippomenes contra eam currere paratus est.**
5. **Multi spectabant et eum incitabant.**
6. **Signum datum est.**
7. **Atalanta celeritatem suam demonstrabat. Paene volabat.**
8. **Quam longe ante eum currit!**
9. **Sed Venus Hippomeni viam ad victoriam docuerat. Ei poma aurea dederat.**
10. **Hippomenes pomum ad terram misit.**
11. **Atalanta ad moram movebatur.**
12. **Hippomenes celeritatem suam auxit.**
13. **Finis erat propinquus.**
14. **Venus, dea amoris, eum bene iuverat.**
15. **Hippomenes consilio donoque deae puellam superaverat.**

Atalanta

1. Atalanta was a girl of Greece and truly beautiful.
2. Many men had raced against her, but she had great speed and had not been surpassed.
3. Venus had a plan. The girl was the reward of victory and she ordered them to run on foot.
4. Hippomenes was prepared to run against her.
5. Many were watching and urging him on.
6. The signal is given.
7. Atalanta was showing her speed. She was almost flying.
8. How far in front of him she runs!
9. But Venus had shown Hippomenes the way to victory. She had given him golden apples.
10. Hippomenes threw an apple to the ground.
11. Atalanta was moved toward delay.
12. Hippomenes increased his speed.
13. The end was near.
14. Venus, goddess of love, had helped him well.
15. Hippomenes had overtaken the girl by the plan and gift of the goddess.

READING VOCABULARY

Nouns

mora, morae, f., delay (moratorium)
nox, noctis, f., night (noctium) (nocturnal)
causa, causae, f., cause, reason (causeless)
iter, itineris, n., journey, march, way (itinerary)
umerus, umeri, m., shoulder (humerus)
pes, pedis, m., foot (pedal)
signum, signi, n., signal, standard (signify)
Atalanta, Atalantae, f., Atalanta
Hippomenes, Hippomenis, m., Hippomenes

Verbs

duco, ducere, duxi, ductus, lead (conduct, aqueduct)
mitto, mittere, misi, missus, send (mission, manumit)
peto, petere, petivi, petitus, seek, ask (petition)
curro, currere, cucurri, cursus, run (current)
dico, dicere, dixi, dictus, say, speak (diction)

Adverb

paene, almost, nearly

Pronoun and Adjective

is, ea, id, he, she, it; this, that

READING GRAMMAR

A. **e/i-conjugation** Verbs follow the same principles as those you have met so far, except in the Future Tense. The predominant vowels are **e** and **i.**

1. Principal Parts: **duco, ducere, duxi, ductus,** lead
2. Present Tense:

ACTIVE		PASSIVE	
I lead, am leading, do lead		I am being led, am led	
duco	**ducimus**	**ducor**	**ducimur**
ducis	**ducitis**	**duceris**	**ducimini**
ducit	**ducunt**	**ducitur**	**ducuntur**

3. Imperfect Tense:

ACTIVE		PASSIVE	
I was leading, led		I was being led, was led	
ducebam	**ducebamus**	**ducebar**	**ducebamur**
ducebas	**ducebatis**	**ducebaris**	**ducebamini**
ducebat	**ducebant**	**ducebatur**	**ducebantur**

4. Future Tense:

ACTIVE		PASSIVE	
I shall lead		I shall be led	
ducam	**ducemus**	**ducar**	**ducemur**
duces	**ducetis**	**duceris**	**ducemini**
ducet	**ducent**	**ducetur**	**ducentur**

5. Perfect Tense:

ACTIVE	PASSIVE
I have led, led	I have been led
duxi	**ductus, a, um sum**
duxisti, etc.	**ductus, a, um es, etc.**

6. Pluperfect Tense:

ACTIVE	PASSIVE
I had led	I had been led
duxeram	**ductus, a, um eram**
duxeras, etc.	**ductus, a, um eras,** etc.

7. Future Perfect Tense:

ACTIVE	PASSIVE
I shall have led	I shall have been led
duxero	**ductus, a, um ero**
duxeris, etc.	**ductus, a, um eris,** etc.

B. 1. **is, ea, id** is used as either a Pronoun or an Adjective. As a Pronoun it has the same gender and number as the Noun it replaces, but its case is determined by its use in the sentence.

Puerum video, I see the boy. **Eum video,** I see him.
Is in casa est, He is in the house.

As a Pronoun, the singular means *he, she,* or *it* and the plural means *they.*

Nom.	**is**	he	**ea**	she	**id**	it
Gen.	**eius**	his	**eius**	her, hers	**eius**	its
Dat.	**ei**	to, for him	**ei**	to, for her	**ei**	to, for it
Acc.	**eum**	him	**eam**	her	**id**	it
Abl.	**eo**	from, with, by, in him	**ea**	from, with, by, in her	**eo**	from, with, by, in it
Nom.	**ei or ii**		**eae**		**ea**	they
Gen.	**eorum**		**earum**		**eorum**	their
Dat.	**eis or iis**		**eis or iis**		**eis or iis**	to, for them
Acc.	**eos**		**eas**		**ea**	them
Abl.	**eis or iis**		**eis or iis**		**eis or iis**	from, with, by, in them

2. As an Adjective, **is, ea, id** must be in the same gender, number and case as the noun it modifies.

is puer, this boy, that boy **ea puella,** this girl, that girl **id bellum,** this war, that war

As an Adjective, the singular means *this* or *that* and the plural means *these* or *those.*

Nom.	this, that	these, those
Gen.	of this, of that	of these, of those
Dat.	to, for this; to, for that	to, for these; to, for those
Acc.	this, that	these, those
Abl.	from, with, by, in this; from, with, by, in that	from, with, by, in these; from, with, by, in those

C. 1. The possessive form of the Pronoun **eius** does not refer to the subject.

Pomum eius videmus. We see his apple.

2. When the possessor is the same as the subject, the Adjective **suus** is used.

Pomum suum habet. He has his (own) apple.

ASSIMILATION

Some prefixes take on the first letter of the word to which they are attached. This process is called assimilation. Assimilation occurs with these prefixes:

ad **ad** and **pono** become **appono,** put to, put near
con **con** and **mitto** become **committo,** send together
in **in** and **mortalis** become **immortalis,** immortal

Sometimes there is a change to a different letter:

in and **porto** become **importo,** carry in, bring in
con and **pono** become **compono,** put together

You will notice that assimilation is a natural process leading to more ease in pronunciation.

PRACTICE EXERCISES

No. 96. Translate these Verb forms.

1. **mittunt**
2. **doctus sum**
3. **petimur**
4. **debet**
5. **moniti eratis**
6. **parati erunt**
7. **duxit**
8. **liberavisti**
9. **adorabam**
10. **miserit**
11. **iubebit**
12. **spectabamur**
13. **demonstratis**
14. **rogabunt**
15. **ducebas**
16. **mittet**
17. **servavi**
18. **timueras**
19. **petiveratis**
20. **manserunt**

No. 97. Translate these phrases.

1. **ob iniuriam**
2. **ex proeliis**
3. **sex horas**
4. **in itinere**
5. **e finibus**
6. **ad Galliam**
7. **ab colle**
8. **in litteris**
9. **ab hominibus**
10. **in ripam**

No. 98. Translate the following.

1. **Eas peto.**
2. **eorum librorum**
3. **hortus eius**
4. **Ea eis dedi.**
5. **Is pugnabat.**
6. **Eum vidistis.**
7. **in eis locis**
8. **patri eius**
9. **Ab eo mittuntur.**
10. **Eos misisti.**
11. **ea hora**
12. **sua signa**
13. **ex eis urbibus**
14. **eam mulierem**
15. **Ab eis ducimur.**
16. **eorum poma**
17. **suos reges**
18. **cum eis**
19. **id iter**
20. **eam causam**

No. 99. Change these Verb forms to the Active or Passive.

1. **ducit**	6. **misisti**	11. **petiverunt**	16. **current**
2. **duxi**	7. **mittebantur**	12. **petiti erimus**	17. **cucurrit**
3. **ducebar**	8. **mittemini**	13. **petet**	18. **curritur**
4. **ducti sunt**	9. **missus es**	14. **petitur**	19. **currebant**
5. **ducam**	10. **miserat**	15. **petebaris**	20. **cursum erat**

FIFTH REVIEW SECTION (CHAPTERS 18–21)

VOCABULARY REVIEW

NOUNS

1. **amor**	15. **Hippomenes**	29. **murus**	1. love	15. Hippomenes	29. wall
2. **Apollo**	16. **hora**	30. **nomen**	2. Apollo	16. hour	30. name
3. **Atalanta**	17. **hortus**	31. **nox**	3. Atalanta	17. garden	31. night
4. **Atlas**	18. **ignis**	32. **pes**	4. Atlas	18. fire	32. foot
5. **audacia**	19. **iter**	33. **pomum**	5. boldness, bravery, daring	19. journey, march, way	33. apple
6. **causa**	20. **Iuno**	34. **pretium**	6. cause, reason	20. Juno	34. price
7. **collis**	21. **lex**	35. **pugna**	7. hill	21. law	35. fight
8. **corpus**	22. **liber**	36. **Pythia**	8. body	22. book	36. Pythia
9. **Eurystheus**	23. **locus**	37. **rex**	9. Eurystheus	23. place	37. king
10. **finis**	24. **mille passus**	38. **serpens**	10. end, border	24. a mile	38. snake, serpent
11. **fines**	25. **milia passuum**	39. **signum**	11. territory	25. miles	39. signal, standard
12. **flumen**	26. **mons**	40. **Tarquinius**	12. river	26. mountain, mount	40. Tarquin
13. **Hercules**	27. **mora**	41. **umerus**	13. Hercules	27. delay	41. shoulder
14. **Hesperides**	28. **mulier**	42. **Venus**	14. the Hesperides	28. woman	42. Venus

ADJECTIVES

1. **aureus**	5. **septem**	9. **ultimus**	1. golden	5. seven	9. last, farthest
2. **duodecim**	6. **sex**	10. **is, ea, id**	2. twelve	6. six	10. this, that
3. **novem**	7. **Sibyllinus**		3. nine	7. Sibylline	
4. **proximus**	8. **superbus**		4. next, nearest	8. proud, haughty	

VERBS

1. **augeo**	5. **doceo**	9. **peto**	1. increase, enlarge	5. teach, show	9. seek
2. **curro**	6. **duco**	10. **rogo**	2. run	6. lead	10. ask, ask for
3. **demonstro**	7. **iubeo**		3. point out, show	7. order, command	
4. **dico**	8. **mitto**		4. speak, say	8. send	

ADVERBS

1. **domi**	3. **postea**	5. **ruri**	1. at home	3. afterwards	5. in the country
2. **paene**	4. **quam diu**		2. almost, nearly	4. how long	

PRONOUNS

1. **is**	2. **ea**	3. **id**	1. he	2. she	3. it

PREPOSITION

1. **in**	1. into, onto; in, on

CONJUNCTION

1. **postquam**	1. after, when

PRACTICE EXERCISES

No. 100. Give the English for these phrases.

1. **in pedibus**	4. **ex agris**	7. **de corpore**	10. **Romam**
2. **ab colli**	5. **in ignem**	8. **ruri**	11. **domi**
3. **ad flumina**	6. **in muris**	9. **Roma**	12. **ex nocte**

No. 101. Translate these Perfect Tenses.

1. **fuerat**	6. **locaverunt**	11. **movimus**	16. **rogatus sum**
2. **regnavimus**	7. **data sunt**	12. **fuimus**	17. **stetit**
3. **rogatus est**	8. **misistis**	13. **incitati erant**	18. **vocavisti**
4. **portaveris**	9. **petitum erit**	14. **properaveratis**	19. **laudati erimus**
5. **dederunt**	10. **auctum erat**	15. **fuerint**	20. **habuerat**

No. 102. Give the English for these phrases.

1. **proximo anno**	4. **multo anno**	7. **eas noctes**	10. **ea hora**
2. **horas septem**	5. **sex annos**	8. **eos annos**	
3. **proximis horis**	6. **eo nocte**	9. **eo anno**	

No. 103. Give the English for these Pronouns.

1. **eius**	4. **ei**	7. **ea**	10. **eum**
2. **eos**	5. **id**	8. **eorum**	11. **ii**
3. **eae**	6. **eas**	9. **eis**	12. **eo**

No. 104. Translate these Adjective phrases.

1. **eum amorem**	5. **eis finibus**	9. **id corpus**	13. **eas leges**
2. **eius audaciae**	6. **eorum itinerum**	10. **eius loci**	14. **eo monte**
3. **ea nomina**	7. **ea poma**	11. **ei regi**	15. **eius signi**
4. **eas causas**	8. **ei mulieri**	12. **eam noctem**	

MARCUS VALERIUS MARTIALIS

Martial was born in Spain about 40 A.D. and went to Rome as a young man. He was a master of the epigram, and his poems, depicting scenes of everyday life, are full of wit, freshness, and satire. Martial died about 103 A.D., after returning to Spain.

Non amo te, Sabidi, nec possum dicere quare;	I do not love thee, Sabidius, nor can I tell you why;
hoc tantum possum dicere: non amo te.	this only I can say: I do not love thee.
Epigrammaton Liber I, xxxii	Epigrams, 1, 32

Cras te victurum, cras dicis, Postume, semper.	Tomorrow you will live, tomorrow you always say, Postumus.
Dic mihi, cras istud, Postume, quando venit?	Tell me, when, Postumus, is that tomorrow coming?
Quam longe cras istud, ubi est? aut unde petendum?	How far away is your tomorrow, where is it? or where must it be sought?
Numquid apud Parthos Armeniosque latet?	It doesn't lie hidden among the Parthians and Armenians, does it?
Iam cras istud habet Priami vel Nestoris annos.	Already that tomorrow of yours has the years of Priam or Nestor.
Cras istud quanti, dic mihi, posset emi?	Tell me, for how much could that tomorrow of yours be bought?
Cras vives? Hodie iam vivere, Postume, serum est;	You will live tomorrow? Today it is already too late to live, Postumus;
ille sapit, quisquis, Postume, vixit heri.	he is wise, whoever has lived yesterday, Postumus.
Epigrammaton Liber V, lviii	Epigrams, 5, 58

Omnia tempus habent,	To every thing there is a season,
et suis spatiis transeunt universa sub caelo.	and a time to every purpose under the heaven:
Tempus nascendi et tempus moriendi,	A time to be born, and a time to die;
tempus plantandi et tempus evellendi quod plantatum est,	a time to plant, and a time to pluck that which is planted;
tempus occidendi et tempus sanandi,	A time to kill, and a time to heal;
tempus destruendi et tempus aedificandi,	a time to break down, and a time to build up;
tempus flendi et tempus ridendi,	A time to weep, and a time to laugh;
tempus plangendi et tempus saltandi,	a time to mourn, and a time to dance;
tempus spargendi lapides et tempus colligendi,	A time to cast away stones, and a time to gather stones together;
tempus amplexandi et tempus longe fieri ab amplexibus,	a time to embrace, and a time to refrain from embracing;
tempus adquirendi et tempus perdendi,	A time to get, and a time to lose;
tempus custodiendi et tempus abiciendi,	a time to keep, and a time to cast away;
tempus scindendi et tempus consuendi,	A time to rend, and a time to sew;
tempus tacendi et tempus loquendi,	a time to keep silence, and a time to speak;
tempus dilectionis et tempus odii,	A time to love, and a time to hate;
tempus belli et tempus pacis.	a time of war, and a time of peace.
Quid habet amplius homo de labore suo?	What profit hath he that worketh in that wherein he laboureth?
Liber Ecclesiastes III, i–ix	Ecclesiastes 3, 1–9

CHAPTER 22

READING

Midas et Aurum

1. **Temporibus antiquis erat rex, Midas.**
2. **Nomen eius regis erat clarum quod amicus Bacchi erat.**
3. **Silenus Bacchum docebat, sed ab hostibus captus erat.**
4. **A Mida liberatus erat. Bacchus vero fuit laetus.**
5. **Bacchus ei nuntiavit: "Donum dabo."**
6. **Midas bonam fortunam, sed non multam sapientiam habebat.**
7. **Rex id donum accepit: Postea ea proxima ei in aurum vertebantur.**
8. **Rex donum dei bene amabat.**
9. **Midas aurum facere properavit.**
10. **In aurum arbores altas atque terram aquamque in eis locis ubi stabat aut ambulabat vertit.**
11. **Ob donum suum deum laudavit.**
12. **Rex superbus auro suo factus erat.**
13. **Nunc Midas domi est. Magno cum studio multa in aurum vertit.**
14. **Tum cibus aquaque ante eum a servo suo ponebantur.**
15. **Ea petivit, sed sine mora in aurum versa sunt.**
16. **Tum Midas timore magno capiebatur. Suam mortem vero timebat.**
17. **In locis ultimis proximisque aurum videbat.**
18. **Ad Bacchum vocavit: "Id donum rogavi, sed non est donum bonum. Est poena magna malaque. Nunc auxilium peto."**
19. **Deus ei auxilium mox dedit.**
20. **Corpus caputque in flumine ponere eum iussit.**
21. **Midas magna cum diligentia id fecit. Mox liberatus est, sed flumini suum donum dederat.**

Midas and the Gold

1. In ancient times there was a king, Midas.
2. The name of this king was famous because he was a friend of Bacchus.
3. Silenus taught Bacchus, but he had been captured by the enemy.
4. He had been freed by Midas. Bacchus was indeed happy.
5. Bacchus told him: "I shall give a gift."
6. Midas had good fortune, but not much wisdom.
7. The king received this gift: Afterwards those things nearest to him were turned into gold.
8. The king liked the gift of the god very much.
9. Midas hurried to make gold.
10. He turns into gold the high trees and also the land and water in those places where he was standing or walking.
11. He praised the god because of his gift.
12. The king had been made proud by his gold.
13. Now Midas is at home. With great eagerness he turns many things into gold.
14. Then food and water were placed in front of him by his servant.
15. He sought these things, but without delay they were turned into gold.
16. Then Midas was seized with great fear. He indeed feared his death.
17. He saw gold in the farthest and nearest places.
18. He called on Bacchus: "I asked for this gift, but it is not a good gift. It is a great and evil punishment. Now I seek help."
19. The god soon gave him help.
20. He ordered him to place his body and head in a river.
21. Midas did this with great care. Soon he was freed, but he had given his own gift to the river.

Midas et Aurum

22. **Post id tempus arenae fluminis erant aureae.**
23. **Bacchus laetus erat quod nunc liber erat et arena ab eo tempore erat pulchra.**

Midas and the Gold

22. After that time the sands of the river were golden.
23. Bacchus was happy because now he was free and the sand was beautiful from that time on.

READING VOCABULARY

Nouns

studium, studii or **studi, n.,** zeal, eagerness (studio)
diligentia, diligentiae, f., diligence, care (diligent)
timor, timoris, m., fear, dread (timorous)
mors, mortis, f., death **(mortium)** (mortality)
poena, poenae, f., punishment, fine (penal)
arena, arenae, f., sand (arena)
cibus, cibi, m., food
tempus, temporis, n., time (temporary, ex tempore)
aurum, auri, n., gold (auriferous)
arbor, arboris, f., tree (arboretum)
Bacchus, Bacchi, m., Bacchus (bacchanalian)
Midas, Midae, m., Midas
Silenus, Sileni, m., Silenus

Verbs

pono, ponere, posui, positus, put, place (position, postpone)
capio, capere, cepi, captus, take, seize, capture (caption)
verto, vertere, verti, versus, turn (vertical)
facio, facere, feci, factus, make, do (factory)

Preposition

propter, because of, on account of

READING GRAMMAR

A. Some **e/i-conjugation** Verbs have **-io** in the first principal part. These also have an **-i-** in most forms of the present, imperfect, and future tenses.

Present tense:

ACTIVE		PASSIVE	
I lead; I seize		I am led; I am seized	
duco	**capio**	**ducor**	**capior**
ducis	**capis**	**duceris**	**caperis**
ducit	**capit**	**ducitur**	**capitur**
ducimus	**capimus**	**ducimur**	**capimur**
ducitis	**capitis**	**ducimini**	**capimini**
ducunt	**capiunt**	**ducuntur**	**capiuntur**

Imperfect tense:

ACTIVE		PASSIVE	
I was leading; I was seizing		I was led; I was seized	
ducebam	**capiebam**	**ducebar**	**capiebar**
ducebas	**capiebas**	**ducebaris**	**capiebaris**
ducebat	**capiebat**	**ducebatur**	**capiebatur**
ducebamus	**capiebamus**	**ducebamur**	**capiebamur**
ducebatis	**capiebatis**	**ducebamini**	**capiebamini**
ducebant	**capiebant**	**ducebantur**	**capiebantur**

Future tense:

ACTIVE		PASSIVE	
I shall lead; I shall seize		I shall be led; I shall be seized	
ducam	**capiam**	**ducar**	**capiar**
duces	**capies**	**duceris**	**capieris**
ducet	**capiet**	**ducetur**	**capietur**
ducemus	**capiemus**	**ducemur**	**capiemur**
ducetis	**capietis**	**ducemini**	**capiemini**
ducent	**capient**	**ducentur**	**capientur**

The perfect tenses are all regular.

B. When **cum** is used to show how something was done, it often follows the Adjective.

Cum diligentia laborat.	He works with diligence.
Magna cum diligentia laborat.	He works with great diligence.

C. The cause of an action may be shown by either the Ablative Case alone or by **ob** or **propter** and the Accusative Case.

timore,	because of (on account of) fear
ob timorem,	because of (on account of) fear
propter timorem,	because of (on account of) fear

LATIN IN THE CONSTITUTION OF THE UNITED STATES

The following Latin phrases are used in the Constitution:

In Section 3, dealing with Officers of the Senate:

"The Senate shall choose their officers, and also a president **pro tempore**, in the absence of the Vice-President, or when he shall exercise the office of President of the United States." **pro tempore** means *for the time.*

In Section 9, dealing with Powers Forbidden to the United States:

"The privilege of the writ of **habeas corpus** shall not be suspended, unless when in cases of rebellion or invasion the public safety may require it." **habeas corpus** means *thou shalt have the body*. A writ of habeas corpus is a legal document making it mandatory that an accused person be told in court the reason for his detention.

"No bill of attainder or **ex-post-facto** law shall be passed." **ex post facto** means *from what is done afterwards.* An ex post facto law is one passed after a crime has been committed. Thus, a person who has committed a crime must be tried under the laws as they existed at the time of the commission of the crime.

PRACTICE EXERCISES

No. 105. Translate these phrases, showing cause or reason.

1. **ob moram**	4. **propter timorem**	7. **celeritate**	10. **tempore**
2. **cura mea**	5. **ob mortem**	8. **ob audaciam**	
3. **propter pericula**	6. **diligentia**	9. **propter moras**	

No. 106. Translate these phrases, showing manner.

1. **cum studio**
2. **magna cura**
3. **magna cum diligentia**
4. **magno cum timore**
5. **cum celeritate**
6. **studio multo**
7. **magno cum studio**
8. **cum mora**
9. **magna celeritate**
10. **magna cum mora**

No. 107. Complete these principal parts.

1. **pono, ponere, __________, positus**
2. **supero, __________, superavi, superatus**
3. **do, dare, __________, datus**
4. **capio, __________, cepi, captus**
5. **servo, servare, servavi, __________**
6. **__________, facere, feci, factus**
7. **verto, vertere, __________, versus**
8. **terreo, terrere, __________, territus**
9. **__________, ducere, duxi, ductus**
10. **paro, parare, paravi, __________**

No. 108. Translate these Verb forms.

1. **iussit**
2. **duxisti**
3. **demonstraverunt**
4. **rogabam**
5. **fecimus**
6. **docetur**
7. **mitteris**
8. **capimini**
9. **spectabit**
10. **augebimus**
11. **petent**
12. **volabant**
13. **obtinebas**
14. **vertebatur**
15. **terruerat**
16. **petiveratis**
17. **ceperant**
18. **moti erunt**
19. **ducti eramus**
20. **capiebat**

No. 109. Translate these prepositional phrases.

1. **ob horam**
2. **propter telum**
3. **ante castra**
4. **a timore**
5. **de arbore**
6. **ab rege**
7. **ex arboribus**
8. **in eum locum**
9. **cum patre**
10. **cum cura**
11. **in aqua**
12. **sub oceano**
13. **circum muros**
14. **contra eum**
15. **inter oppida**
16. **per agrum**
17. **post castra**
18. **sine eis**
19. **trans mare**
20. **de viris**

CHAPTER 23

READING

Hannibal

1. **Adulescens, Hannibal, erat inimicus Romanis quod a patre suo ductus est.**
2. **In Africa habitaverunt, sed mox Hannibal cum suis trans aquam in navibus multis ad Hispaniam navigavit.**
3. **Ipse multas copias et classem bonam habuit.**
4. **In Hispania multa oppida oppugnavit et praedam captivosque cepit.**
5. **Tum ad Italiam viros suos duxit, sed inter Hispaniam Italiamque erant montes.**

Hannibal

1. The youth, Hannibal, was unfriendly to the Romans because he had been led by his father.
2. They lived in Africa, but soon Hannibal with his men sailed across the water in many ships to Spain.
3. He himself had many troops and a good fleet.
4. In Spain he attacked many towns and took booty and captives.
5. Then he led his men to Italy, but between Spain and Italy there were mountains.

Hannibal

6. **Eidem montes pedites equitesque eius minime iuverunt.**
7. **Multa impedimenta portabantur. Ad imperatorem Romanorum id nuntium portatum est.**
8. **Romani ad hostes iter facere properaverunt.**
9. **Romani proelio hostes non vicerunt, sed bellum ad Africam mox portatum est et Romani ad victoriam ab imperatore suo ibi ducti sunt.**

Hannibal

6. These same mountains did not help his foot-soldiers and horsemen at all.
7. They were carrying much baggage. This message was carried to the general of the Romans.
8. The Romans hurried to travel toward the enemy.
9. The Romans did not conquer the enemy in battle, but soon the war was carried to Africa and the Romans were led to victory there by their general.

Theseus et Minotaurus

1. **Populus Graeciae contra populum insulae Cretae multos annos bellum gesserat.**
2. **Graeci magno cum animo diu contendebant, sed ab copiis Minois, regis Cretae, victi erant.**
3. **Haec fuerat causa belli: Filius Minois a Graecis interfectus erat. Itaque rex ob iniuriam illam ab his poenam petebat.**
4. **Septem puellas et septem pueros rogavit.**
5. **Graeci erant miseri, sed illos miserunt.**
6. **Minos, rex, labyrinthum habebat. In labyrintho animal barbarum, Minotaurum, tenebat.**
7. **In labyrinthum puellas puerosque duxit.**
8. **In illo loco terrebantur quod contra eum sine armis pugnare non poterant et mortem acceperunt.**

Theseus and the Minotaur

1. The people of Greece had waged war against the people of the island of Crete for many years.
2. The Greeks fought for a long time with great spirit, but they had been conquered by the forces of Minos, the king of Crete.
3. This was the cause of the war: The son of Minos had been killed by the Greeks. And so the king sought punishment from them because of that injury.
4. He asked for seven girls and seven boys.
5. The Greeks were unhappy, but they sent them.
6. Minos, the king, had a labyrinth. In the labyrinth he kept a savage animal, the Minotaur.
7. He led the girls and boys into the labyrinth.
8. In that place they were terrified because they were not able to fight against him without weapons and they accepted death.

READING VOCABULARY

Nouns

animus, animi, m., mind, spirit (animosity)
labyrinthus, labyrinthi, m., labyrinth (labyrinthal)
iniuria, iniuriae, f., injury, harm (injurious)
adulescens, adulescentis, m., youth (**adulescentium**) (adolescent)
classis, classis, f., a fleet (**classium**) (class)
imperator, imperatoris, m., general, commander, emperor (imperative)
impedimentum, impedimenti, n., hindrance In the plural, baggage (impediment)
eques, equitis, m., horseman, knight (equestrian)
pedes, peditis, m., foot soldier
navis, navis, f., ship (**navium**) (navy)
Minotaurus, Minotauri, m., the Minotaur
Minos, Minois, m., Minos
Hannibal, Hannibalis, m., Hannibal
Africa, Africae, f., Africa

Adjectives

hic, haec, hoc, this
ille, illa, illud, that
idem, eadem, idem, the same (identical)
ipse, ipsa, ipsum, himself, herself, itself; very

Pronouns

hic, haec, hoc, he, she, it
ille, illa, illud, he, she, it
idem, eadem, idem, he, she, it
ipse, ipsa, ipsum, he (himself), she (herself), it (itself)

Verbs

vinco, vincere, vici, victus, conquer
contendo, contendere, contendi, contentus, hasten, strive, contend (contender)
interficio, interficere, interfeci, interfectus, kill
gero, gerere, gessi, gestus, carry on, wage

Conjunction

itaque, and so, therefore

READING GRAMMAR

A. These words are used as both Pronouns and Adjectives in the same way as **is, ea, id.**

	PRONOUN	ADJECTIVE
hic, haec, hoc	he, she, it (here)	this
ille, illa, illud	he, she, it (there)	that
idem, eadem, idem	he, she, it (the same)	the same
ipse, ipsa, ipsum	he, she, it (-self)	himself, herself, itself; very

hic vir, this man	**hic,** he
ille homo, that man	**ille,** he
idem homo, the same man	**idem,** he
vir ipse, the man himself	**ipse,** he

The declension of these words is very much the same as **is, ea, id:**

Nom.	**hic**	he	**haec**	she	**hoc**	it	this
Gen.	**huius**	his	**huius**	her	**huius**	its	of this
Dat.	**huic**	to him	**huic**	to her	**huic**	to it	to this
Acc.	**hunc**	him	**hanc**	her	**hoc**	it	this
Abl.	**hoc**	by him	**hac**	by her	**hoc**	by it	by this
Nom.	**hi**		**hae**		**haec**	they	these
Gen.	**horum**		**harum**		**horum**	their	of these
Dat.	**his**		**his**		**his**	to them	to these
Acc.	**hos**		**has**		**haec**	them	these
Abl.	**his**		**his**		**his**	by them	by these

	SINGULAR			PLURAL		
Nom.	**ille**	**illa**	**illud**	**illi**	**illae**	**illa**
Gen.	**illius**	**illius**	**illius**	**illorum**	**illarum**	**illorum**
Dat.	**illi**	**illi**	**illi**	**illis**	**illis**	**illis**
Acc.	**illum**	**illam**	**illud**	**illos**	**illas**	**illa**
Abl.	**illo**	**illa**	**illo**	**illis**	**illis**	**illis**

ille, illa, illud has the same meanings (he, she, it) as **is, ea, id** or **hic, haec, hoc** when used as a Pronoun. As an Adjective, **ille, illa, illud** means *that.*

ipse, ipsa, ipsum is declined just like **is, ea, id** or **ille, illa, illud** after the first few forms:

Nom.	**ipse**	**ipsa**	**ipsum**
Gen.	**ipsius**	**ipsius**	**ipsius**
Dat.	**ipsi**	**ipsi**	**ipsi**
Acc.	**ipsum**	**ipsam**	**ipsum**
Abl.		regular	

As a Pronoun, **ipse, ipsa, ipsum** means *he* (himself), *she* (herself), *it* (itself). As an Adjective, it means *himself, herself, itself, very.*

idem, eadem, idem is based on **is, ea, id** and declined in much the same way:

Nom.	**idem**	**eadem**	**idem**	**eidem, iidem**	**eaedem**	**eadem**
Gen.	**eiusdem**	**eiusdem**	**eiusdem**	**eorundem**	**earundem**	**eorundem**
Dat.	**eidem**	**eidem**	**eidem**	**eisdem, iisdem**	in all genders	
Acc.	**eundem**	**eandem**	**idem**	**eosdem**	**easdem**	**eadem**
Abl.	**eodem**	**eadem**	**eodem**	**eisdem, iisdem**	in all genders	

As a Pronoun, **idem, eadem, idem** means (the same) *he,* (the same) *she,* (the same) *it.* As an Adjective it means *same.*

B. **possum, posse, potui,** *to be able, can,* is based on **sum, esse, fui.**

Present tense

possum	I am able, can	**possumus**	we are able, can
potes	you are able, can	**potestis**	you are able, can
potest	he, she, it is able, can	**possunt**	they are able, can

Imperfect tense

poteram I was able, could
poteras you were able, could
etc.

Future tense

potero I shall be able, can
poteris you will be able, can
etc.

Perfect tense

potui I have been able, could
potuisti you have been able, could
etc.

Pluperfect tense

potueram I had been able, could
potueras you had been able, could
etc.

Future Perfect tense

potuero I shall have been able, could
potueris you will have been able, could
etc.

possum, posse, potui must always have a completing infinitive.

ducere potest, he is able to lead, he can lead
vincere posse debet, he ought to be able to conquer

THE PRONUNCIATION OF CHURCH LATIN

The pronunciation of Church Latin may follow the classical Latin pronunciation, or the general pattern of the Italian pronunciation. The rules are by no means fixed and standardized, but, with widened oral communication, the Italian pronunciation of liturgical Latin has increased in the Roman Catholic Church, as it has also in the singing of all Church Latin.

1. Vowels.
   The vowels have the same pronuciation, except that **u** becomes **ou.** meus, meous
2. Consonants.
   The most noticeable difference is that **c** before **e** or **i** is not **k**, but **ch.** cibus, chibous

   If **c** before **e** or **i** is preceded by an **s**, the **s** is dropped. scio, chio

   ti between two vowels is **tsi.** nationem, natsionem

   ti after a consonant (except **s**, **t**, or **x**) is **ci.** amanti, amanci

   g before **e** or **i** is soft, like **j.** gens, jens

   All double consonants are pronounced definitely, with equal stress on each. anno, an-no

PRACTICE EXERCISES

No. 110. Translate these phrases which use **hic** and **ille.**

1. **hic murus**
2. **illam urbem**
3. **in illo loco**
4. **hi duces**
5. **illis militibus**
6. **illi legato**
7. **hos imperatores**
8. **illa consilia**
9. **illius oceani**
10. **horum hominum**
11. **in illo horto**
12. **illa dea**
13. **illius peditis**
14. **de hoc domino**
15. **ex illa arbore**
16. **hunc impedimentum**
17. **his patribus**
18. **has naves**
19. **ille liber**
20. **illi puellae**
21. **haec arma**
22. **harum partium**
23. **de illa pace**
24. **illarum arenarum**
25. **his annis**
26. **illam horam**
27. **illud signum**
28. **huius equi**
29. **ad has feminas**
30. **illos nuntios**

No. 111. Translate these Pronouns.

1. **huius**
2. **ille**
3. **illi**
4. **hos**
5. **illis**
6. **harum**
7. **hoc**
8. **huic**
9. **illa**
10. **hi**
11. **haec**
12. **hanc**
13. **has**
14. **illum**
15. **illos**

No. 112. Translate these phrases which use **idem** and **ipse.**

1. **dea ipsa**
2. **ex templis ipsis**
3. **urbem eandem**
4. **homines ipsos**
5. **ab eodem adulescenti**
6. **idem nomen**
7. **eiusdem nationis**
8. **cum eisdem equitibus**
9. **eadem itinera**
10. **iisdem viris**
11. **ex agro ipso**
12. **annis ipsis**
13. **pueri ipsi**
14. **legati ipsius**
15. **eadem hora**
16. **lex ipsa**
17. **mons ipse**
18. **puellae ipsae**
19. **idem iter**
20. **ab mulieribus ipsis**
21. **eodem tempore**
22. **eorundem imperatorum**
23. **eadem oppida**
24. **in urbibus ipsis**
25. **eiusdem populi**
26. **iidem homines**
27. **ex iisdem locis**
28. **iisdem annis**
29. **nocte ipsa**
30. **pax ipsa**

No. 113. Translate these Pronouns.

1. ipsi	**4. ipsa**	**7. eundem**	**10. ipsius**
2. eiusdem	**5. ipsos**	**8. eorundem**	
3. idem	**6. eadem**	**9. ex iisdem**	

No. 114. Give the English for these forms of possum.

1. ducere poterant	**6. necare non potuimus**	**11. iuvare poterimus**
2. manere potes	**7. iubere potueram**	**12. pugnare poteris**
3. adorare non potuit	**8. docere potes**	**13. vocare non potuerunt**
4. liberare poterit	**9. rogare poteramus**	**14. laborare non possum**
5. curare possunt	**10. augere non potui**	**15. manere potuistis**

CHAPTER 24

READING

Theseus et Minotaurus (concl'd.)	Theseus and the Minotaur (concl'd.)
1. Interea in Graecia Theseus fortuna misera puerorum puellarumque Graecorum incitatus est.	1. Meanwhile in Greece Theseus was aroused by the unhappy fortune of the Greek boys and girls.
2. Rogavit: "Estne nullum auxilium pro his filiis civium nostrorum?"	2. He asked: "Is there no help for these children of our citizens?"
3. Itaque ad Cretam cum sociis suis navi contendit.	3. And so he hurried to Crete by ship with his comrades.
4. Ariadne, filia regis, eum vidit et ob virtutem eius illum amavit.	4. Ariadne, the daughter of the king, saw him and loved him because of his courage.
5. Sine mora illa de labyrintho eum docuit.	5. Without delay she showed him about the labyrinth.
6. Tum Theseus solus ad labyrinthum properavit. Arma portabat et bonum consilium Ariadnes memoria tenebat.	6. Then Theseus alone hurried to the labyrinth. He carried weapons and he remembered the good advice of Ariadne.
7. Mox Minotaurum spectabat. Cum illo animali diu contendebat, sed id interficere potuit.	7. Soon he saw the Minotaur. He struggled with that animal for a long time, but was able to kill it.
8. Minotaurus necatus erat. Pueri puellaeque liberati erant.	8. The Minotaur had been killed. The boys and girls had been freed.
9. Totos annos postea populus Graeciae laetus erat quod regi malo Cretae nullas poenas dabat.	9. For all the years afterwards the people of Greece were happy because they paid no penalties to the evil king of Crete.

Ulixes et Cyclops	Ulysses and the Cyclops
1. **Homerus, poeta antiquus, de bello inter viros Graeciae Troiaeque in suo magno opere scripsit.**	1. Homer, an ancient poet, wrote in his great work about the war between the men of Greece and Troy.
2. **Post multos annos longos Troia ab Graecis capta erat.**	2. After many long years Troy had been captured by the Greeks.
3. **Graeci ab illo loco navigabant. Apud eos erat Ulixes, homo audax, sed brevi tempore navis eius tempestate ad aliam partem maris portata est.**	3. The Greeks were sailing away from that place. Among them was Ulysses, a bold man, but in a short time his ship was carried by a storm to another part of the sea.
4. **Ex navi ad terram cum sociis suis Ulixes contendit.**	4. Ulysses hurried from his ship to the land with his comrades.
5. **Non longe ab illo loco ubi stabant corpus magnum Polyphemi, Cyclopis, mox viderunt. Ille in colli habitabat.**	5. Not far from that place where they were standing they soon saw the large body of Polyphemus, the Cyclops. He lived on a hill.
6. **Graeci iniuriam timebant.**	6. The Greeks feared injury.
7. **Polyphemus eos a mari celeribus pedibus duxit.**	7. Polyphemus led them away from the sea at a swift pace.
8. **Viri cibum exspectabant, sed Cyclops pro cibo suo unum hominem, tum alterum, et alium cepit.**	8. The men waited for food, but the Cyclops, for his own food, took one man, then another, and another.
9. **Alii pro sociis suis dolebant.**	9. The others grieved for their comrades.
10. **Illine ab Polyphemo fugere poterunt?**	10. Will they be able to flee from Polyphemus?

READING VOCABULARY

Nouns

civis, civis, m. or f., citizen (civium) (civic)
Theseus, Thesei, m., Theseus
Ariadne, Ariadnes, f., Ariadne (a Greek noun)
opus, operis, n., work (opera)
tempestas, tempestatis, f., storm, bad weather (tempest)
poeta, poetae, m., poet (poetical)
Polyphemus, Polyphemi, m., Polyphemus
Cyclops, Cyclopis, m., Cyclops
Homerus, Homeri, m., Homer
Ulixes, Ulixis, m., Ulysses

Verbs

scribo, scribere, scripsi, scriptus, write (scribe)
fugio, fugere, fugi, flee, run away, escape (fugitive)

Adverb

interea, meanwhile

Adjectives

celer, celeris, celere, quick, swift (celerity)
acer, acris, acre, sharp, active, keen (acrid)
omnis, omne, all, every (omnibus)
audax, audacis, bold **audacis** is the Gen. Case (audacious)
brevis, breve, short, brief (brevity)
alius, alia, aliud, other, another (alien)
unus, una, unum, one (unite)
alter, altera, alterum, the one, the other (alternate)
nullus, nulla, nullum, no, none (null)
solus, sola, solum, alone, only (solitude)
totus, tota, totum, all, whole (total)

Prepositions

apud, among, in the presence of With the Acc. Case
pro, in front of; for, instead of With the Abl. Case

READING GRAMMAR

A. Some Adjectives that belong to the **a-** and **o-declensions** have the Genitive singular ending in **-ius** and the Dative singular ending in **-i**. Otherwise, they are regular.

Nom.	**unus**	**una**	**unum**
Gen.	**unius**	**unius**	**unius**
Dat.	**uni**	**uni**	**uni**
Acc.	**unum**	**unam**	**unum**
etc.			

These Adjectives are declined like **unus**:

alius, alia, aliud, other, another
alter, altera, alterum, the one, the other
neuter, neutra, neutrum, neither
nullus, nulla, nullum, no, none
solus, sola, solum, alone, only
totus, tota, totum, whole, all
ullus, ulla, ullum, any
uter, ultra, utrum, which (of two)

B. Sometimes **alius** or **alter** may be in pairs:

alius...alius, one...another **alii...alii,** some...others
alter...alter, the one...the other (of two)

Alterum iter longum est, alterum non est.	One road is long, the other is not.
Alii sunt boni, alii sunt mali.	Some are good, some are bad.

C. Those Adjectives that do not belong to the **a-** or **o-declensions** belong to the **i-declension.** These are of three kinds, according to the number of spellings in the Nominative singular, but all have the **i-declension** endings. The masculine and feminine genders are declined like **urbs**; the neuter like **mare**. See Chapter 15. The three kinds are:

1. one spelling for all genders:

	M.	F.	N.
Nom.	**audax**	**audax**	**audax**
Gen.	**audacis**	**audacis**	**audacis**
Dat.	**audaci**	**audaci**	**audaci**
etc.			

2. two spellings—one for the masculine and feminine, one for the neuter:

	M.	F.	N.
Nom.	**omnis**	**omnis**	**omne**
Gen.	**omnis**	**omnis**	**omnis**
Dat.	**omni**	**omni**	**omni**
etc.			

3. three spellings—one for each gender:

	M.	F.	N.
Nom.	**celer**	**celeris**	**celere**
Gen.	**celeris**	**celeris**	**celeris**
Dat.	**celeri**	**celeri**	**celeri**
etc.			

SUFFIXES

Some of the more common suffixes used to form Adjectives are:

-eus, denoting the material. English, of **aureus,** of gold

-osus, denoting fullness. English, full of **periculosis,** full of danger

-bilis, denoting possibility. English, able **amabilis,** able to be loved, lovable

-anus, -icus, -alis, -inus, denoting connection.

-anus becomes -ane or -an in English. **Romanus,** Roman

-icus becomes -ic in English. **publicus,** public

-alis becomes -al in English. **mortalis,** mortal

-inus becomes -in or -ine in English. **Latinus,** Latin

PRACTICE EXERCISES

No. 115. Give the English for these phrases.

1. **uno anno**
2. **nullam curam**
3. **utrius doni**
4. **ulli navi**
5. **totos annos**
6. **cum patre solo**
7. **nullarum mortium**
8. **neutri nationi**
9. **in altera via**
10. **alio nomine**
11. **ad utrum flumen**
12. **ullius collis**
13. **uni libro**
14. **ob nullas causas**
15. **ab neutro homine**

No. 116. Translate these Verb forms.

1. **timuerant**
2. **fuistis**
3. **mittent**
4. **cepit**
5. **timebit**
6. **spectabant**
7. **tenebuntur**
8. **mittar**
9. **laudati sunt**
10. **factum erat**
11. **navigabas**
12. **dabantur**
13. **gerit**
14. **fuerant**
15. **habuerunt**

No. 117. Give the English for the following.

1. **alter puer est, alter non est**
2. **nullo tempore**
3. **ullius belli**
4. **ad utra castra**
5. **mulieres ipsae solae**
6. **neutrius adulescentis**
7. **alias urbes**
8. **unam partem**
9. **de neutra puella**
10. **aliud iter**

No. 118. Give the English for these phrases.

1. **hora breve**
2. **servi audacis**
3. **eques celer**
4. **in flumine celeri**
5. **ab viris audacibus**
6. **tempora omnia**
7. **a legato acri**
8. **vita brevis**
9. **omnibus horis**
10. **in navi celeri**
11. **opus audax**
12. **brevi tempore**
13. **copiae acres**
14. **equi celeris**
15. **acres feminae**
16. **mortem celerem**
17. **itinera brevia**
18. **audaci homini**
19. **brevem annum**
20. **omni in loco**

CHAPTER 25

READING

Ulixes et Cyclops (concl'd.)	Ulysses and the Cyclops (concl'd.)
1. Postquam Cyclops haec fecerat, Graeci fortes mortem exspectabant, sed Ulixes Polyphemum interficere in animo habebat.	1. After the Cyclops had done these things, the brave Greeks waited for death, but Ulysses had in mind to kill Polyphemus.
2. Ob magnitudinem viri non erat ullum iter facile ex periculo eorum, sed consilium parabant et suos animos bonos tenebant.	2. Because of the great size of the man there was not any easy way out of their danger, but they prepared a plan and kept their good spirits.
3. Ante hoc tempus alia pericula gravia superaverant et hoc periculum novum superare in animo habuerunt.	3. Before this time they had overcome other serious dangers and they had in mind to overcome this new danger.
4. Uterque Cyclopem timebat, sed Polyphemus inimicus omnibus erat.	4. Each feared the Cyclops, but Polyphemus was unfriendly to all.
5. Eum incitare non debebant. Itaque Ulixes suum consilium eis demonstravit.	5. They ought not to arouse him. And so Ulysses showed them his plan.
6. Partem arboris in igni posuerunt. Post breve tempus finis arboris erat acer.	6. They placed part of a tree in the fire. After a short time the end of the tree was sharp.
7. Hoc erat telum eorum contra Cyclopem. Id magna cum diligentia paraverant.	7. This was their weapon against the Cyclops. They had prepared it with great care.
8. Hoc telo Cyclops poenas dabit.	8. With this weapon the Cyclops will pay the penalty.
9. Polyphemus unum oculum solum habuit. Magna cum audacia Ulixes et socii sui in oculo eius finem arboris posuerunt.	9. Polyphemus had only one eye. With great boldness Ulysses and his comrades put the end of the tree in his eye.
10. Iniuria erat gravis et Cyclops postea videre non poterat.	10. The injury was serious and the Cyclops was not able to see after that.
11. Polyphemus etiam multa animalia habebat.	11. Polyphemus also had many animals.
12. Ante portam ille saxum grave et magnum posuerat.	12. He had put a heavy and large stone in front of the door.
13. Id a Graecis moveri non potuit, sed Cyclops ab porta saxum movebat, cum animalia cibum petebant.	13. This could not be moved by the Greeks, but the Cyclops moved the stone away from the door, when the animals sought food.
14. Hoc erat consilium: Ulixes et sui amici fugam suam noctu paraverunt.	14. This was the plan: Ulysses and his friends prepared their flight at night.
15. Cyclops eos videre non potuit.	15. The Cyclops was not able to see them.
16. Saxum ab porta movit.	16. He moved the stone away from the door.
17. Animalia per portam cucurrerunt. Sub animalibus erant Graeci.	17. The animals ran through the door. Under the animals were the Greeks.
18. Graeci simulabant et Polyphemus eos non cognovit.	18. The Greeks pretended and Polyphemus did not recognize them.
19. Tum Ulixes clamavit. Itaque Cyclops fugam eorum cognovit.	19. Then Ulysses shouted. And so the Cyclops learned of their flight.

Ulixes et Cyclops (concl'd.)

20. **Cyclops ad mare properavit. Saxum magnum ad Graecos iecit.**
21. **Polyphemus dixit: "Quis es?"**
22. **Ulixes clamavit: "Nullus homo sum.", sed Graeci in navi erant et laeti erant quod a Polyphemo fugerant et ad Graeciam navigabant.**
23. **Postea de oculo suo Polyphemus dicebat: "Nullus id fecit."**

Ulysses and the Cyclops (concl'd.)

20. The Cyclops hurried to the sea. He threw a large stone toward the Greeks.
21. Polyphemus said: "Who are you?"
22. Ulysses shouted: "I am no man.", but the Greeks were on the ship and were happy because they had escaped from Polyphemus and were sailing to Greece.
23. Afterwards Polyphemus said about his eye: "No one did it."

READING VOCABULARY

Nouns

oculus, oculi, m., eye (oculist)
porta, portae, f., gate, door, entrance (portal)
saxum, saxi, n., stone, rock (saxatile)
fuga, fugae, f., flight, escape (fugue)
telum, teli, n., weapon

Adjectives

facilis, facile, easy (facility)
fortis, forte, brave, strong (fort)
gravis, grave, heavy, severe, serious (gravity)
novus, nova, novum, new (novel)
uterque, utraque, utrumque, each, every

Pronoun

quis, quid, who?, what?

Verbs

simulo, simulare, simulavi, simulatus, pretend (simulate)
clamo, clamare, clamavi, clamatus, shout, cry (clamor)
iacio, iacere, ieci, iactus, throw (project)
cognosco, cognoscere, cognovi, cognitus, learn, recognize, know (cognizance)

Adverb

noctu, at night (noctambular)

READING GRAMMAR

A. **uterque, utraque, utrumque** is declined just like **uter, utra, utrum.**

uterque vir, each man	**utriusque viri**, of each man
utrique viro, to each man	**utrumque virum**, each man

B. The declension of **quis, quid**, who?, what?, is quite similar to that of **is, ea, id.**

	SINGULAR			PLURAL			
	M.	F.	N.	M.	F.	N.	
Nom.	**quis**	**quis**	**quid**	**qui**	**quae**	**quae**	who?, what?
Gen.	**cuius**	**cuius**	**cuius**	**quorum**	**quarum**	**quorum**	of whom?, whose?, of what?
Dat.	**cui**	**cui**	**cui**	**quibus**	**quibus**	**quibus**	to, for whom?, to, for what?
Acc.	**quem**	**quem**	**quid**	**quos**	**quas**	**quae**	whom?, what?
Abl.	**quo**	**quo**	**quo**	**quibus**	**quibus**	**quibus**	from, with, by, in whom?, what?

Quis est? Who is it?	**Qui sunt?** Who are they?
Cuius est? Whose is it?	**Quorum est?** Whose is it?
Quem vides? Whom do you see?	**Quid vides?** What do you see?

C. When **cum** is used with the Ablative case, it is generally added to the end.

quocum, with whom **quibuscum,** with whom

D. The Present Passive Infinitive of the **a-** and **e-conjugations** is like the Present Active Infinitive except that it ends in **-i.**

amare, to love	**amari,** to be loved
habere, to have	**haberi,** to be had

In the **e/i-conjugation,** the **-i** is added directly to the stem.

ducere, to lead	**duci,** to be led
capere, to take	**capi,** to be taken

FAMILIAR QUOTATIONS

Nil homini certum est, Nothing is certain to man. Ovid

Virtus praemium est optimum, Virtue is the best reward. Plautus

Omnia praeclara rara, All the best things are rare. Cicero

Possunt quia posse videntur, They can because they think they can. Virgil

Alea iacta est, The die is cast. Caesar

Mens sana in corpore sano, A sound mind in a sound body. Juvenal

Carmina morte carent, Songs do not die. Ovid

PRACTICE EXERCISES

No. 119. Translate these Adjective phrases.

1. **solis aurei**
2. **ex neutro loco**
3. **summo in monte**
4. **itineris facilis**
5. **ullae horae**
6. **poenas graves**
7. **nationum proximarum**
8. **civem audacem**
9. **corpus robustum**
10. **fluminum celerium**
11. **libros latinos**
12. **homines alii**
13. **navis vestra**
14. **patrum multorum**
15. **utriusque regis**

No. 120. Give the English for these Interrogative phrases and clauses.

1. **Qui estis?**
2. **Cui ea dedit?**
3. **Quos videbo?**
4. **cuius oculi?**
5. **Quae cognoscit?**
6. **Quocum ambulat?**
7. **A quo captus est?**
8. **Quis clamat?**
9. **Quis pugnat?**
10. **quorum tela?**
11. **Quid habes?**
12. **Quem necavit?**
13. **Quibus id dabo?**
14. **Quid rogatum est?**
15. **Cui donum misisti?**
16. **Quem amas?**
17. **Quis fugit?**
18. **Quid facile est?**
19. **Cuius est?**
20. **quibuscum?**
21. **Quos mittet?**
22. **Quid facit?**
23. **Qui contendunt?**
24. **A quo gestum est?**
25. **Quis vocat?**

No. 121. Give the Active form of these Present Passive Infinitives.

1. **pugnari**	5. **laudari**	9. **cognosci**	13. **haberi**	17. **augeri**
2. **mitti**	6. **rogari**	10. **necari**	14. **moveri**	18. **servari**
3. **regi**	7. **scribi**	11. **capi**	15. **parari**	19. **vinci**
4. **dari**	8. **videri**	12. **timeri**	16. **duci**	20. **terreri**

No. 122. Give the Passive form of these Present Active Infinitives.

1. **demonstrare**	6. **armare**	11. **mittere**	16. **interficere**
2. **ducere**	7. **amare**	12. **gerere**	17. **iuvare**
3. **movere**	8. **facere**	13. **accipere**	18. **tenere**
4. **iubere**	9. **docere**	14. **timere**	19. **cognoscere**
5. **vertere**	10. **occupare**	15. **vocare**	20. **simulare**

SIXTH REVIEW SECTION (CHAPTERS 22–25)

VOCABULARY REVIEW

NOUNS

1. **adulescens**	15. **fuga**	29. **pedes**	1. youth	15. flight, escape	29. foot soldier
2. **Africa**	16. **Hannibal**	30. **poena**	2. Africa	16. Hannibal	30. punishment, fine
3. **animus**	17. **Homerus**	31. **poeta**	3. mind, spirit	17. Homer	31. poet
4. **arbor**	18. **impedimentum**	32. **Polyphemus**	4. tree	18. hindrance	32. Polyphemus
5. **arena**	19. **imperator**	33. **porta**	5. sand	19. commander, general, emperor	33. gate, door, entrance
6. **Ariadne**	20. **iniuria**	34. **saxum**	6. Ariadne	20. injury, harm	34. stone, rock
7. **aurum**	21. **labyrinthus**	35. **Silenus**	7. gold	21. labyrinth	35. Silenus
8. **Bacchus**	22. **Midas**	36. **studium**	8. Bacchus	22. Midas	36. zeal, eagerness
9. **cibus**	23. **Minos**	37. **telum**	9. food	23. Minos	37. weapon
10. **civis**	24. **Minotaurus**	38. **tempestas**	10. citizen	24. the Minotaur	38. storm, bad weather
11. **classis**	25. **mors**	39. **tempus**	11. fleet	25. death	39. time
12. **Cyclops**	26. **navis**	40. **Theseus**	12. Cyclops	26. ship	40. Theseus
13. **diligentia**	27. **oculus**	41. **timor**	13. diligence, care	27. eye	41. fear, dread
14. **eques**	28. **opus**	42. **Ulixes**	14. horseman, knight	28. work	42. Ulysses

PRONOUNS

1. **hic, haec, hoc**	4. **ipse, ipsa, ipsum**	1. he, she, it	4. he himself, she herself, it itself
2. **idem, eadem, idem**	5. **quis, quid**	2. he, she, it	5. who?, what?
3. **ille, illa, illud**		3. he, she, it	

ADJECTIVES

1. **acer**	11. **idem**	1. sharp, active, keen	11. the same
2. **alius**	12. **ille**	2. other, another	12. that
3. **alter**	13. **ipse**	3. the one, the other	13. very, himself, herself, itself
4. **audax**	14. **novus**	4. bold	14. new
5. **brevis**	15. **nullus**	5. short, brief	15. no, none
6. **celer**	16. **omnis**	6. quick, swift	16. all, every
7. **facilis**	17. **solus**	7. easy	17. alone, only
8. **fortis**	18. **totus**	8. brave, strong	18. all, whole
9. **gravis**	19. **unus**	9. heavy, severe, serious	19. one
10. **hic**	20. **uterque**	10. this	20. each, every

VERBS

1. **capio**	8. **iacio**	1. take, seize, capture	8. throw
2. **clamo**	9. **interficio**	2. shout, cry	9. kill
3. **cognosco**	10. **pono**	3. learn, recognize, know	10. put, place
4. **contendo**	11. **scribo**	4. hasten, strive, contend	11. write
5. **facio**	12. **simulo**	5. make, do	12. pretend
6. **fugio**	13. **verto**	6. flee, run away, escape	13. turn
7. **gero**	14. **vinco**	7. carry on, wage	14. conquer

ADVERBS

1. interea	**2. noctu**	**1. meanwhile**	**2. at night**

PREPOSITIONS

1. apud	**3. propter**	**1. among, in the presence of**	**3. because of, on account of**
2. pro		**2. in front of; for, instead of**	

CONJUNCTION

1. itaque	**1. and so, therefore**

PRACTICE EXERCISES

No. 123. Translate these Verbs.

1. **capiunt**
2. **cognitum erat**
3. **victi sunt**
4. **vertent**
5. **interficiebamus**
6. **fecerunt**
7. **ceperas**
8. **fugiebat**
9. **ponetur**
10. **gesserint**
11. **scribit**
12. **iacis**
13. **contendent**
14. **positi sunt**
15. **gestum est**

No. 124. Translate these Phrases.

1. **propter mortem**
2. **ob iniuriam**
3. **diligentia magna**
4. **ob imperatorem**
5. **propter cibum**
6. **ob classes**
7. **parva cum poena**
8. **magno cum studio**
9. **ob impedimentum**
10. **propter arenam**

No. 125. Translate these Pronouns.

1. **hunc**
2. **huius**
3. **illos**
4. **illud**
5. **ipse**
6. **illorum**
7. **eadem**
8. **eiusdem**
9. **hic**
10. **ipsorum**
11. **quem**
12. **quid**
13. **cuius**
14. **cui**
15. **quocum**

No. 126. Translate these Verb forms.

1. **clamare potuit**
2. **capere poterant**
3. **facere potes**
4. **ponere possumus**
5. **vincere potuistis**
6. **contendere poterit**
7. **scribere potuerunt**
8. **cognoscere poteramus**
9. **vertere potes**
10. **gerere possunt**

No. 127. Translate these Adjective phrases.

1. **unius operis**
2. **omnium civium**
3. **aliud impedimentum**
4. **nova tela**
5. **brevi tempore**
6. **toti saxo**
7. **nullius timoris**
8. **ullam iniuriam**
9. **audaces equites**
10. **celeris poena**

MARCUS TULLIUS CICERO

Cicero was born near Arpinum, in Latium, the province in which Rome was located, in 106 B.C., of an upper middle class family. He studied law, philosophy, and rhetoric in Rome, Athens, and Rhodes, and became consul in 63 B.C. It was in this office that he disclosed Catiline's conspiracy to overthrow the government and, in four orations delivered in the Senate, persuaded the Senators to decree the death penalty for the conspirators. After Caesar's assassination in 44 B.C. and the formation of the Second Triumvirate, Cicero was murdered in 43 B.C., while trying to escape from his political enemies.

O tempora! O mores! Senatus haec intellegit, consul videt; hic tamen vivit. Vivit? Immo vero etiam in senatum venit, fit publici consili particeps, notat et designat oculis ad caedem unum quemque nostrum. Nos autem, fortes viri, satis facere rei publicae videmur, si istius furorem ac tela vitamus. Ad mortem te, Catilina, duci iussu consulis iam pridem oportebat; in te conferri pestem, quam tu in nos machinaris.	Oh what times these are! Oh what habits we have! The Senate knows these things, the consul sees them; this man, however, lives. Does he live? Indeed, he even comes into the Senate, he becomes a participant in the public plans, he notes and designates with his eyes each single one of us for murder. We, however, brave men, seem to do enough for the Republic, if we avoid the fury and weapons of this man. You, Catiline, should have been led to your death by the order of the consul long ago; the destruction that you are plotting against us should have been brought against you.
In Catilinam Oratio Prima, ii	First Oration Against Catiline, 2

These two stories were written by Odo de Cerinton, who lived in the twelfth century and composed a work called **NARRATIONES**, which drew stories from various fables and other sources, giving a mystical interpretation to tales about animals.

De Hydro	About the Hydra
Quoddam animal dicitur hydrus, cuius natura est se involvere luto, ut melius posset labi. Tandem in os crocodili, quando dormit, intrat et sic, ventrem eius ingrediens, cor eius mordet et sic crocodilum interimit.	There is a certain animal called the hydra, whose nature it is to bury itself in the mud so that it might be better able to glide. Finally it enters the mouth of a crocodile, when it is sleeping, and thus, entering its stomach, it eats its heart and thus kills the crocodile.
Mistice: Hydrus significat filium Dei, qui assumpsit lutum nostrae carnis ut facilius laberetur in os diaboli, et sic, ventrem eius ingrediens et cor eius mordens, ipsum interficit.	Mystical interpretation: The hydra signifies the son of God, who has assumed the mud of our flesh so that it might slip more easily into the mouth of the devil, and thus, entering his stomach and eating his heart, he kills him.

De Antilope	About the Antelope
Quoddam animal est quod vocatur antilops; quod cum virgultis ludit cum cornibus, tandem cornua eius implicantur cum virgultis quod non potest ea extrahere et tunc incipit clamare; quo audito veniunt venatores et interficiunt eum.	There is a certain animal that is called the antelope; when this animal plays in a thicket with its horns, finally its horns are entangled with the thicket so that it is not able to extricate them and then it begins to cry aloud; when this is heard, hunters come and kill him.
Mistice: Sic contigit quod plerique delectati sunt et ludunt cum negotiis huius mundi et sic in eisdem implicantur quod evelli non possunt et sic a venatoribus, id est a daemonibus, capiuntur et interficiuntur.	Mystical interpretation: Thus it happens that many people are delighted and play with the occupations of this world and thus are entangled in these things so that they can not be torn away and thus by hunters, that is by demons, they are taken and killed.

CHAPTER 26

READING

Orpheus et Eurydice

1. Orpheus erat vir fortis, sed dolebat quod Eurydice morte capta erat et eum solum et miserum reliquerat.
2. Orpheus animalia omnia et naturam bene amabat et laetus esse simulabat, sed Eurydicen semper petebat.
3. Orpheus ipse sine ea esse non poterat. Itaque auxilium ab deis petivit.
4. Nihil ab Iove faci poterat. Eurydice ab terra discesserat et apud Inferos nunc habitabat.
5. Iter ad regnum Plutonis erat difficile.
6. Pluto suos non saepe tradit, sed Orpheus erat audax et paene nullum timorem habebat.
7. Sub terram magna cum celeritate contendit. Ante regem, Plutonem, mox stat.
8. Orpheus ab Plutone petivit: "Cur Eurydicen hic tenes? Non solum ei amorem summum semper docebam sed etiam mors ei non est idonea. Eurydice ipsa nihil fecerat."
9. Tum Pluto ipse pro illo acriter dolebat, sed Orpheum iussit: "Eam tradam, sed iter ex regno Inferorum difficile est. Illa ad terram tuam reduci poterit, sed eam spectare non debes. Cum primus eam ad terram educes, tum eam spectare poteris."
10. Ab Plutone grate discesserunt et iter ab illo loco malo celeriter faciebant.
11. Primo ille fortiter ambulabat, sed Orpheus amore regebatur. Non diu postea ad eam oculos suos vertit.
12. Ob eam causam Pluto magna cum celeritate illam cepit et eam ad Inferos reduxit.
13. Ab illo tempore in terra non visa est.

Orpheus and Eurydice

1. Orpheus was a brave man, but he grieved because Eurydice had been taken by death and had left him alone and wretched.
2. Orpheus loved all animals and nature very much and he pretended to be happy, but he always looked for Eurydice.
3. Orpheus himself could not be without her. And so he sought help from the gods.
4. Nothing could be done by Jupiter. Eurydice had departed from the earth and was now living among Those Below.
5. The journey to the kingdom of Pluto was difficult.
6. Pluto does not often give up his own, but Orpheus was bold and had almost no fear.
7. He hurries below the earth with great speed. He soon stands before the king, Pluto.
8. Orpheus asked Pluto: "Why do you keep Eurydice here? Not only did I always show the greatest love for her, but also death is not suitable to her. Eurydice herself had done nothing."
9. Then Pluto himself felt keenly sorry for him, but he instructed Orpheus: "I shall give her up, but the way out of the kingdom of Those Below is difficult. She can be led back to your land, but you ought not to look at her. When you, going first, lead her back to earth, then you can look at her."
10. They departed from Pluto gratefully and quickly made the journey away from that evil place.
11. At first he walked bravely, but Orpheus was ruled by love. Not long afterwards he turns his eyes toward her.
12. For this reason Pluto seized her with great speed and led her back to Those Below.
13. From that time she was not seen on the earth.

READING VOCABULARY

Nouns

regnum, regni, n., kingdom (interregnum)
natura, naturae, f., nature (natural)
nihil or **nil, n.,** nothing **nihil** (or **nil**) has the same spelling in all Cases. (nihilist)
Orpheus, Orphei, m., Orpheus
Eurydice, Eurydices, f., Eurydice (a Greek noun)

Adjectives

difficilis, difficile, difficult, hard (difficulty)
primus, prima, primum, first (prime, primary)

Adverbs

parum, too little, not enough
magnopere, greatly

Verbs

relinquo, relinquere, reliqui, relictus, leave, leave behind (relinquish)
discedo, discedere, discessi, discessus, withdraw, go away, leave
trado, tradere, tradidi, traditus, give up, surrender (tradition)
rego, regere, rexi, rectus, rule (regent)
educo, educere, eduxi, eductus, lead out (educate)
reduco, reducere, reduxi, reductus, lead back (reduce)

READING GRAMMAR

A. Adverbs are generally formed from Adjectives.

1. Adverbs based on **a-** and **o-declension** Adjectives end in **-e.**

altus, high	**alte,** high, on high
latus, wide	**late,** widely
longus, long	**longe,** far, distant
miser, wretched	**misere,** wretchedly
pulcher, beautiful	**pulchre,** beautifully

2. Adverbs based on **i-declension** Adjectives end in **-ter.**

acer, keen	**acriter,** keenly
audax, bold	**audacter,** boldly
celer, swift	**celeriter,** swiftly
fortis, brave	**fortiter,** bravely

3. Some Adverbs are irregular.

bonus, good	**bene,** well
difficilis, difficult	**difficile,** with difficulty
facilis, easy	**facile,** easily
magnus, great	**magnopere,** greatly
malus, bad	**male,** badly
parvus, little	**parum,** too little, not enough
primus, first	**primum,** first, or **primo,** at first
solus, alone	**solum,** alone, only

4. Other Adverbs are not based on any Adjective. **nunc, semper, non,** etc.

B. **i-conjugation** Verbs have **i** as the predominant vowel.

1. Principal Parts: **audio, audire, audivi, auditus,** hear

2. Present Tense:

ACTIVE		PASSIVE	
I hear, do hear, am hearing		I am being heard, am heard	
audio	**audimus**	**audior**	**audimur**
audis	**auditis**	**audiris**	**audimini**
audit	**audiunt**	**auditur**	**audiuntur**

3. Imperfect Tense:

ACTIVE	PASSIVE
I was hearing, heard	I was being heard, was heard
audiebam	audiebar
audiebas	audiebaris
audiebat	audiebatur
audiebamus	audiebamur
audiebatis	audiebamini
audiebant	audiebantur

4. Future Tense:

ACTIVE		PASSIVE	
I shall hear		I shall be heard	
audiam	**audiemus**	**audiar**	**audiemur**
audies	**audietis**	**audieris**	**audiemini**
audiet	**audient**	**audietur**	**audientur**

5. Perfect Tense:

ACTIVE	PASSIVE
I have heard, heard	I have been heard
audivi	**auditus, a, um sum**
audivisti, etc.	**auditus, a, um es, etc.**

6. Pluperfect Tense:

ACTIVE	PASSIVE
I had heard	I had been heard
audiveram	**auditus, a, um eram**
audiveras, etc.	**auditus, a, um eras, etc.**

7. Future Perfect Tense:

ACTIVE	PASSIVE
I shall have heard	I shall have been heard
audivero	**auditus, a, um ero**
audiveris, etc.	**auditus, a, um eris, etc.**

FAMILIAR PHRASES

status quo or **status in quo**, the state in which. That is, the existing conditions.
mirabile dictu, wonderful to tell, relate.
per se, by itself, of itself; by its own force.
cum grano salis, with a grain of salt.
modus vivendi, manner of living (often temporary).
post scriptum, written after. Abbreviated, **P.S.** or **p.s.**
inter nos, among us, among ourselves.
sine qua non, something indispensable or necessary. Literally, without which not.

PRACTICE EXERCISES

No. 128. Form the Adverbs and give the English meanings.

1. **pulcher**
2. **longus**
3. **magnus**
4. **novus**
5. **acer**
6. **gravis**
7. **brevis**
8. **altus**
9. **gratus**
10. **audax**
11. **miser**
12. **proximus**
13. **fortis**
14. **celer**
15. **liber**

No. 129. Translate these Verb forms.

1. **portas**
2. **habeo**
3. **ducunt**
4. **iacit**
5. **audivistis**
6. **liberatus est**
7. **visi erant**
8. **auditi sunt**
9. **acceptus es**
10. **auditus eram**
11. **audiebant**
12. **paratus erit**
13. **audiet**
14. **petiverunt**
15. **audiunt**
16. **iuvabamini**
17. **audiebamur**
18. **vertebamus**
19. **capientur**
20. **audieris**
21. **audiris**
22. **fecit**
23. **rogabunt**
24. **audivimus**
25. **auditi erant**

No. 130. Give the English for these phrases, and clauses.

1. **fortiter pugnant**
2. **proxime vidimus**
3. **difficile gessit**
4. **late accipientur**
5. **bene docemur**
6. **longe ambulat**
7. **bene stant**
8. **facile cognovit**
9. **magnopere amabat**
10. **parum acriter**

No. 131. Translate these sentences.

1. **Locus facile defendetur.**
2. **Primo nihil parari poterat.**
3. **Ob timorem non fortiter contendistis.**
4. **Utramque portam amas?**
5. **Terra natura difficile defensa est.**
6. **Non solum rex sed etiam regina id audivit.**
7. **De quo audacter scripsit?**
8. **Illo anno multa parabamus.**
9. **Eurydice sub terra misere habitabat.**
10. **Longe ab hoc loco eos duxit.**

CHAPTER 27

READING

Hero et Leander	Hero and Leander
1. **Sunt multae fabulae de amore Leandri Herusque.**	1. There are many stories about the love of Hero and Leander.
2. **Haec fuit puella pulchra, quae in Graecia habitabat et quae omnia in templo, quod erat in oppido suo, curabat.**	2. She was a beautiful girl, who used to live in Greece and who took care of everything in the temple, that was in her town.
3. **Ille in altera regione, quae erat trans Hellespontum, pontem Graeciae, habitabat, sed, cum eam videre cupiebat, trans mare quod non erat latum natabat.**	3. He lived in another region, which was across the Hellespont, the sea of Greece, but, when he wished to see her, he used to swim across the sea, which was not wide.
4. **Ob leges templi cum ea videri non poterat, sed illa lex eum non impedivit. Itaque ad eam semper noctu veniebat.**	4. Because of the laws of the temple he could not be seen with her, but that law did not hinder him. And so he used to come to her always at night.
5. **Etiam longum et difficile iter trans aquam ab puella eum non prohibuit.**	5. Even the long and difficult journey across the water did not keep him from the girl.
6. **Hero ad mare de alto turri omnibus noctibus spectabat.**	6. Hero used to watch every night from a high tower toward the sea.
7. **Leander sine periculo ullo saepe veniebat et tum Hero ipsa vero laeta erat, quod eum bene amabat.**	7. Leander often came without any danger and then Hero herself was truly happy, because she loved him well.
8. **Diu Leander bonam fortunam habebat et omnibus noctibus ad Graeciam facile natabat atque ad illam terram sine ullo periculo pervenit.**	8. For a long time Leander had good fortune and swam easily to Greece every night and came to that land without any danger.

Hero et Leander	Hero and Leander
9. **Nullam inopiam celeritatis aut studi habebat. Ut accidit tamen uno tempore, cum natabat, tempestate magna victus est.**	9. He had no lack of speed or eagerness. As it happened, however, one time, when he was swimming, he was overcome by a great storm.
10. **Primo trans aquam turris Herus ab illo videri poterat, sed iam iter erat difficile et mox tempestate sub mare mittebatur.**	10. At first Hero's tower could be seen by him across the water, but already the way was difficult and soon he was sent under the sea by the storm.
11. **Hero totam noctem eum misere exspectabat.**	11. Hero waited for him unhappily all night.
12. **Tum ad mare contendit et corpus illius petebat. Id primo non conspexit.**	12. Then she hurried to the sea and sought his body. She did not see it at first.
13. **Tum in loco non longe ab mari corpus Leandri repperit.**	13. Then in a place not far from the sea she found the body of Leander.
14. **Misera Hero in mare cucurrit et illa eum morte sua repperit.**	14. The unhappy Hero ran into the sea and she found him by her own death.

READING VOCABULARY

Nouns

turris, turris, f., tower **(turrium)** (turret)
regio, regionis, f., region, boundary (regional)
Hero, Herus, f., Hero (a Greek noun)
Leander, Leandri, m., Leander
Hellespontus, Hellesponti, m., Hellespont
inopia, inopiae, f., want, scarcity

Prounoun and Adjective

qui, quae, quod, who, which, that; which, what

Adverbs

tamen, however, nevertheless
iam, already, now

Conjunction

ut, as

Verbs

impedio, impedire, impedivi, impeditus, hinder (impede)
prohibeo, prohibere, prohibui, prohibitus, keep off, hinder, prohibit, prevent (prohibition)
cupio, cupere, cupivi, cupitus, desire, wish, want (cupidity)
venio, venire, veni, ventus, come (venture)
pervenio, pervenire, perveni, perventus, arrive
accido, accidere, accidi, happen (accident)
conspicio, conspicere, conspexi, conspectus, observe (conspectus)
reperio, reperire, repperi, repertus, find, discover (repertory)

READING GRAMMAR

A. A Relative Clause is used to tell something about its antecedent. It is, therefore, introduced by a Relative Pronoun in the same number and gender as its antecedent.

vir qui, the man, who **puella quae,** the girl, who
bellum quod, the war, that

The case of a Relative Pronoun, however, is determined by its use, in its own clause.

vir quem video, the man, whom I see
puella quam video, the girl, whom I see

	SINGULAR			PLURAL			
	M.	F.	N.	M.	F.	N.	
Nom.	**qui**	**quae**	**quod**	**qui**	**quae**	**quae**	who, which, that
Gen.	**cuius**	**cuius**	**cuius**	**quorum**	**quarum**	**quorum**	whose, of which
Dat.	**cui**	**cui**	**cui**	**quibus**	**quibus**	**quibus**	to, for whom, which
Acc.	**quem**	**quam**	**quod**	**quos**	**quas**	**quae**	whom, which, that
Abl.	**quo**	**qua**	**quo**	**quibus**	**quibus**	**quibus**	from, with, by, in which, whom

Cum is added to the end of the Ablative: **quocum, quacum, quibuscum**

B. An Interrogative Adjective modifies a noun and asks a question. It is therefore in the same gender, number, and case as the noun it modifies.

qui vir? which man? **quae puella?** which girl?
quod bellum? what war?

The Interrogative Adjective in Latin is spelled the same as the Relative Pronoun. Only its use is different.

PREFIXES

prae, before. **praepono,** put before.
re, again, back. **remitto,** send back.
con, together, with; very, thoroughly.
convoco, call together.
conficio, finish (do thoroughly).
pro, out, forth. **provoco,** call forth.

PRACTICE EXERCISES

No. 132. In the following sentences translate (1) the relative clause, and (2) the whole sentence.

1. **Homines qui cum copiis suis iter faciunt sunt fortes.**
2. **Turris quam aedificavit ex oppido barbaros prohibebat.**
3. **Femina quacum ambulabam mater mea est.**
4. **Navis cuius nomen conspicere non possumus ad Italiam navigat.**
5. **Puer cui litteras dedi celeriter veniet.**
6. **Timor quem habebitis mox non memoria tenebitur.**
7. **Flumen ad quod fugiebant erat altum latumque.**
8. **Locus de quo scripsit longe est ab urbe.**
9. **Omnia quae habuit nunc mea sunt.**
10. **Viri quorum pueros vides sunt amici.**

No. 133. Translate these phrases containing interrogative adjectives.

1. **in quibus locis?**	6. **qua celeritate?**	11. **cum quibus militibus?**
2. **qui homo?**	7. **quo anno?**	12. **quorum civium?**
3. **quod oppidum?**	8. **cuius nominis?**	13. **quae impedimenta?**
4. **quae praeda?**	9. **qua hora?**	14. **cuius magnitudinis?**
5. **quos viros?**	10. **quo tempore?**	15. **quo consilio?**

No. 134. Give the English for these Verb forms.

1. **faciunt**	6. **currebat**	11. **auditis**	16. **prohibuerunt**
2. **iubebit**	7. **fuerat**	12. **pervenisti**	17. **erunt**
3. **repperisti**	8. **cepit**	13. **contendebat**	18. **videbor**
4. **perveniet**	9. **conspexerunt**	14. **dederant**	19. **rogari**
5. **haberi**	10. **accidebat**	15. **videri**	20. **habebo**

No. 135. Translate these phrases and clauses.

1. **non potuit**	6. **fortis populus**	11. **proximo anno**
2. **illius loci**	7. **ob tempestatem**	12. **mi amice**
3. **filios tuos**	8. **magno studio**	13. **omnes homines**
4. **alii veniunt**	9. **domi mansit**	14. **nihil timet**
5. **venire cupit**	10. **eius nationis**	15. **non solum mater tua**

CHAPTER 28

READING

Equus Troiae

1. **Graeci novem annos Troiam oppugnaverant et iam domi esse cupiebant.**
2. **Bellum diu et fortiter gesserant, sed neque urbem ceperant neque illum locum relinquere potuerant.**
3. **Itaque consilium ceperunt. Magno studio laboreque equum magnum fecerunt. Multi milites Graeci, qui bene pugnare poterant, a sociis suis in equo ipso noctu locati sunt.**

The Trojan Horse

1. The Greeks had attacked Troy for nine years and now they wanted to be at home.
2. They had carried on war for a long time and bravely, but they had neither captured the city nor had they been able to leave that place.
3. And so they decided on a plan. With great zeal and work they made a large horse. Many Greek soldiers, who were able to fight well, were placed in the horse itself by their comrades at night.

Equus Troiae

4. **Exercitus urbis Troiae, qui post muros urbis erat, equum illa nocte non vidit.**
5. **Cives Troiae tamen, adventu solis in caelo, equum viderunt et eum in urbem duxerunt, sed mox Graeci, qui in equo positi erant, clamabant et in cives exercitumque Troiae impetum faciebant.**
6. **Populus terrebatur.**
7. **Graeci telis suis et igni urbem ceperunt. Tum Graeci ad mare, ubi alii Graeci naves suas instruxerant, cucurrerunt.**
8. **Post breve tempus, manus Graecorum cum captivis multis a Troia navigavit.**

The Trojan Horse

4. The army of the city of Troy, which was behind the walls of the city, did not see the horse that night.
5. The citizens of Troy, however, at the arrival of the sun in the sky, saw the horse and led it into the city, but soon the Greeks, who had been placed in the horse, shouted and made an attack on the citizens and army of Troy.
6. The people were terrified.
7. With their weapons and fire the Greeks took the city. Then the Greeks ran to the sea, where the other Greeks had drawn up their ships.
8. After a short time, the band of Greeks sailed from Troy with many captives.

Proelium Marathonium

1. **Anno XD Ante Christum, Graecia ab exercitu Persarum graviter oppugnabatur.**
2. **Persae trans mare ad Graeciam navigaverant et multa oppida occupaverant.**
3. **Hostes ad locum, qui non multa milia passuum Athenis erat, iam iter fecerant, et ob hanc rem cives Athenarum et in aliis urbibus propinquis illi loco adventum hostium timebant.**
4. **Populus Athenarum ad Spartam virum misit.**
5. **Ille totum iter cucurrit et ab populo Spartae auxilium petivit, sed Sparta legem habebat. Hac lege, illi sine luna in caelo bellum gerere non poterant, et illo tempore luna non erat.**
6. **Itaque milites soli Athenarum aciem suam instruxerunt et sagittis ac telis gravibus hostes vicerunt. Illo die populus Athenarum spem victoriae magnae videbat.**
7. **Postea ob virtutem viri, qui Athenis Spartam cucurrerat, ludos habebant. His ludis nomen proeli, quod in agro Marathonio fuerat, dederunt.**
8. **Etiam hodie ludo pedibus id nomen damus.**

The Battle of Marathon

1. In the year 490 B.C., Greece was heavily attacked by the army of the Persians.
2. The Persians had sailed across the sea to Greece and had seized many towns.
3. The enemy had already made the journey to a place, which was not many miles from Athens, and for this reason the citizens of Athens and in other cities near to that place feared the arrival of the enemy.
4. The people of Athens sent a man to Sparta.
5. He ran the whole way and sought help from the people of Sparta, but Sparta had a law. By this law, they were not able to carry on war without a moon in the sky, and at that time there was no moon.
6. And so the soldiers of Athens drew up their battle line alone and conquered the enemy with arrows and heavy weapons. On that day the people of Athens saw the hope of a great victory.
7. Afterwards because of the courage of the man, who had run from Athens to Sparta, they held games. To these games they gave the name of the battle, that had been on the field of Marathon.
8. Even today we give this name to a contest on foot.

READING VOCABULARY

Nouns

domus, domus, f., house, home (domicile)
exercitus, exercitus, m., army (exercise)
cornu, cornus, n., horn, wing (of an army) (cornucopia)
adventus, adventus, m., arrival, approach (advent, adventure)
impetus, impetus, m., attack (impetuous)
manus, manus, f., hand, group (manual)
passus, passus, m., pace (passage)
dies, diei, m. or f., day (Diet)
res, rei, f., thing (re)
spes, spei, f., hope
acies, aciei, f., line of battle
Persae, Persarum, m., the Persians
Athenae, Athenarum, f., Athens
Sparta, Spartae, f., Sparta

Adjective

Marathonius, Marathonia, Marathonium, of Marathon

Verb

instruo, instruere, instruxi, instructus, draw up, form, train (instruct)

Conjunction

neque, and . . . not **neque . . . neque,** neither . . . nor

READING GRAMMAR

A. Nouns that end in **-us** in the Genitive singular are **u-declension.** Those that end in **-us** in the Nominative singular are masculine, with a few exceptions; those in **-u** are neuter.

Nom.	**exercitus**	the army	**cornu**	the horn, wing
Gen.	**exercitus**	of the army	**cornus**	of the horn, wing
Dat.	**exercitui**	to, for the army	**cornu**	to, for the horn, wing
Acc.	**exercitum**	the army	**cornu**	the horn, wing
Abl.	**exercitu**	from, with, by, in the army	**cornu**	from, with, by, in the horn, wing
Nom.	**exercitus**	the armies	**cornua**	the horns, wings
Gen.	**exercituum**	of the armies	**cornuum**	of the horns, wings
Dat.	**exercitibus**	to, for the armies	**cornibus**	to, for the horns, wings
Acc.	**exercitus**	the armies	**cornua**	the horns, wings
Abl.	**exercitibus**	from, with, by, in the armies	**cornibus**	from, with, by, in the horns, wings

B. Nouns that end in **-ei** in the Genitive singular are **e-declension.** They are all feminine, except **dies** (day), which is generally masculine.

Nom.	**res**	the thing	**res**	the things
Gen.	**rei**	of the thing	**rerum**	of the things
Dat.	**rei**	to, for the thing	**rebus**	to, for the things
Acc.	**rem**	the thing	**res**	the things
Abl.	**re**	from, with, by, in the thing	**rebus**	from, with, by, in the things

C. **Domus** (house, home) has endings in both the **o-declension** and the **u-declension.**

Nom.	**domus**	house	**domus**	houses
Gen.	**domus, domi**	of the house	**domuum, domorum**	of the houses
Dat.	**domui, domo**	to, for the house	**domibus**	to, for the houses
Acc.	**domum**	house	**domos, domus**	houses
Abl.	**domo, domu**	from, with, by, in the house	**domibus**	from, with, by, in the houses

FAMILIAR ABBREVIATIONS

A.D., Anno Domini, in the year of (our) Lord.
a.m., ante meridiem, before noon.
p.m., post meridiem, after noon.
cf., confer, compare.
et al., et alibi, and elsewhere; **et alii,** and others.
vs., versus, against.
c., circ., circa, circum, about. Used with dates.
@, ad, to or at.

PRACTICE EXERCISES

No. 136. Give the English for these phrases.

1. **multos passus**
2. **vestra manus**
3. **longum impetum**
4. **ob adventum eius**
5. **utrumque cornu**
6. **exercituum nostrorum**
7. **in cornu tuo**
8. **ex exercitu**
9. **in domum**
10. **sex milia passuum**
11. **contra exercitus**
12. **ob adventum tuum**
13. **impetus hostium**
14. **manus militum**
15. **ab exercitu**

No. 137. Give the English for these phrases.

1. **acies suas**
2. **multo die**
3. **proximo die**
4. **ob has res**
5. **ullius spei**
6. **totam rem**
7. **unam diem**
8. **quarum rerum?**
9. **nostrae acies**
10. **quas res?**
11. **in qua acie?**
12. **utriusque diei**
13. **ob eam rem**
14. **in his aciebus**
15. **multam spem**

No. 138. Translate these Verb forms.

1. **ambulavit**
2. **videmur**
3. **erant**
4. **fecerat**
5. **fugiebat**
6. **reperit**
7. **datum erat**
8. **potest**
9. **instructum est**
10. **videri**
11. **relicti sunt**
12. **pugnabunt**
13. **instruxit**
14. **iter facit**
15. **audientur**

No. 139. Translate these sentences.

1. **Omnes res faciles esse videntur.**
2. **Post sex dies neuter miles ullam spem habebat.**
3. **Captivi quos reduxisti ex eorum exercitu venerunt.**
4. **Quis fortem impetum magnopere impedivit?**
5. **Una hora homines domum venient.**
6. **Quam ob rem aciem suam in colli instruebat?**
7. **Inter has res quas habemus est parva copia aquae.**
8. **Milites in illo cornu equos suos ad agrum vertunt.**
9. **Neque cornu neque acies spem videbat.**
10. **Qui inter hos populos regnum tenent?**

CHAPTER 29

READING

Proelium Thermopylarum

1. Post decem annos Persae ad Graeciam navibus suos reduxerunt.
2. Proelium Marathonium anno XD Ante Christum fuerat.
3. Hic annus erat XXD Ante Christum et hoc proelium appellatur Proelium Thermopylarum.
4. Persae magnam copiam et cibi et frumenti, quam trans mare portare in animo habebant, decem annos paraverant atque exercitum fortem acremque habuerunt.
5. Illi in impetu hoc omnem spem suam posuerant, sed illo tempore erat apud Graecos nulla pax. Alia civitas contra aliam contendebat.
6. Itaque Athenae Spartaque Graeciam totam aegre defendere poterant.
7. Exercitus hostium ad partem montium quae Thermopylae appellata est pervenit.
8. Hic locus natura fortis est quod iter parvum inter montes ab non multis militibus teneri poterat.
9. In eo loco manus parva Graecorum conlocata erat et adventum hostium exspectabat.
10. Graeci in montibus facile pugnare poterant. Ei enim patriam suam bene sciebant.
11. Iter per montes erat et difficile et angustum. Itaque Graeci praesidium ibi conlocaverant.
12. Hi contra milites fortes hostium, qui spem iam relinquebant, diu et fortiter contenderunt, sed erat unus homo, qui Persis auxilium dedit.
13. Hic vir hostibus iter, quod erat post locum ubi praesidium Graecum instructum erat, trans montes demonstravit.

The Battle of Thermopylae

1. After ten years the Persians led their men back to Greece by ship.
2. The Battle of Marathon had been in the year 490 B.C.
3. This year was 480 B.C. and this battle is called the Battle of Thermopylae.
4. The Persians for ten years had prepared a great supply both of food and grain, which they intended to carry across the sea, and they also had a brave and keen army.
5. They had placed all their hope in this attack, but at that time there was no peace among the Greeks. One state was fighting against another.
6. And so Athens and Sparta were able to defend all Greece with difficulty.
7. The army of the enemy came to the part of the mountains which is called Thermopylae.
8. This place is strong by nature because the small road between the mountains was able to be held by a few soldiers.
9. In this place a small group of Greeks had been stationed and was waiting for the arrival of the enemy.
10. The Greeks were able to fight easily in the mountains. For they knew their native country well.
11. The way through the mountains was both difficult and narrow. And so the Greeks had stationed a garrison there.
12. They fought for a long time and bravely against the brave soldiers of the enemy, who were already giving up hope, but there was one man, who gave help to the Persians.
13. This man pointed out to the enemy a way across the mountains, which was in back of the place where the Greek guard had been drawn up.

Proelium Thermopylarum	The Battle of Thermopylae
14. **Exercitus hostium ad locum post aciem Graecam noctu iter fecit.**	14. The army of the enemy made its way at night to a place in back of the Greek battle line.
15. **Alii Graeci fugere potuerunt, sed alii milites Spartae et sociorum eius nullum timorem demonstraverunt.**	15. Some Greeks were able to escape, but other soldiers of Sparta and her allies showed no fear.
16. **Hi gladiis et aliis telis diu pugnabant, sed post breve tempus Graeci omnes ab hostibus interfecti erant et Persae trans corpora eorum Athenas iter fecerunt.**	16. These men fought for a long time with swords and other weapons, but after a short time all the Greeks had been killed by the enemy and the Persians made their way to Athens over their bodies.

READING VOCABULARY

Nouns

civitas, civitatis, f., state
Thermopylae, Thermopylarum, f. pl., Thermopylae
praesidium, praesidii or praesidi, n., guard, garrison (presidial)

Pronouns

ego, mei, I (egotist)
nos, nostrum, we (nostrum)
tu, tui, you (sing.)
vos, vestrum, you (pl.)

Verbs

appello, appellare, appellavi, appellatus, address, call, name (appellation)
conloco, conlocare, conlocavi, conlocatus, place, station (collocate)
scio, scire, scivi, scitus, know (sciolist)

Adjective

decem, ten (decimal)

Conjunction

enim, for Never the first word in a Latin sentence.

READING GRAMMAR

A. Personal Pronouns are used to show emphasis or to make a clear distinction.

Emphasis: **ego scio**, I (myself) know
Clarity: **ego et tu scimus**, I and you know

1. Personal Pronouns of the First Person.

	SINGULAR		PLURAL	
Nom.	**ego**	I	**nos**	we
Gen.	**mei**	of me	**nostrum or nostri**	of us
Dat.	**mihi**	to, for me	**nobis**	to, for us
Acc.	**me**	me	**nos**	us
Abl.	**me**	from, with, by, in me	**nobis**	from, with, by, in us

2. Personal Pronouns of the Second Person.

	SINGULAR		PLURAL	
Nom.	**tu**	you	**vos**	you
Gen.	**tui**	of you	**vestrum** or **vestri**	of you
Dat.	**tibi**	to, for you	**vobis**	to, for you
Acc.	**te**	you	**vos**	you
Abl.	**te**	from, with, by, in you	**vobis**	from, with, by, in you

3. You have already met the Personal Pronouns of the Third Person.

SINGULAR		PLURAL	
is, ea, id	he, she, it	**ei, eae, ea**	they
ille, illa, illud	he, she, it	**illi, illae, illa**	they
hic, haec, hoc	he, she, it	**hi, hae, haec**	they

B. Adjectives are more commonly used to show possession than is the Genitive Case of the Personal Pronouns, except in the Third Person.

1st Person	**meus, mea, meum**	my, mine
	noster, nostra, nostrum	our, ours
2nd Person	**tuus, tua, tuum**	your, yours
	vester, vestra, vestrum	your, yours

But

3rd Person	**eius, eius, eius**	his, her, its
	eorum, earum, eorum	their
or		
	illius, illius, illius	his, her, its
	illorum, illarum, illorum	their
or		
	huius, huius, huius	his, her, its
	horum, harum, horum	their

When the Third Person possessor is the same as the subject:

suus, sua, suum his, her, its, their (own)

Cum is added to the end of the Personal Pronouns.

mecum, with me **nobiscum**, with us
tecum, with you **vobiscum**, with you

C. Reflexive Pronouns reflect back to the subject and therefore have no Nominative Case.

Me video, I see myself **Te vides**, you see yourself

1. Reflexive Pronouns of the First Person.

	SINGULAR		PLURAL	
Gen.	**mei**	of myself	**nostri**	of ourselves
Dat.	**mihi**	to, for myself	**nobis**	to, for ourselves
Acc.	**me**	myself	**nos**	ourselves
Abl.	**me**	from, with, by, in myself	**nobis**	from, with, by, in ourselves

2. Reflexive Pronouns of the Second Person.

	SINGULAR		PLURAL	
Gen.	**tui**	of yourself	**vestri**	The meanings are the
Dat.	**tibi**	to, for yourself	**vobis**	same as the singular.
Acc.	**te**	yourself	**vos**	
Abl.	**te**	from, with, by, in yourself	**vobis**	

3. Reflexive Pronouns of the Third Person.

	SINGULAR	
Gen.	**sui**	of himself, herself, itself
Dat.	**sibi**	to, for himself, herself, itself
Acc.	**se**	himself, herself, itself
Abl.	**se**	from, with, by, in himself, herself, itself

In the plural, the Latin is the same—**sui, sibi, se, se**—but the meaning is plural—themselves.

LEGAL TERMS

a vinculo matrimoni, from the bond of marriage. Used in a decree of absolute divorce.

caveat emptor, let the buyer beware. The buyer buys at his own risk.

inter vivos, between the living. Used to indicate a gift from a living person to another living person.

compos mentis, sound or sane of mind. **non compos mentis** or **non compos,** not sound or sane of mind.

nolo contendere, I do not wish to contend. A plea by which a defendant is subject to conviction, but does not admit his guilt.

nolle prosequi, to be unwilling to prosecute. Abbr. **nol pros.** A court record stating that the prosecutor will not carry his suit further.

non prosequitur, he does not prosecute. Abbr. **non pros.** Used to indicate a decision against a plaintiff who does not appear in court to prosecute.

obiter dictum, something said along the way. Used of remarks made by a judge that are not part of the legal decision, but are his personal comments and observations on matters relating to the case and decision.

nisi, if not, unless. Used to indicate that an order or decree will go into effect at a specified time unless modified by further evidence or cause presented before that time.

sui iuris or **suo iure,** of one's own right or in one's own right. Used of a person who has full capacity and ability to act for himself in legal proceedings.

PRACTICE EXERCISES

No. 140. Give the English for these Personal Pronouns.

1. **vos**	7. **te**	13. **vobis**	19. **illorum**	25. **illis**
2. **nos**	8. **ego**	14. **eos**	20. **ad vos**	26. **de his**
3. **a te**	9. **eum**	15. **illud**	21. **tibi**	27. **illa**
4. **eorum**	10. **mihi**	16. **huic**	22. **vestrum**	28. **cum ea**
5. **ea**	11. **nobiscum**	17. **eius**	23. **nostri**	29. **horum**
6. **ei**	12. **tu**	18. **tecum**	24. **de me**	30. **illos**

No. 141. Give the English for these Reflexive Pronouns.

1. **sibi**	3. **a me**	5. **se**	7. **mihi**	9. **me**
2. **te**	4. **vos**	6. **vobis**	8. **nobis**	10. **nos**

No. 142. Translate these sentences.

1. **Homo ipse nos scit.**
2. **Ego tibi auxilium misi.**
3. **Nos in hoc loco te repperimus.**
4. **Venietisne vos mecum?**
5. **Tu nobis libros das.**
6. **Vos eum non auditis.**
7. **Illi ad nos fugiebant.**
8. **Is mihi haec misit.**
9. **Tecum domum ambulare non poterit.**
10. **Haec est patria nostra.**
11. **Tu id illis narrabis.**
12. **Nos hanc domum reducemus.**
13. **Illi ab his pacem petebant.**
14. **Ego a te et tuo gladio terrebar.**
15. **Nos illo tempore nos servaveramus.**
16. **Nonne tu nos iuvare potes?**
17. **Ille urbem eorum vidit.**
18. **Nos ipsi eos venire iubebimus.**
19. **Vos nobis ea demonstrabitis.**
20. **Animus eius me non diu terrebat.**

SEVENTH REVIEW SECTION (CHAPTERS 26–29)

VOCABULARY REVIEW

NOUNS

1.	acies	line of battle
2.	adventus	arrival, approach
3.	Athenae	Athens
4.	civitas	state
5.	cornu	horn, wing
6.	dies	day
7.	domus	house, home
8.	Eurydice	Eurydice
9.	exercitus	army
10.	Hellespontus	Hellespont
11.	Hero	Hero
12.	impetus	attack
13.	inopia	want, scarcity
14.	Leander	Leander
15.	manus	hand, group
16.	natura	nature
17.	nihil, nil	nothing
18.	Orpheus	Orpheus
19.	passus	pace
20.	Persae	the Persians
21.	praesidium	guard, garrison
22.	regio	region, boundary
23.	regnum	kingdom
24.	res	thing
25.	Sparta	Sparta
26.	spes	hope
27.	Thermopylae	Thermopylae
28.	turris	tower

ADJECTIVES

1.	decem	ten
2.	difficilis	difficult, hard
3.	Marathonius	of Marathon
4.	primus	first

PRONOUNS

1.	ego	I
2.	nos	we
3.	qui	who, which, that; which, what
4.	tu	you(s.)
5.	vos	you(pl.)

VERBS

1.	accido	happen
2.	appello	address, call, name
3.	conloco	place, station
4.	conspicio	observe
5.	cupio	desire, wish, want
6.	discedo	withdraw, go away, leave
7.	educo	lead out
8.	impedio	hinder
9.	instruo	draw up, form, train
10.	pervenio	arrive
11.	prohibeo	keep off, hinder, prohibit, prevent
12.	reduco	lead back
13.	rego	rule
14.	relinquo	leave, leave behind
15.	reperio	find, discover
16.	scio	know
17.	trado	give up, surrender
18.	venio	come

ADVERBS

1.	iam	now, already
2.	magnopere	greatly
3.	parum	too little, not enough
4.	primum, primo	first, at first
5.	solum	alone, only
6.	tamen	however, nevertheless

CONJUNCTIONS

1.	enim	for
2.	neque	and not
3.	neque . . . neque	neither . . . nor
4.	ut	as

PRACTICE EXERCISES

No. 143. Give the Adverbs of these Adjectives, with their meanings.

1. **latus**
2. **acer**
3. **difficilis**
4. **miser**
5. **longus**
6. **magnus**
7. **laetus**
8. **liber**
9. **parvus**
10. **angustus**

No. 144. Translate these Verbs.

1. **veniam**
2. **sciebat**
3. **auditus est**
4. **perveniebamus**
5. **impedientur**
6. **reperiunt**
7. **audiebaris**
8. **scitum erat**
9. **cupiverunt**
10. **audieris**

No. 145. Translate these Pronouns.

1. **cuius**
2. **quem**
3. **quae**
4. **qui**
5. **quibuscum**
6. **nos**
7. **mihi**
8. **me**
9. **vestrum**
10. **tibi**
11. **tecum**
12. **eius**
13. **eorum**
14. **illum**
15. **hanc**

No. 146. Translate these Nouns.

1. **exercitui**
2. **res**
3. **cornus**
4. **aciem**
5. **spem**
6. **manuum**
7. **die**
8. **impetibus**
9. **adventum**
10. **domum**
11. **rebus**
12. **cornua**
13. **exercituum**
14. **manui**
15. **spei**

PUBLIUS VERGILIUS MARO

Virgil was born in 70 B.C. near Mantua, in the north of Italy, and was educated in Milan, Rome, and Naples, where he studied philosophy and rhetoric. During the latter part of his life, he lived near Naples, where he composed his epic poem, **The Aeneid.** Virgil died in 19 B.C. at Brundisium, while returning from Greece.

Ibant obscuri, sola sub nocte, per umbram	They walked obscured by darkness, in the lonely night, through the shadows
perque domos Ditis vacuas, et inania regna;	and through the vacant kingdoms of Pluto, and the empty homes;
quale per incertam lunam sub luce maligna	just as under the dim light of a wavering moon
est iter in silvis, ubi caelum condidit umbra	is a journey in the woods, when Jupiter has hidden the sky in shadows
Iuppiter, et rebus nox abstulit atra colorem.	and black night has taken away the color from things.
Vestibulum ante ipsum primisque in faucibus Orci	Before the very entrance and in the very jaws of Orcus
Luctus et ultrices posuere cubilia Curae,	Grief and avenging Cares have placed their couches,
pallentesque habitant Morbi, tristisque Senectus,	and pale Diseases dwell, and sad Old Age,
et Metus, et malesuada Fames, ac turpis Egestas,	and Fear, and Hunger persuading-evil, also base Want,
terribiles visu formae, Letumque Labosque,	forms terrible to see, both Death and Toil,
tum consanguineus Leti Sopor, et mala mentis	then Sleep the kinsman of Death, and evil Pleasures
Gaudia, mortiferumque adverso in limine Bellum,	of the mind, and death-bearing War on the threshold opposite,
ferreique Eumenidum thalami, et Discordia demens,	and the iron chambers of the Furies, and mad Discord,
vipereum crinem vittis innexa cruentis.	entwining her snaky hair with bloody fillets.
Aeneidos VI, 268–281	Aeneid 6, 268–281

These two stories are found in the sermons of James of Vitry, who was the Cardinal Bishop of Tusculum and died in 1240 A.D. The stories were used to illustrate a point as well as to entertain the listeners.

De Arbore In Qua Se Suspendebant Mulieres

De quodam alio audivi, qui habebat arborem in horto suo, in qua duae eius uxores suspenderant semetipsas. Cui quidam eius vicinus ait: "Valde fortunata est arbor illa et bonum omen habet. Habeo autem uxorem pessimam; rogo te, da mihi surculum ex ea, ut plantem in horto meo."

About a Tree on Which Women Were Hanging

I have heard about a certain other man, who had a tree in his garden, on which two of his wives had hung themselves. A certain one of his neighbors said to him: "Certainly that tree is lucky and holds a good omen. I, however, have a very bad wife; I ask you, give me a young shoot from it, so that I may plant it in my garden."

De Bachone Qui Pendebat In Quadam Villa

Aliquando transivi per quandam villam in Francia, ubi suspenderant pernam seu bachonem in platea hac condicione ut, qui vellet iuramento firmare quod uno integro anno post contractum matrimonium permansisset cum uxore ita quod de matrimonio non paenituisset, bachonem haberet. Et cum per decem annos ibi pependisset non est unus solus inventus qui bachonem lucraretur, omnibus infra annum de matrimonio contracto paenitentibus.

About a Side of Bacon Which Was Hanging in a Certain Town

Once I passed through a certain town in France, where they had hung a ham or side of bacon in the street with this condition that, whoever might wish to swear on oath that he had lived one whole year with his wife after the marriage had been contracted in such a way that he had not regretted the marriage, might have the side of bacon. And although it had hung there for ten years not one single man was found who might win the side of bacon, because all inside of a year from the contract of marriage regretted it.

CHAPTER 30

READING

Aeneas in Igni Troiae

1. **Aeneas in vias Troiae una nocte cucurrit et multitudinem militum Graecorum, qui vero laeti erant, quod urbem vicerant, ibi videbat.**
2. **Aeneas cum parva manu sociorum suorum contra hostes primo contendit, sed nihil faci poterat.**
3. **Tum patrem suum, qui domi erat, memoria tenuit et domum properavit.**

Aeneas in the Fire of Troy

1. Aeneas ran into the streets of Troy one night and he saw there a great number of Greek soldiers, who were truly happy, because they had conquered the city.
2. Aeneas with a small band of his comrades at first struggled against the enemy, but nothing could be done.
3. Then he remembered his father, who was at home, and he hurried home.

Aeneas in Igni Troiae

4. Troia eo tempore acriter incendebatur. Populus Troiae dediderat. Bellum contra Graecos pugnatum erat.

5. Aeneas patrem suum secum venire coegit et in umeris suis totum onus corporis eius portabat. Hi tres, Aeneas atque pater suus atque suus filius parvus, ex igni contendebant.

6. Ob victoriam hostium magnopere opprimebantur.

7. Post breve tempus, Aeneas matrem fili sui, Creusam, memoria tenuit. Illa enim erat in urbe. Itaque in urbem celeriter cucurrit.

8. Bis centum tempora eam appellabat, sed illa ibi non erat. A Morte educta erat.

Aeneas in the Fire of Troy

4. Troy at that time was being fiercely burned. The people of Troy had surrended. The war against the Greeks had been finished.

5. Aeneas forced his father to come with him and he carried the whole burden of his body on his shoulders. These three, Aeneas and his father and his small son, hurried from the fire.

6. Because of the victory of the enemy they were greatly oppressed.

7. After a short time, Aeneas remembered the mother of his son, Creusa. For she was in the city. And so he ran quickly into the city.

8. He called her twice a hundred times, but she was not there. She had been carried off by Death.

Iter Ulixis

1. Decem annos Ulixes ab portu Troiae ad patriam suam navigabat. Ipse et socii sui ad multa loca illo tempore pervenerunt.

2. Primus locus erat eis acriter gratus idoneusque.

3. Secundus locus erat terra in qua Polyphemus habitabat.

4. Tertio in loco, venti eis ab rege ventorum dati sunt.

5. Quarto in loco, multi viri ab illo, quem ibi reppererunt, necati sunt.

6. Ob feminam pulchram ab quinto loco difficile se recipere potuerunt.

7. Sexto in loco, omnes qui apud Inferos convenerant viderunt.

8. Septimo in loco, multas res pulchras audiverunt et ibi manere cupiverunt.

9. Ab octavo loco celeriter fugerunt. Nam duo animalia ibi habitabant. Unum ex his erat serpens et alterum erat magnum saxum.

10. Nono in loco animalia dei solis tenebantur.

11. Tum omnes socii eius in mari necati sunt. Itaque ille solus ad decimum locum pervenit.

12. Iter difficile susceperat, sed post decem aestates atque decem hiemes servatus erat et domum venit.

The Journey of Ulysses

1. Ulysses sailed for ten years from the harbor of Troy to his native country. He and his comrades arrived at many places during that time.

2. The first place was keenly pleasing and suitable to them.

3. The second place was the land in which Polyphemus lived.

4. In the third place, winds were given to them by the king of the winds.

5. In the fourth place, many of the men were killed by him, whom they found there.

6. They were able to depart from the fifth place with difficulty because of a beautiful woman.

7. In the sixth place, they saw all those who had come together among Those Below.

8. In the seventh place, they heard many beautiful things and wished to stay there.

9. They fled from the eighth place quickly. For two animals lived there. One of these was a serpent and the other was a large rock.

10. In the ninth place the animals of the god of the sun were held.

11. Then all his comrades were killed on the sea. And so he arrived alone at the tenth place.

12. He had undertaken a difficult journey, but after ten summers and ten winters he had been saved and he came home.

READING VOCABULARY

Nouns

multitudo, multitudinis, f., great number, multitude (multitudinous)
Creusa, Creusae, f., Creusa
onus, oneris, n., burden, weight (onerous)
aestas, aestatis, f., summer
ventus, venti, m., wind (vent)
hiems, hiemis, f., winter
portus, portus, m., harbor, port

Adverb

bis, twice (bicycle)

Conjunction

nam, for

Verbs

incendo, incendere, incendi, incensus, set fire to, burn (incendiary)
opprimo, opprimere, oppressi, oppressus, overcome, crush (oppressive)
dedo, dedere, dedidi, deditus, give up, surrender
cogo, cogere, coegi, coactus, collect, drive, compel (cogent)
recipio, recipere, recepi, receptus, take back, receive (reception)
convenio, convenire, conveni, conventus, come together, assemble (convention)
suscipio, suscipere, suscepi, susceptus, take up, undertake (susceptible)

READING GRAMMAR

A. The Cardinal Numbers one to twenty, one hundred, and one thousand:

1—unus, una, unum	**11—undecim**
2—duo, duae, duo	**12—duodecim**
3—tres, tria	**13—tredecim**
4—quattuor	**14—quattuordecim**
5—quinque	**15—quindecim**
6—sex	**16—sedecim**
7—septem	**17—septendecim**
8—octo	**18—duodeviginti**
9—novem	**19—undeviginti**
10—decem	**20—viginti**

100—centum
1000—mille

These Cardinal Numbers are declined:

1—

	M.	F.	N.
Nom.	**unus**	**una**	**unum**
Gen.	**unius**	**unius**	**unius**
Dat.	**uni**	**uni**	**uni**
Acc.	**unum**	**unam**	**unum**
Abl.	**uno**	**una**	**uno**

2—

	M.	F.	N.
Nom.	**duo**	**duae**	**duo**
Gen.	**duorum**	**duarum**	**duorum**
Dat.	**duobus**	**duabus**	**duobus**
Acc.	**duos, duo**	**duas**	**duo**
Abl.	**duobus**	**duabus**	**duobus**

3—

	M. and F.	N.
Nom.	**tres**	**tria**
Gen.	**trium**	**trium**
Dat.	**tribus**	**tribus**
Acc.	**tres, tris**	**tria**
Abl.	**tribus**	**tribus**

1000—

	SINGULAR	PLURAL
Nom.	**mille**	**milia**
Gen.	**mille**	**milium**
Dat.	**mille**	**milibus**
Acc.	**mille**	**milia**
Abl.	**mille**	**milibus**

1. **Mille** is an Adjective in the singular and a Noun in the plural.

mille homines, a thousand men
milia hominum, thousands of men

2. The other Cardinal Numbers may be used as Adjectives or Nouns.

tres homines, three men
tres hominum, three of the men
tres de hominibus, three (from the) men
tres ex hominibus, three (from the) men

B. The Ordinal Numbers first to tenth:

first—**primus, prima, primum**
second—**secundus, secunda, secundum**
third—**tertius, tertia, tertium**
fourth—**quartus, quarta, quartum**
fifth—**quintus, quinta, quintum**
sixth—**sextus, sexta, sextum**
seventh—**septimus, septima, septimum**
eighth—**octavus, octava, octavum**
ninth—**nonus, nona, nonum**
tenth—**decimus, decima, decimum**

All Ordinal Numbers are **a-** and **o-declension** Adjectives.

sexto die, on the sixth day
quartum annum, for the fourth year

LATIN MOTTOES

E Pluribus Unum, One from Many, United States
Nil sine numine, Nothing without divine power, Colorado
Qui transtulit sustinet, He who has transplanted sustains, Connecticut
Scuto bonae voluntatis tuae coronasti nos, You have crowned us with the shield of Thy Will, Maryland
Si quaeris peninsulam amoenam circumspice, If you seek a pleasant peninsula, look around, Michigan
Crescit eundo, It increases as it goes, New Mexico
Esse quam videri, To be rather than to seem, North Carolina
Labor omnia vincit, Labor conquers all, Oklahoma
Alis volat propriis, It flies on its own wings, Oregon
Animis opibusque parati, Prepared in mind and resources, South Carolina
Sic semper tyrannis, Thus always to tyrants, Virginia

PRACTICE EXERCISES

No. 147. Give the meanings of these Cardinal Numbers.

1. **quindecim**
2. **novem**
3. **viginti**
4. **quinque**
5. **sedecim**
6. **decem**
7. **tres**
8. **septendecim**
9. **quattuor**
10. **undecim**
11. **centum**
12. **quattuordecim**
13. **octo**
14. **undeviginti**
15. **duo**
16. **tredecim**
17. **septem**
18. **unus**
19. **duodeviginti**
20. **mille**
21. **duodecim**
22. **sex**

No. 148. Give the meanings of these Ordinal Numbers.

1. **quartus**
2. **octavus**
3. **decimus**
4. **tertius**
5. **septimus**
6. **secundus**
7. **quintus**
8. **nonus**
9. **primus**
10. **sextus**

No. 149. Translate these phrases which contain Cardinal Numbers.

1. **mille naves**	8. **quinque annos**	15. **tria loca**
2. **tres homines**	9. **sex de militibus**	16. **duae de provinciis**
3. **milium militum**	10. **septem horis**	17. **duodecim diebus**
4. **quattuordecim dies**	11. **centum annis**	18. **sex animalium**
5. **unius viri**	12. **octo ex pueris**	19. **duodeviginti ex regibus**
6. **viginti milia passuum**	13. **duos dies**	20. **tribus annis**
7. **centum pueros**	14. **decem legum**	

No. 150. Translate these phrases which contain Ordinal Numbers.

1. **decimae puellae**	4. **septima navis**	7. **decima hieme**	10. **primo anno**
2. **octavo die**	5. **quinta aestate**	8. **septimus impetus**	
3. **sexta hora**	6. **tertium diem**	9. **nonae horae**	

CHAPTER 31

READING

Cupido et Psyche	Cupid and Psyche
1. **Erant olim tres sorores pulchrae, quae erant filiae regis reginaeque. Harum Psyche erat clarissima. Itaque fama eius in regionibus, quae finitimae erant domui suae, erat aequa illi Veneris.**	1. There were once three beautiful sisters, who were daughters of the king and queen. Of these Psyche was the most famous. And so her reputation in the regions, that were neighboring to her home, was equal to that of Venus.
2. **Venus non solum immortalis sed etiam superbissima erat. Itaque contra puellam, quae neque dea neque immortalis erat, poenam reperire constituit.**	2. Venus was not only immortal but also very proud. And so she decided to find a punishment against the girl, who was neither a goddess nor immortal.
3. **Dea pulchra nullam inopiam consili habebat. Postquam ipsa iter ex hac difficultate delegerat, filium suum, Cupidem, deum amoris, ad se vocavit.**	3. The beautiful goddess had no lack of plan. After she had chosen a way out of this difficulty, she called her son, Cupid, the god of love, to her.
4. **Ei difficultatem suam demonstrat et dicit: "Omnes Psychen petunt et illi nunc me adorare non etiam simulant. Ob iniurias, quas matri tuae fecit, poenas dare debet. Hoc opus tibi idoneum est."**	4. To him she pointed out her difficulty and said: "All seek Psyche and they do not even pretend to worship me now. Because of the injuries, which she has done to your mother, she ought to pay penalties. This work is suitable to you."
5. **Cupido matrem suam iuvare celeriter parabat.**	5. Cupid quickly prepared to help his mother.
6. **Ad hortum Veneris, in quo erant duo fontes, quorum alter dulcis erat alterque non dulcis, properavit.**	6. He hurried to the garden of Venus, in which there were two fountains, one of which was sweet and the other not sweet.

Cupido et Psyche

7. **Postquam ex utroque fonte aquam obtinuerat, Psychen, quae domi dormiebat, petivit.**
8. **Ipse, ubi illam vidit, paene motus est quod pulcherrima erat, sed deus matrem memoria tenebat et puellam aqua, quae non dulcis erat, et sagitta sua tetigit.**
9. **Psyche incitata est, sed Cupidinem videre non poterat. Ipse territus est et in illa aquam dulcem posuit.**
10. **Postea Psyche, quamquam pulchra erat, miserrima quoque erat. Quod illa a Venere non amabatur nullus eam in matrimonium ducere cupiebat.**
11. **Itaque Psyche domi manebat et pater materque puellae simillimam inopiam spei demonstrabant.**
12. **Hoc ab oraculo dictum erat: "Non a viro, sed ab uno contra quem nullus stare potest tu in matrimonium duceris."**

Cupid and Psyche

7. After he had obtained water from each fountain, he sought Psyche, who was asleep at home.
8. He himself, when he saw her, was almost moved because she was very pretty, but the god remembered his mother and touched the girl with the water, that was not sweet, with his arrow.
9. Psyche was aroused, but she was not able to see Cupid. He was frightened and placed the sweet water on her.
10. Afterwards Psyche, although she was pretty, was also very unhappy. Because she was not loved by Venus, no one wanted to marry her.
11. And so Psyche remained at home and the father and mother of the girl showed a very similar lack of hope.
12. This had been said by the oracle: "You will be married not by a man, but by one against whom no one can stand."

READING VOCABULARY

Nouns

fons, fontis, m., spring, fountain (fontium) (font)
matrimonium, matrimonii or matrimoni, n., marriage (matrimony) **in matrimonium ducere,** marry
oraculum, oraculi, n., oracle (oracular)
soror, sororis, f., sister (sorority)
difficultas, difficultatis, f., difficulty
Cupido, Cupidinis, m., Cupid (cupidity)
Psyche, Psyches, f., Psyche (a Greek noun) (psychic)

Adjectives

similis, simile, like, similar (similarity)
dulcis, dulce, sweet (dulcet)
aequus, aequa, aequum, equal, level, fair (equality)
immortalis, immortale, immortal (immortality)

Verbs

dormio, dormire, dormivi, dormitus, sleep (dormant, dormitory)
tango, tangere, tetigi, tactus, touch (tangent)
deligo, deligere, delegi, delectus, choose, select
constituo, constituere, constitui, constitutus, decide, establish (constitution)

Adverbs

olim, formerly, once upon a time
quoque, also

Conjunction

quamquam, although

READING GRAMMAR

A. Adjectives have three degrees of comparison—positive, comparative, and superlative.

1. The Positive degree is always the simple form of the Adjective.

longus, longa, longum, long
fortis, forte, brave
miser, misera, miserum, wretched
pulcher, pulchra, pulchrum, pretty
acer, acris, acre, keen
facilis, facile, easy

2. The Comparative degree of all Adjectives ends in **-ior** or **-ius.**

longior, longius, longer, rather long, too long, quite long
fortior, fortius, braver, rather brave, too brave, quite brave
miserior, miserius, more wretched, rather wretched, quite wretched
pulchrior, pulchrius, prettier, more pretty, rather pretty, quite pretty
acrior, acrius, keener, more keen, rather keen, quite keen
facilior, facilius, easier, more easy, rather easy, quite easy

3. The Superlative degree endings are:

a. for those Adjectives that end in **-er,**

miserrimus, a, um, very wretched, most wretched
pulcherrimus, a, um, very pretty, most pretty, prettiest
acerrimus, a, um, very keen, most keen, keenest

b. for **facilis, difficilis,** and **similis,**

facillimus, a, um, very easy, most easy, easiest
difficillimus, a, um, very difficult, most difficult
simillimus, a, um, very similar, most similar

c. for all other Adjectives, the ending is **-issimus, a, um**

longissimus, a, um, very long, most long, longest
fortissimus, a, um, very brave, bravest, most brave

B. 1. The Positive degree of an Adjective is declined regularly in the **a-** and **o-declensions** or in the **i-declension.**

2. The Comparative degree is declined:

	SINGULAR		PLURAL	
	M. and F.	**N.**	**M. and F.**	**N.**
Nom.	**longior**	**longius**	**longiores**	**longiora**
Gen.	**longioris**	**longioris**	**longiorum**	**longiorum**
Dat.	**longiori**	**longiori**	**longioribus**	**longioribus**
Acc.	**longiorem**	**longius**	**longiores**	**longiora**
Abl.	**longiore**	**longiore**	**longioribus**	**longioribus**

3. The Superlative degree is declined regularly in the **a-** and **o-declensions.**

FAMILIAR QUOTATIONS

Laudator temporis acti. A praiser of past times. Horace

Abeunt studia in mores. Pursuits pass over into habits. Ovid

Factum fieri infectum non potest. What is done can not be undone. Terence

O tempora! O mores! Oh the times! Oh the customs! Cicero

Tu ne cede malis. Do not yield to misfortunes. Virgil

Docendo discitur. We learn by teaching. Seneca

In hoc signo vinces. By this sign thou shalt conquer. Constantine

Non datur ad Musas currere lata via. It is not granted to run to the Muses on a wide road. Propertius

Est modus in rebus. There is a middle course in things. Horace

Forsan et haec olim meminisse iuvabit. Perhaps some time it will be pleasant to remember even these things. Virgil

PRACTICE EXERCISES

No. 151. Translate these Positive degree Adjectives.

1. **iter difficile**
2. **domum miseram**
3. **virorum liberorum**
4. **timores acres**
5. **exercitus similes**
6. **diem longum**
7. **in monte alto**
8. **flumina celeria**
9. **vias latas**
10. **puellarum pulchrarum**

No. 152. Translate these Comparative degree Adjectives.

1. **viae angustiores**
2. **puer altior**
3. **puellarum laetiorum**
4. **populus amicior**
5. **iter longius**
6. **in locis gratioribus**
7. **sororum clariorum**
8. **hiemem longiorem**
9. **flumina latiora**
10. **virum audaciorem**

No. 153. Translate these Superlative degree Adjectives.

1. **fontis dulcissimi**
2. **ex hortis pulcherrimis**
3. **templum angustissimum**
4. **ob memorias miserrimas**
5. **oracula clarissima**
6. **civis laetissimus**
7. **ex agro latissimo**
8. **cum matribus pulcherrimis**
9. **in navi novissima**
10. **nomina brevissima**

No. 154. Translate these sentences.

1. **Is est locus miserrimus.**
2. **Fortissimi homines ad insulam pervenerunt.**
3. **Acerrimi equi erant inter primos.**
4. **Quid ad Graeciam est iter facilius?**
5. **Populus Italiae est liberrimus.**
6. **Haec est angustior pars aquae.**
7. **Hae res sunt quoque simillimae.**
8. **Flumen altissimum et latius vidimus.**
9. **Nostri ad urbem viam breviorem delegerunt.**
10. **Aedificium altum ab hoc loco videre potestis.**

CHAPTER 32

READING

Cupido et Psyche (cont'd.)

1. Locus, quem oraculum demonstraverat et in quo maritus illam exspectabat, summo in monte erat.
2. Illa ipsa etiam miserior aut patre aut matre erat. Itaque ad suam fortunam malam se dedere constituit.
3. Mox postea puella, cum matre patreque atque multis ex amicis suis, ad montem a populo oppidi, in quo habitabat, ducta est.
4. Hi eam solam ibi reliquerunt, quamquam pro ea magnopere dolebant, et se receperunt.
5. Psyche, quae summo in monte diu steterat et omnia in eo loco timebat, ab uno ex ventis, Zephyro, a monte ad terram pulcherrimam celeriter portata est.
6. Postquam breve tempus dormiverat, circum se spectabat et in silvam, quae propinqua erat agro, in quo a Zephyro relicta erat, audacter ambulavit.
7. In silva domum, quae pulchrior erat ulla quam antea viderat, repperit. Ad domum cucurrit.
8. Omnia in domo ei erant gratissima et ipsa tum vero laetissima erat.
9. Mox vocem audivit, sed neque virum neque mulierem vidit. Vox dixit: "Haec domus tua est et nos servi tui erimus. Omnia quae rogabis faciemus."
10. Postea in domo habitabat et laetior erat quam ulla puella in terra illa. Nil cupiebat.
11. Domum, servos, omnia bona, et maritum habebat, sed hunc non videbat. Noctu veniebat et ab ea ante diem properabat.

Cupid and Psyche (cont'd.)

1. The place, which the oracle had pointed out and in which her husband was waiting for her, was on the top of a mountain.
2. She herself was more unhappy than either her father or mother. And so she decided to surrender herself to her bad fortune.
3. Soon afterwards the girl, with her mother and father and many of her friends, was led to the mountain by the people of the town, in which she lived.
4. They left her there alone, although they felt very sorry for her, and departed.
5. Psyche, who had stayed on the top of the mountain for a long time and was afraid of everything in that place, was carried quickly from the mountain to a very beautiful land by one of the winds, Zephyr.
6. After she had slept for a short time, she looked around her and boldly walked into the forest, which was near the field, in which she had been left by Zephyr.
7. In the forest she found a house, which was prettier than any that she had seen before. She ran toward the house.
8. All the things in the house pleased her very much and she herself was then truly very happy.
9. Soon she heard a voice, but she saw neither man nor woman. The voice said: "This house is yours and we shall be your servants. We shall do everything that you ask."
10. Afterwards she lived in the house and she was happier than any girl in that land. She wished for nothing.
11. She had a house, servants, all good things, and a husband, but she did not see him. He came at night and hurried away from her before day.

Cupido et Psyche (cont'd.)

12. **Quam ob rem maxime dolebat, sed maritum suum bene amabat. Ipse dixit: "Me nunc amas quod aequi sumus. Hoc iter optimum est."**
13. **Diu tamen laetissima erat, sed posteriore tempore matrem patremque sororesque quoque memoria tenebat et oppressa est quod ibi non erant.**
14. **Una nocte, ubi maritus eius venit, ab eo viam e difficultate sua petivit.**

Cupid and Psyche (cont'd.)

12. For this reason she grieved greatly, but she loved her husband well. He said: "You love me now because we are equal. This way is best."
13. For a long time, however, she was very happy, but at a later time she remembered her mother and father and also her sisters and was oppressed because they were not there.
14. One night, when her husband came, she sought from him a way out of her difficulty.

READING VOCABULARY

Nouns

maritus, mariti, m., husband (marital)
Zephyrus, Zephyri, m., Zephyr, west wind
vox, vocis, f., voice (vocal)

Adjective

posterus, postera, posterum, next, following (posterior)

Adverbs

quam, than
antea, before
multo, much, by much
magis, more
maxime, most, especially (maximum)

Conjunction

aut . . . aut, either . . . or

READING GRAMMAR

A. There are two ways to show the comparison between two things.

1. **quam,** with the same case for the two things being compared.

   Ego altior sum quam tu, I am taller than you
   amicior illi quam huic, more friendly to that one than this

2. the Ablative Case after the Comparative degree, without **quam.**

   Ego altior sum te, I am taller than you
   amicior illi hoc, more friendly to that one than this

B. Some Adjectives have an irregular comparison.

bonus, a, um good	**melior, melius** better	**optimus, a, um** best
magnus, a um large	**maior, maius** larger	**maximus, a, um** largest
malus, a, um bad	**peior, peius** worse	**pessimus, a, um** worst
parvus, a, um small	**minor, minus** smaller	**minimus, a, um** smallest

multus, a, um	——, **plus**	**plurimus, a, um**
much	more	most
multi, ae, a	**plures, plura**	**plurimi, ae, a**
many	more	most

The Superlative degree of **posterus** is **postremus, a, um,** or **postumus, a, um.**

C. Most Adjectives ending in a vowel and **-us** are compared this way:

idoneus, a, um	**magis idoneus, a, um**	**maxime idoneus, a, um**
suitable	more suitable	most suitable

D. **Plus** is a neuter noun in the singular; an adjective in the plural.

		M. and F.	N.
Nom.	**plus**	**plures**	**plura**
Gen.	**pluris**	**plurium**	**plurium**
Dat.	——	**pluribus**	**pluribus**
Acc.	**plus**	**plures, pluris**	**plura**
Abl.	**plure**	**pluribus**	**pluribus**

MATHEMATICAL TERMS BASED ON LATIN

plus, more, increased by.
minus, less, diminished by.
multiplication, from **multiplicare,** to make manifold or many fold.
division, from **dividere,** divide.
subtraction, from **subtrahere,** withdraw, draw from beneath.
addition, from **addere,** add to, or **additio,** adding.
ratio, from **ratio,** reason.
quotient, from **quotiens,** how often, how many times.
sum, from **summa,** sum or total, or **summus,** highest.
number and numeral, from **numerus,** number.
integer, from **integer,** whole, untouched.
fraction, from **frangere,** break.
percent and per centum, from **per centum,** by the hundred, in the hundred.

PRACTICE EXERCISES

No. 155. Translate these sentences.

1. **Hae turres altiores sunt quam illae.**
2. **Es altior patre tuo.**
3. **Illa itinera aliis faciliora non sunt.**
4. **Patri tuo quam matri similior es.**
5. **Homines multo fortiores mulieribus sunt.**
6. **Domus eius ruri novior est illa in urbe.**
7. **Puer laetior est quam soror.**
8. **Barbari multo audaciores sunt finitimis suis.**
9. **Ille vobis amicior quam mihi erit.**
10. **Estne manus celerior quam oculus?**

No. 156. Give the English for these Verb forms.

1. **erunt**
2. **demonstratum est**
3. **constituit**
4. **parabitur**
5. **ducebant**
6. **relictus est**
7. **mittetur**
8. **portaris**
9. **videbamus**
10. **ambulavit**

No. 157. Give the English for these Adjectives.

1. **plura**
2. **melior**
3. **pessimorum**
4. **maioris**
5. **minorum**
6. **plurimorum**
7. **pluribus**
8. **posteros**
9. **magis idonei**
10. **maxime idoneum**

No. 158. Translate these Adjective phrases.

1. **in pluribus urbibus**	8. **rei pessimae**	15. **soror minima**
2. **ex fontibus minoribus**	9. **ad partem meliorem**	16. **plurium difficultatum**
3. **virtutem maximam**	10. **cum maiore exercitu**	17. **iter melius**
4. **vox optima**	11. **die longiore**	18. **aestatis pessimae**
5. **de muris altioribus**	12. **plurimas civitates**	19. **dona plurima**
6. **plus aquae**	13. **finem peiorem**	20. **navis minoris**
7. **tempus magis idoneum**	14. **annos optimos**	

CHAPTER 33

READING

Cupido et Psyche (cont'd.)	Cupid and Psyche (cont'd.)
1. **Postridie ad Zephyrum quam celerrime contendit et illi id quod maritus suus dixerat narrabat.**	1. On the next day she hurried as quickly as possible to Zephyr and told him what her husband had said.
2. **Imperia Cupidinis facillime confecit et brevi tempore duae sorores eius ad domum eius a Zephyro celeriter portatae sunt.**	2. He very easily carried out the commands of Cupid and in a short time her two sisters were carried quickly to her house by Zephyr.
3. **Psyche adventu earum laetissima erat et illis omnia sua demonstravit. Ipsae tamen postquam domum atque servos illius viderant inopiam eius bonae fortunae acerrime cognoverunt.**	3. Psyche was very happy at their arrival and showed them all her possessions. They, however, after they had seen her house and servants, clearly recognized her lack of good fortune.
4. **Multa rogabant: "Esne uxor laeta?" "Quis es maritus tuus?"**	4. They asked many things: "Are you a happy wife?" "Who is your husband?"
5. **Magno cum studio verba eius audiebant. Vita eius melior quam vita earum esse videbatur.**	5. They listened to her words with great eagerness. Her life seemed to be better than their life.
6. **Eam miserrime conspiciebant. Eodem tempore spem maiorem videbant: "Num tu maritum tuum umquam vidisti? Maritus quem uxor numquam vidit optimus maritus esse non potest. Nonne verba oraculi memoria tenes? Ille aut serpens aut animal est."**	6. They looked at her most unhappily. At the same time they saw a greater hope: "You haven't ever seen your husband, have you? A husband whom his wife has never seen can not be the best husband. You remember the words of the oracle, don't you? He is either a serpent or an animal."
7. **Psyche consilio sororum suarum coacta est quod ab eis semper facillime ducebatur. Itaque lucem ac gladium cepit et haec in loco idoneo conlocavit.**	7. Psyche was convinced by the plan of her sisters because she was always very easily influenced by them. And so she took a light and a sword and placed these things in a suitable place.

Cupido et Psyche (cont'd.)

8. **Psyche consilium sororum suarum minime amabat, sed verba earum quam verba sua plus poterant. Illae plus facile quam ipsa dicere poterant.**
9. **Itaque ipsa lucem gladiumque paravit et maritus eius ad eam noctu venit. Ipsa maxime timebat, sed ei timorem suum non demonstrabat.**
10. **Dum ille dormit, lucem cepit et supra eum id tenebat. Quid vidit? Neque serpentem neque animal ante se conspexit. Erat unus ex deorum pulcherrimus atque gratissimus.**
11. **A timore liberata erat. Eum non diutius timebat, sed magis amabat.**
12. **Ut accidit tamen umerum eius luce tetigit et ille excitatus est. Ipse nullum verbum dixit, sed oculis suis eam monuit et alis celeribus eam reliquit.**
13. **Psyche ad terram cecidit. Cupido supra eam breve tempus volabat et dixit: "Contra imperia matris meae te amavi. Immortales mortales non saepe amant, sed te in matrimonium duxi et me interficere nunc cupis. Amor tuus minus fortis meo est."**
14. **His verbis puellam miserrimam reliquit et ad caelum volavit.**

Cupid and Psyche (cont'd.)

8. Psyche did not like her sisters' plan at all, but their words were more powerful than her own. They were able to talk more easily than she.
9. And so she got the light and the sword ready and her husband came to her at night. She was very much afraid, but she did not show her fear to him.
10. While he slept, she took the light and held it above him. What did she see? She saw in front of her neither a serpent nor an animal. He was one of the most handsome and pleasing of the gods.
11. She had been freed from fear. She no longer feared him, but loved him more.
12. As it happened, however, she touched his shoulder with the light and he was aroused. He said no word, but warned her with his eyes and left her on swift wings.
13. Psyche fell to the ground. Cupid flew above her for a short time and said: "I have loved you against the commands of my mother. Immortals do not often love mortals, but I married you and now you want to kill me. Your love is less strong than mine."
14. With these words he left the very unhappy girl and flew to the sky.

READING VOCABULARY

Nouns

imperium, imperii or **imperi, n.,** command (imperial)
uxor, uxoris, f., wife (uxorial)
verbum, verbi, n., word (verb)
lux, lucis, f., light (lucent)

Adjective

mortalis, mortale, mortal (mortality)

Conjunction

dum, while With the Present tense.

Verbs

excito, excitare, excitavi, excitatus, arouse, stir up (excitement)
cado, cadere, cecidi, casurus, fall (cadence)
conficio, conficere, confeci, confectus, finish, complete, carry out (confection)
plus posse, be more powerful
plurimum posse, be most powerful

Adverbs

supra, over, above Also a Preposition with the Accusative Case.
quam, as possible With the Superlative degree.
numquam, never
umquam, ever
postridie, on the next day

READING GRAMMAR

A. Adverbs are compared in much the same way as Adjectives, but have only one form for each degree.

1. Regular Adverbs are compared:

longe far	**longius** farther	**longissime** farthest
misere unhappily	**miserius** more unhappily	**miserrime** most unhappily
pulchre beautifully	**pulchrius** more beautifully	**pulcherrime** most beautifully
acriter keenly	**acrius** more keenly	**acerrime** most keenly
fortiter bravely	**fortius** more bravely	**fortissime** most bravely
facile easily	**facilius** more easily	**facillime** most easily

2. These Adverbs are irregular:

bene well	**melius** better	**optime** best
magnopere greatly	**magis** more	**maxime** most
male badly	**peius** worse	**pessime** worst
multum much	**plus** more	**plurimum** most
parum little	**minus** less	**minime** least
diu long	**diutius** longer	**diutissime** longest
saepe often	**saepius** more often	**saepissime** most often

B. When **quam** is used with the superlative degree of an Adjective or Adverb it means *as . . . as possible.*

quam pulcherrimus, as pretty as possible
quam pulcherrime, as beautifully as possible

GEOMETRICAL TERMS BASED ON LATIN

perpendicular, from **per,** through, and **pendere,** hang.
circumference, from **circum,** around, and **ferre,** carry.
circle, from **circus,** circle.
radius, from **radius,** staff, rod, ray.
arc, from **arcus,** bow, arc.
tangent, from **tangere,** touch.
angle, from **angulus,** angle, corner.
obtuse, from **obtundere,** strike.
acute, from **acuere,** sharpen.
triangle, from **tri,** three, and **angulus,** angle.
rectangle, from **rectus,** right, and **angulus,** angle.
square, from **ex,** out, and **quadra,** square.
Q.E.D., abbreviation of **quod erat demonstrandum,** which was to be demonstrated.

PRACTICE EXERCISES

No. 159. Give the English for these Adjectives and Adverbs.

1. **latus**	9. **liberior**	17. **pulchrius**	25. **acer**
2. **late**	10. **liberrimus**	18. **pulcherrime**	26. **acriter**
3. **latior**	11. **liberius**	19. **celer**	27. **acrior**
4. **latius**	12. **liberrime**	20. **celeriter**	28. **acrius**
5. **latissimus**	13. **pulcher**	21. **celerior**	29. **acerrimus**
6. **latissime**	14. **pulchrior**	22. **celerius**	30. **acerrime**
7. **liber**	15. **pulcherrimus**	23. **celerrimus**	
8. **libere**	16. **pulchre**	24. **celerrime**	

No. 160. Translate these sentences, containing Adverbs.

1. **Gravissime oppugnabantur.**
2. **Fortius pugnat.**
3. **Celeriter incensi sunt.**
4. **Multo brevius dicent.**
5. **Audacissime monebitur.**
6. **Difficile aciem instruxerunt.**
7. **Acrius bellum gessit.**
8. **Superbe ambulant.**
9. **Gratius dabat.**
10. **Altissime laudatur.**
11. **Latius missi sunt.**
12. **Liberrime dedit.**
13. **Longissime navigat.**
14. **Miserius movet.**
15. **Nove videbantur.**
16. **Pulchrius movent.**
17. **Acerrime timebit.**
18. **Audacter capti sunt.**
19. **Brevissime dicebat.**
20. **Fortiter pugnant.**

No. 161. Give the English for these Adverbs.

1. **bene**	6. **diu**	11. **melius**	16. **plurimum**	21. **minime**
2. **magnopere**	7. **saepe**	12. **peius**	17. **diutissime**	
3. **male**	8. **diutius**	13. **minus**	18. **saepissime**	
4. **multum**	9. **plus**	14. **saepius**	19. **optime**	
5. **parum**	10. **magis**	15. **maxime**	20. **pessime**	

No. 162. Translate these sentences, containing Adverbs.

1. **Saepius perveniunt.**
2. **Quam diutissime pugnavit.**
3. **Magis excitatus est.**
4. **Plus impediebatur.**
5. **Optime amatus es.**
6. **Id saepissime auditum est.**
7. **Minus difficile ambulat.**
8. **Apud nos plurimum possunt.**
9. **Plus celeriter volat.**
10. **Multum diutius manebit.**

EIGHTH REVIEW SECTION (CHAPTERS 30–33)

VOCABULARY REVIEW

NOUNS

1. **aestas**	8. **lux**	15. **portus**	1. **summer**	8. **light**	15. **harbor, port**
2. **Creusa**	9. **maritus**	16. **Psyche**	2. **Creusa**	9. **husband**	16. **Psyche**
3. **Cupido**	10. **matrimonium**	17. **soror**	3. **Cupid**	10. **marriage**	17. **sister**
4. **difficultas**	11. **multitudo**	18. **uxor**	4. **difficulty**	11. **great number, multitude**	18. **wife**
5. **fons**	12. **onus**	19. **ventus**	5. **spring, fountain**	12. **burden, weight**	19. **wind**
6. **hiems**	13. **oraculum**	20. **verbum**	6. **winter**	13. **oracle**	20. **word**
7. **imperium**	14. **plus**	21. **vox**	7. **command**	14. **more**	21. **voice**
		22. **Zephyrus**			22. **Zephyr, west wind**

ADJECTIVES

1. aequus	7. minimus	13. plurimus	1. equal, level, fair	7. smallest	13. most		
2. dulcis	8. minor	14. posterus	2. sweet	8. smaller	14. next, following		
3. immortalis	9. mortalis	15. postumus	3. immortal	9. mortal	15. next, following		
4. maior	10. optimus	16. similis	4. larger	10. best	16. like, similar		
5. maximus	11. peior		5. largest	11. worse			
6. melior	12. pessimus		6. better	12. worst			

VERBS

1. cado	9. excito	1. fall	9. arouse, stir up
2. cogo	10. incendo	2. collect, drive, compel	10. set fire to, burn
3. conficio	11. opprimo	3. finish, complete, carry out	11. overcome, crush
4. constituo	12. plurimum posse	4. decide, establish	12. be most powerful
5. convenio	13. plus posse	5. come together, assemble	13. be more powerful
6. dedo	14. recipio	6. give up, surrender	14. take back, receive
7. deligo	15. suscipio	7. choose, select	15. take up, undertake
8. dormio	16. tango	8. sleep	16. touch

ADVERBS

1. antea	7. olim	1. before	7. formerly, once upon a time
2. bis	8. postridie	2. twice	8. on the next day
3. magis	9. quam	3. more	9. as possible; than
4. maxime	10. supra	4. most, especially	10. over, above
5. multo	11. umquam	5. much, by much	11. ever
6. numquam		6. never	

CONJUNCTIONS

1. aut . . . aut	3. nam	5. quoque	1. either . . . or	3. for	5. also
2. dum	4. quamquam		2. while	4. although	

PRACTICE EXERCISES

No. 163. Translate these phrases.

1. una ex sororum
2. tria flumina
3. duos annos
4. mille anni
5. duas uxores
6. centum verba
7. unius vocis
8. viginti fontes
9. quarta hora
10. quinto die
11. secundo anno
12. septimum verbum
13. primum oraculum
14. in quarto portu
15. ex sexta porta

No. 164. Translate these Adjective phrases.

1. longiorem hiemem
2. pulcherrima aestas
3. longissimorum annorum
4. dulcius verbum
5. onus simillimum
6. vocis immortalis
7. iter facilius
8. luces clariores
9. difficultatis acerrimae
10. maritorum fortiorum

No. 165. Give the English for these Adjectives.

1. dulcis, dulcior, dulcissimus
2. acer, acrior, acerrimus
3. longus, longior, longissimus
4. similis, similior, simillimus
5. altus, altior, altissimus
6. liber, liberior, liberrimus
7. celer, celerior, celerrimus
8. latus, latior, latissimus
9. clarus, clarior, clarissimus
10. audax, audacior, audacissimus

No. 166. Give the English for these Adjectives.

1. **magnus, maior, maximus**
2. **parvus, minor, minimus**
3. **bonus, melior, optimus**
4. **malus, peior, pessimus**
5. **multus, plus, plurimus**
6. **multi, plures, plurimi**
7. **idoneous, magis idoneus, maxime idoneus**

No. 167. Translate into English.

1. **longius ambulabat**
2. **misere oppressus est**
3. **parum dormit**
4. **diutissime incendet**
5. **acrius excitati sunt**
6. **magis tangebant**
7. **facilius dediderunt**
8. **plurimum possunt**
9. **plus poterit**
10. **minus facile cogentur**

PHAEDRUS

Phaedrus was a freedman of Augustus, who lived in the first half of the first century A.D. Five books of his **Fables** are extant. These are based on early folk tales and on the Greek fables of Aesop. Phaedrus, in turn, furnished the material for the French fabulist, La Fontaine.

Qui se laudari gaudet verbis subdolis,	He who rejoices that he is praised by words of flattery,
sera dat poenas turpes paenitentia.	too late pays his penalty with lowly repentance.
Cum de fenestra corvus raptum caseum	When a crow started to eat the cheese
comesse vellet, celsa residens arbore,	he snatched from a window, perching in a lofty tree,
vulpes hunc vidit; deinde sic coepit loqui:	a wolf saw him; thus, with flattery, he began to speak:
"O qui tuarum, corve, pinnarum est nitor.	"Oh what a brightness, crow, your feathers have.
Quantum decoris corpore et vultu geris.	What grace of body, what charm of looks you possess.
Si vocem haberes, nulla prior ales foret."	If you should have a voice, no bird would be above you."
At ille stultus, dum vult vocem ostendere,	Then he, foolish one, while he tried to show off his voice,
emisit ore caseum, quem celeriter	dropped the cheese from his mouth. This quickly
dolosa vulpes avidis rapuit dentibus.	the tricky fox snatched in his greedy teeth.
Tum demum ingemuit corvi deceptus stupor.	Then the crow, deceived by his stupidity, groaned, but too late.
Phaedrus I, xiii	Phaedrus I, 13

The **Stabat Mater** was composed by an unknown author, although Saint Bonaventure is sometimes given the credit for its composition, probably in the thirteenth century, and has been set to music by many musicians since the eighteenth century.

Stabat mater dolorosa	At the Cross her station keeping,
iuxta crucem lacrimosa,	Stood the mournful Mother weeping,
dum pendebat filius,	Close to Jesus at the last.
cuius animam gementem,	Through her soul, of joy bereaved,
contristantem et dolentem	Bowed with anguish, deeply grieved,
pertransivit gladius.	Now at length the sword hath passed.

O quam tristis et afflicta
fuit illa benedicta
mater unigenti,
quae maerebat et dolebat
et tremebat, dum videbat
nati poenas incliti!

Oh how sad and sore distressed
Was that Mother, highly blest,
Of the sole begotten One!
Oh that silent, ceaseless mourning,
Oh those dim eyes, never turning
From that wondrous, suffering Son!

Quis est homo qui non fleret,
matrem Christi si videret
in tanto supplicio?
Quis non posset contristari
piam matrem contemplari
dolentem cum filio?

Who on Christ's dear Mother gazing,
In her trouble so amazing,
Born of woman, would not weep?
Who on Christ's dear Mother thinking,
Such a cup of sorrow drinking,
Would not share her sorrow deep?

Pro peccatis suae gentis
vidit Iesum in tormentis
et flagellis subditum;
vidit suum dulcem natum
morientem, desolatum,
dum emisit spiritum.

For the sins of his own nation,
Saw him hang in desolation
Till his Spirit forth he sent;
Bruised, derided, cursed, defiled,
She beheld her tender Child,
All with bloody scourges rent.

Eia mater, fons amoris!
Me sentire vim doloris
fac, ut tecum lugeam.
Fac ut ardeat cor meum
in amando Christum Deum,
ut sibi complaceam.

O, thou Mother, fount of love!
Touch my spirit from above,
Make my heart with thine accord.
Make me feel as thou hast felt;
Make my soul to glow and melt
With the love of Christ my Lord.

Sancta mater, istud agas,
crucifixi fige plagas
cordi meo valide;
tui nati vulnerati,
tam dignati pro me pati,
poenas mecum divide.

Holy Mother, pierce me through.
In my heart each wound renew
Of my Saviour crucified;
Let me share with thee his pain,
Who for all my sins was slain,
Who for me in torment died.

Fac me vere tecum flere,
crucifixo condolere,
donec ego vixero;
iuxta crucem tecum stare,
meque tibi sociare
in planctu desidero.

Let me mingle tears with thee,
Mourning him who mourned for me,
All the days that I may live.
By the cross with thee to stay,
There with thee to weep and pray,
Is all I ask of thee to give.

Virgo virginum praeclara,
mihi iam non sis amara,
fac me tecum plangere;
fac ut portem Christi mortem,
passionis fac consortem
et plagas recolere.

Virgin of all virgins blest,
Listen to my fond request:
Let me share thy grief divine.
Let me to my latest breath,
In my body bear the death
Of that dying Son of thine.

Fac me plagis vulnerari,
cruce hac inebriari,
et cruore filii;
per te, Virgo, sim defensus
inflammatus et accensus,
in die iudicii.

Wounded with his every wound,
Steep my soul till it hath swooned
In his very blood away.
Be to me, O Virgin, nigh,
Lest in flames I burn and die
In his awful judgment day.

Fac me cruce custodiri
morte Christi praemuniri,
confoveri gratia.
Quando corpus morietur,
fac ut animae donetur
paradisi gloria.

Christ, when thou shalt call me hence,
Be thy Mother my defense,
Be thy cross my victory.
While my body here decays
May my soul thy goodness praise
Safe in Paradise with thee.

CHAPTER 34

READING

Cupido et Psyche (cont'd.)

1. Postquam Cupido uxorem suam tam celeriter reliquerat, illa circum se spectavit. Omnis spes ab ea interea cecidit atque sua vita laeta discessit, nam horti pulchri ac domus magna nunc ibi non erant.
2. Non longe ab urbe, ubi antea habitaverat, erat sola. Maxime dolebat.
3. Sorores fabulam eius magno cum studio audiverunt. Sibi dixerunt: "Cupido unam ex nobis nunc certe deliget."
4. Prima luce postridie illae duae ad montem properaverunt et Zephyrum audacissime appellabant. Utraque tamen ad terram sub monte cecidit et interfecta est, quod deus venti eam non iuvit.
5. Psyche interea maritum suum noctu dieque petebat. Montem altissimum, in quo templum magnum erat, conspexit. Eratne templum Cupidinis?
6. In templo aliud genus rei invenit. Omnibus in partibus aedifici frumentum videbat.
7. Quo modo multa genera frumenti in ordine ponere poterit.
8. Nunc etiam magis dolebat, sed erat puella fortissima.

Cupid and Psyche (cont'd.)

1. After Cupid had left his wife so quickly, she looked around her. All hope fell from her meanwhile and her happy life departed, for the beautiful gardens and large house were not there now.
2. She was alone, not far from the city, where she had lived before. She grieved very much.
3. Her sisters heard her story with great eagerness. They said to themselves: "Cupid will now certainly choose one of us."
4. At dawn the next day those two hurried to the mountain and very boldly called Zephyr by name. Each, however, fell to the ground at the foot of the mountain and was killed, because the god of the wind did not help her.
5. Psyche meanwhile sought her husband night and day. She saw a very high mountain, on which there was a large temple. Was it the temple of Cupid?
6. In the temple she found another kind of thing. In all parts of the building she saw grain.
7. How will she be able to put many kinds of grain in order?
8. Now she grieved even more, but she was a very brave girl.

Cupido et Psyche (cont'd.)

9. **Dum illa laborat, Ceres, dea frumenti, in templum venit, nam id erat templum Cereris. Ceres puellam miserrimam iuvare cupiebat quod Psyche bene laboraverat et frumentum in templo in ordine bene posuerat.**
10. **Dea ei auxilium dare cupiebat quod illa pro ea satis iam fecerat. Dixit: "Venus tibi auxilium non dat. Dea bona est, sed filium suum, maritum tuum, maxime amat et eum dedere non cupit."**
11. **Psyche nullam spem habebat, sed tamen ad domum deae pulcherrimae properavit.**
12. **Ibi Venerem superbam invenit, quae dixit: "Nonne tu me tandem memoria tenes? Maritus tuus vulnus quod tu luce ei dedisti nunc curat. Postquam hunc laborem confecisti tibi eum dare cupio."**
13. **Hoc opus erat: Magnum numerum et multa genera frumenti sine ordine ante se videbat.**
14. **Mors melior quam hoc opus esse videbatur. Ipsa nil fecit. Labor maximus erat, sed Cupido uxorem suam mox vidit et ei auxilium misit.**
15. **Parva formica, quae erat dux sociorum amicorumque suorum, ad eam venit.**
16. **Omnes hae formicae brevissimo tempore frumentum in ordine conlocaverunt. Fugerunt postquam hoc fecerant.**

Cupid and Psyche (cont'd.)

9. While she was working, Ceres, the goddess of grain, came into the temple, for this was the temple of Ceres. Ceres wished to help the very unhappy girl because Psyche had worked well and had put the grain in the temple in order well.
10. The Goddess wished to give help to her because she had already done enough for her. She said: "Venus does not give help to you. The goddess is good, but she loves her son, your husband, very much and does not want to give him up."
11. Psyche had no hope, but nevertheless she hurried to the house of the very beautiful goddess.
12. There she found the proud Venus, who said: "You finally remember me, don't you? Your husband is now caring for the wound that you gave him with the light. After you have finished this work I want to give him to you."
13. This was the task: She saw in front of her a great amount and many kinds of grain without order.
14. Death seemed to be better than this task. She did nothing. The work was very great, but Cupid soon saw his wife and sent help to her.
15. A small ant, that was the leader of his comrades and friends, came to her.
16. All these ants placed the grain in order in a very short time. They fled after they had done this.

READING VOCABULARY

Nouns

dux, ducis, m., leader (duke)
numerus, numeri, m., number (numeral)
vulnus, vulneris, n., wound (vulnerable)
satis, n., enough Same spelling in all cases. (satisfy)
formica, formicae, f., ant (formic)
modus, modi, m., manner, way (mode)
genus, generis, n., kind, class (genus)
ordo, ordinis, m., rank, order (order, ordinal)

Verb

invenio, invenire, inveni, inventus, find, come upon (invent)

Adverbs

tam, so
satis, enough (satisfaction)
tandem, finally (tandem)

READING GRAMMAR

A. All Infinitives are formed on the same pattern.

1. The Present Active Infinitive is the second principal part.

amare, to love	**ducere,** to lead	**esse,** to be
habere, to have	**capere,** to seize	**posse,** to be able
	audire, to hear	

2. The Present Passive Infinitive ends in **-i.** Note the **e/i-conjugation** drops the **-er-.**

amari, to be loved	**duci,** to be led	**audiri,** to be heard
haberi, to be had	**capi,** to be seized	

3. The Perfect Active Infinitive is the third principal part ending in **-isse.**

amavisse, to have loved	**duxisse,** to have led	**fuisse,** to have been
habuisse, to have had	**cepisse,** to have seized	**potuisse,** to have been able
	audivisse, to have heard	

4. The Perfect Passive Infinitive is the fourth principal part in the Accusative case with **esse.**

amatum, am, um esse, to have been loved	**captum, am, um esse,** to have been seized
habitum, am, um esse, to have been had	**auditum, am, um esse,** to have been heard
ductum, am, um esse, to have been led	

5. The Future Active Infinitive is the fourth principal part ending in **-urum** with **esse.**

amaturum, am, um esse, to be about to love	**capturum, am, um esse,** to be about to seize
habiturum, am, um esse, to be about to have	**auditurum, am, um esse,** to be about to hear
ducturum, am, um esse, to be about to lead	**futurum, am, um esse,** to be about to be

B. You have already met the completing Infinitive.

Id capere cupit. He wants to take it.

The Infinitive is also used to express:

1. A Subject.

Id invenire difficile est. It is difficult to find it.

2. A Direct Object.

Natare amat. He likes to swim.

3. An Indirect Statement after a Verb showing mental processes such as saying, thinking, knowing, hearing.

Virum laborare dico. I say that the man is working.

C. All Subjects of Infinitives are in the Accusative case.

virum laborare	**viros laborare**
agrum arari	**agros arari**

D. The Perfect Passive and Future Active Infinitives must be Accusative to agree with their Accusative subjects.

Agrum aratum esse dicit.	He says the field has been plowed.
Agros aratos esse dicit.	He says the fields have been plowed.
Virum laboraturum esse dicit.	He says the man is going to work.
Viros laboraturos esse dicit.	He says the men are going to work.

MEDICAL ABBREVIATIONS

The following are some of the more common medical and pharmaceutical abbreviations of Latin terms.

℞, recipe, take
bib., bibe, drink
d., da, give
cap., capsula, capsule
gtt., guttae, drops
gr., granum, grain
Lb., libra, pound
mist., mistura, mixture
ol., oleum, oil
ung., unguentum, ointment
pulv., pulvis, powder
aq., aqua, water
c̄, cum, with
no., numero, number
os., os, ora, mouth
p.o., per os, by mouth
Q.s., quantum sufficiat, a sufficient quantity
Q.v., quantum vis, as much as you wish
a.c., ante cibum, before food, before meals
p.c., post cibum, after food, after meals
stat., statim, immediately
quotid., quotidie, every day
alt. dieb., alternis diebus, every other day, on alternate days
t.i.d., ter in die, three times a day
q.i.d., quater in die, four times a day
H., hora, hour
h.s., hora somni, at the hour of sleep, bedtime
Q.h., quaque hora, every hour **Q.2h.,** every two hours
omn. hor., omni hora, every hour
noct., nocte, at night
omn. noct., omni nocte, every night
t.i.n., ter in nocte, three times a night, **q.i.n., quater in nocte,** four times a night
rep. repetatur, let it be repeated
non rep., non repetatur, do not repeat
p.r.n., pro re nata, as the occasion arises, as needed
Sig., S., signetur, let it be marked (directions to patient)

PRACTICE EXERCISES

No. 168. Give the English for these Infinitives.

1. **monere**
2. **auxisse**
3. **iaci**
4. **positurum esse**
5. **fugisse**
6. **impedire**
7. **natavisse**
8. **territurum esse**
9. **mansisse**
10. **auditurum esse**
11. **scripsisse**
12. **pugnaturum esse**
13. **laudaturum esse**
14. **excitari**
15. **petitum esse**
16. **mittere**
17. **tangi**
18. **oppugnatum esse**
19. **sciri**
20. **gesturum esse**
21. **accipi**
22. **victum esse**
23. **dici**
24. **ambulaturum esse**
25. **timuisse**

No. 169. Change these Infinitives to the Active, and give the English.

1. **peti**
2. **captum esse**
3. **haberi**
4. **rectum esse**
5. **portari**
6. **vocatum esse**
7. **faci**
8. **datum esse**
9. **instrui**
10. **verti**

No. 170. Change these Infinitives to the Passive, and give the English.

1. **narrare**
2. **defendisse**
3. **videre**
4. **iuvare**
5. **pugnavisse**
6. **movisse**
7. **vocare**
8. **invenire**
9. **necavisse**
10. **relinquere**

No. 171. Give the Future Active Infinitive of these Verbs, and the English.

1. **esse**
2. **iubere**
3. **facere**
4. **defendere**
5. **oppugnare**
6. **properare**
7. **capere**
8. **invenire**
9. **dare**
10. **ponere**

No. 172. Translate these sentences.

1. **Illi milites viros auxilium portaturos esse dixerunt.**
2. **Putatisne opus vestrum factum esse?**
3. **Nos hostes quam celerrime venturos esse sperabamus.**
4. **Puellae laetae esse videntur.**
5. **Hic rex bene regere cupiebat.**
6. **Ille appellari non cupiet.**
7. **Oppidum nostrum defendere optimum est.**
8. **Spem habuisse melius erat quam se recepisse.**
9. **Celeritatem augeri posse nuntiavit.**
10. **Nos locum meliorem invenire iussit.**

CHAPTER 35

READING

Cupido et Psyche (cont'd.)

1. **Venus ad templum suum multo die venit et ad illam partem templi ubi puellam reliquerat sine mora properavit. Ipsa puellam miseram ante se etiam tum laborem difficile habere sperabat.**
2. **Ubi laborem confectum esse vidit, filium suum id fecisse putabat et puellae cibum minimum dedit.**
3. **Postridie puellam ad se venire iussit. Dea ad silvam in qua erant multae oves, quarum lana erat aurea, currere et lanam reportare illam iussit.**
4. **Cum illa ad flumen pervenit non solum oves sed etiam deum fluminis invenit.**
5. **Ille dixit flumen celerrimum esse atque oves die maxime inimicas esse, sed demonstravit oves noctu futuras esse dulciores. Quam ob rem illa ad noctem exspectavit et oves dormire invenit.**
6. **Labor eius facillimus erat quod lana ovium in arboribus erat. Oves non etiam tetigerat, sed auxilio dei multam lanam auream ab arboribus obtinuit et eodem die ad Venerem, dominam suam, properavit, quod pro illa omnia bene facere cupiebat.**
7. **Postquam ad Veneram venerat et sub pedibus illius lanam posuerat, Psyche deam eam liberaturam esse atque se maritum suum recepturam esse sperabat.**

Cupid and Psyche (cont'd.)

1. Venus came to her temple late in the day and hurried without delay to that part of the temple where she had left the girl. She hoped that the unhappy girl had difficult work ahead of her even then.
2. When she saw that the work had been finished, she thought her son had done it and she gave the girl very little food.
3. On the next day she ordered the girl to come to her. The goddess ordered her to run to the forest in which there were many sheep, whose wool was golden, and to bring back the wool.
4. When she came to the river, she found not only the sheep but also the god of the river.
5. He said that the river was very swift and the sheep were especially unfriendly in the daytime, but he pointed out that the sheep would be more gentle at night. For this reason she waited until night and found that the sheep were sleeping.
6. Her work was very easy because the wool of the sheep was on the trees. She had not even touched the sheep, but with the help of the god she obtained much golden wool from the trees and the same day she hurried to Venus, her mistress, because she wished to do everything well for her.
7. After she came to Venus and placed the wool at her feet, Psyche hoped that the goddess would free her and that she would get back her husband.

Cupido et Psyche (cont'd.)

8. **Qua de causa spes eius celeriter fugit nam domina eius illam sine auxilio alterius lanam non obtinuisse dixit.**
9. **Puellam esse utilem cupiebat. Itaque eam apud Inferos iter facere iussit. Ei arcam parvam dedit.**
10. **Psyche miser templum Veneris reliquit et se mortem certe inventuram esse putabat quod dea partem pulchritudinis Proserpinae ex terra mortis ad se reportari cupiebat.**
11. **Psyche tamen fortissima erat et ad turrem altissimam venit. Celerrimum iter ad Inferos petebat, sed vox ex turre eam appellavit et ipsam illo modo se necare non debere dixit.**
12. **Vox quoque id ei futurum esse postremum laborem nuntiavit. Puellae iter facile celereque ad regnum Plutonis demonstravit et illa ex timore ab eodem amico qui eam antea servaverat nunc liberata est.**

Cupid and Psyche (cont'd.)

8. For this reason her hope quickly fled for her mistress said that she had not obtained the wool without the help of another.
9. She wanted the girl to be useful. And so she ordered her to make a journey among Those Below. She gave her a small box.
10. The unhappy Psyche left the temple of Venus and thought that she would certainly find death because the goddess wished a part of Proserpina's beauty to be brought back to her from the land of death.
11. Psyche, however, was very brave and came to a very high tower. She was seeking the fastest way to Those Below, but a voice out of the tower called her and said she ought not to kill herself in that manner.
12. The voice also announced that this would be the last task for her. It pointed out to the girl an easy and quick way to the kingdom of Pluto and she was now freed from fear by the same friend who had saved her before.

READING VOCABULARY

Nouns

lana, lanae, f., wool (lanate, lanolin)
ovis, ovis, f., sheep (ovium) (ovine)
pulchritudo, pulchritudinis, f., beauty (pulchritude)

Adjective

utilis, utile, useful (utility)

Verbs

puto, putare, putavi, putatus, think, believe (putative)
spero, sperare, speravi, speratus, hope (aspire)
reporto, reportare, reportavi, reportatus, carry back, bring back (reporter)

READING GRAMMAR

A. There are three Participles in Latin.

1. The Present Active Participle ends in **-ns.**

amans, loving	**ducens,** leading	**audiens,** hearing
habens, having	**capiens,** seizing	

2. The Perfect Passive Participle is the fourth principal part.

amatus, a, um, having been loved	**captus, a, um,** having been seized
habitus, a, um, having been had	**auditus, a, um,** having been heard
ductus, a, um, having been led	

3. The Future Active Participle is the fourth principal part ending in **-urus.**

amaturus, a, um, about to love	**capturus, a, um,** about to seize
habiturus, a, um, about to have	**auditurus, a, um,** about to hear
ducturus, a, um, about to lead	

B. Participles are Adjectives and must agree with their Nouns in gender, number, and case.

1. The Present Participle is **i-declension:**

	M. and F.	N.		M. and F.	N.
Nom.	**amans**	**amans**	the loving	**amantes**	**amantia**
Gen.	**amantis**	**amantis**	of the loving	**amantium**	**amantium**
Dat.	**amanti**	**amanti**	to the loving	**amantibus**	**amantibus**
Acc.	**amantem**	**amans**	the loving	**amantes**	**amantia**
Abl.	**amanti**	**amanti**	from, with, by, in the loving	**amantibus**	**amantibus**

2. The Perfect and Future Participles are **a-** and **o-declension.**

C. Participles are best translated by a clause in English, beginning with *when, who, because, if,* or *although.*

Miles captus non timebat.	The soldier, although he was captured, was not afraid.
Miles captus timebat.	The soldier, because he was captured, was afraid.
Miles pugnans necatus est.	The soldier, when he was fighting, was killed.
	-or- The soldier, who was fighting, was killed.

FAMILIAR ABBREVIATIONS

i.e., id est, that is.
pro and con, pro et contra, for and against.
etc., et cetera, and the rest; and so forth.
e.g., exempli gratia, for (the sake of) example.
no., numero, by number.
viz., videlicet, namely, that is to say; introduces further explanation.
d.v. or **D.V., Deo volente,** God willing; if God is willing.
vox pop., vox populi, the voice of the people.

PRACTICE EXERCISES

No. 173. Translate these Participles.

1. **vocans**
2. **motus**
3. **missurus**
4. **accipiens**
5. **venturus**
6. **spectatus**
7. **perveniens**
8. **capturus**
9. **ponens**
10. **nuntiatus**
11. **monitus**
12. **timens**
13. **dicturus**
14. **excitatus**
15. **videns**

No. 174. Translate these Participial Phrases.

1. **naves navigantes**
2. **ducem iussurum**
3. **illi oppugnati**
4. **viros perventuros**
5. **petentes pacem**
6. **canem currentem**
7. **urbes captae**
8. **templa aedificata**
9. **portus inventos**
10. **flumina currentia**

No. 175. Translate these sentences.

1. **Populus urbium captarum quam fortissimus erat.**
2. **Viri perventuri iter quam celerrime faciebant.**
3. **Rex patriam vestram nunc regens timidus esse videtur.**
4. **Mulier difficultatem tuam videns auxilium dabit.**
5. **Tempestas non auctura non acerrima erit.**
6. **Pater filios suos visurus magnum gaudium habebat.**
7. **Ei nostros timentes quam celerrime currebant.**
8. **Homines victi maxime territi sunt.**
9. **In oppido perveniens illa fabulam suam narravit.**
10. **Illi portam defendentes amici non erant.**

No. 176. Translate these Adverbs.

1. **fortiter**
2. **quam celerrime**
3. **minime**
4. **diutissime**
5. **acrius**
6. **difficile**
7. **facillime**
8. **melius**
9. **male**
10. **magnopere**
11. **saepius**
12. **miserrime**

CHAPTER 36

READING

Cupido et Psyche (concl'd.)

1. **Psyche, timida videri non cupiens, verba vocis magno cum gaudio audivit et hunc laborem difficillimum futurum esse sperabat.**
2. **Itaque haec omnia, quae ei demonstraverant, facere contendit. Sine plurimo periculo enim ad regnum Inferorum iter facere magnopere cupiebat.**
3. **Cerberus, ante portam quae ad terram mortis ducit positus, canis erat audacissimus qui tria capita habebat, sed Psyche voce monita eum non timebat.**
4. **Charon tum nave minima trans flumen illam, in regnum Plutonis venturam, duxit.**
5. **Ante Proserpinam, reginam pulcherrimam Inferorum, stans illa Venerem donum cupire nuntiavit.**
6. **Regina arcam a puella cepit et in eandem arcam partem parvam suae pulchritudinis posuit. Dea, puellae arcam dans, illam monuit.**

Cupid and Psyche (concl'd.)

1. Psyche, who did not wish to seem timid, heard the words of the voice with great joy and hoped this task would be very difficult.
2. And so she hurried to do all these things, that they had pointed out to her. For she greatly wished to make the journey to the kingdom of Those Below without very great danger.
3. Cerberus, who was placed in front of the door that leads to the land of death, was a very bold dog who had three heads, but Psyche, because she had been warned by the voice, was not afraid of him.
4. Charon then led her, as she was about to come into the kingdom of Pluto, across the river in a very small boat.
5. Standing in front of Proserpina, the very beautiful queen of Those Below, she reported that Venus wanted a gift.
6. The queen took the box from the girl and put a small part of her own beauty into the same box. The goddess, as she gave the box to the girl, warned her.

Cupido et Psyche (concl'd.)	Cupid and Psyche (concl'd.)
7. Illam, in arcam spectantem, in periculum magnum casuram esse dixit, sed Psyche, ex terra Inferorum iter facere cupiens, verbis reginae ad timorem non excitata est.	7. She said that she would fall into great danger, if she looked into the box, but Psyche, who wished to make the journey out of the land of Those Below, was not aroused to fear by the words of the queen.
8. Ad terram mortalium eandem viam cepit, sed postquam ad lucem pervenerat in arcam spectare et pulchritudinem videre atque habere cupiebat, sed nil pulchritudinis ibi invenit, arca aperta.	8. She took the same road to the land of mortals, but after she had arrived at the light she wished to look into the box and to see and have the beauty, but she found no beauty there, when the box was opened.
9. Psyche dolens pulchritudinem ibi non invenit quod id quod Proserpina in arca posuerat somnus altus Inferorum erat.	9. The grieving Psyche did not find beauty there because what Proserpina had placed in the box was the deep sleep of Those Below.
10. Somno ex carcere suo liberato, puella somno celeriter capta est et ipsa sine ulla mora, modo simili corpori quod a Morte delectum erat, media in via cecidit. Nil sciebat atque nil faciebat. Solum dormiebat.	10. When sleep had been freed from its prison, the girl was quickly overcome by sleep and without any delay, in a manner similar to a body that had been chosen by Death, she fell in the middle of the road. She knew nothing and she did nothing. She only slept.
11. Cupido tamen, vulnere eius curato, magno cum gaudio uxorem suam vidit. Ad locum ubi illa dormiebat quam celerrime volavit.	11. Cupid, however, when his wound had been healed, saw his wife with great joy. He flew as quickly as possible to the place where she was sleeping.
12. Ipse, supra illam stans, somnum qui illam opprimebat cepit et, hoc in arca posito, una ex sagittis suis uxorem tetigit.	12. He, standing above her, took the sleep that was oppressing her and, when this had been placed in the box, he touched his wife with one of his arrows.
13. Ipse dixit: "Tu, multis temporibus e morte servata, omnes labores tuos conficere debes. His factis, omnia reliqua faciam."	13. He said: "You, because you have been saved from death many times, ought to finish all your tasks. When these have been done, I shall do all the other things."
14. Illa satis poenae habuerat. Hic ad Iovem properavit et ab eo auxilium petivit. Iuppiter ad Venerem eodem die iter fecit et illa tandem puellam dedidit.	14. She had had enough punishment. He hurried to Jupiter and begged aid from him. Jupiter made the journey to Venus the same day and she at last surrendered the girl.
15. Psyche, ad regnum deorum a Mercurio ducta, immortalis facta est.	15. Psyche, after she had been led to the kingdom of the gods by Mercury, was made immortal.
16. Matrimonium ab illo tempore ad finem temporis omnis, illa immortali facta, laetissimum erat.	16. The marriage from that time to the end of all time was very happy, because she had been made immortal.
17. Mortales hac fabula animum esse immortalem atque se gaudium per omnes difficultates semper inventuros esse docentur.	17. Mortals are taught by this story that the spirit is immortal and that they will always find joy through all difficulties.

READING VOCABULARY

Nouns

carcer, carceris, n., prison (incarcerate)
somnus, somni, m., sleep (insomnia)
gaudium, gaudii or gaudi, n., joy (gaudy)
canis, canis, m. and f., dog (canine)
Cerberus, Cerberi, m., Cerberus
Charon, Charontis, m., Charon

Adjectives

timidus, timida, timidum, timid (timidity)
apertus, aperta, apertum, open (aperture)
reliquus, reliqua, reliquum, remaining, rest of

READING GRAMMAR

A Participle with a Noun or Pronoun, both in the Ablative case, may be used as a clause. The Participle may be replaced by a Noun or an Adjective.

1. The clause must have a Noun or Pronoun subject that is different from the subject of the main part of the sentence.
2. The clause may be translated with *because, when, although,* or *if.*
3. The Verb "to be" must sometimes be supplied in English.

Oppidis captis, pacem petebant. When the towns had been captured, they sought peace.
Hoc viro duce, vincemur. If this man is leader, we shall be conquered.
Navibus gravibus, celerius navigabant. Although the ships were heavy, they were sailing quite quickly.

FAMILIAR QUOTATIONS

Veni, vidi, vici, I came, I saw, I conquered. Caesar
Vae victis, Woe to the vanquished. Livy
In medias res, Into the midst of things. Horace
Finis coronat opus, The end crowns the work. Ovid
Non omnia possumus omnes, We can't all do everything. Virgil
Diem perdidi, I have lost a day. Titus
Pares cum paribus facillime congregantur, Equals very easily congregate with equals. Cicero

PRACTICE EXERCISES

No. 177. Translate these sentences.

1. **Multi, oraculo audito, ad terram nostram venire constituerunt.**
2. **Signo dato, in agrum impetum fecerunt.**
3. **Homines, armis non multis, tamen fortiter pugnaverunt.**
4. **Militibus multis interfectis, pacem petiverunt.**
5. **Viri, praeda magna, magno cum gaudio domi accipientur.**
6. **Hac re gesta, pueri domum venient.**
7. **Illo duce, id sine difficultate faciemus.**
8. **His mihi nuntiatis, ex urbe iter facere cupiebam.**
9. **His necatis, populus melius regetur.**
10. **Die dicto, omnia quam celerrime paraverunt.**
11. **Porta aperta, in casam venire potuit.**
12. **Nullam spem habebat, oppido capto.**
13. **His rebus factis, rex plus poterat.**
14. **Reliquis visis, ad silvam curremus.**
15. **Patre eius duce, omnia audacter faciunt.**
16. **Pace facta, ab insula navigabit.**
17. **Multis timidis, flumina invenire non poterunt.**
18. **Tempore nunc brevi, nullum auxilium perveniet.**
19. **Loco idoneo, hic diutius manere cupitis.**
20. **Auxilio dato, gaudium magnum erat.**

NINTH REVIEW SECTION (CHAPTERS 34–36)

VOCABULARY REVIEW

NOUNS

1. canis	7. gaudium	13. ovis	1. dog	7. joy	13. sheep
2. carcer	8. genus	14. pulchritudo	2. prison	8. kind, class	14. beauty
3. Cerberus	9. lana	15. satis	3. Cerberus	9. wool	15. enough
4. Charon	10. modus	16. somnus	4. Charon	10. manner, way	16. sleep
5. dux	11. numerus	17. vulnus	5. leader	11. number	17. wound
6. formica	12. ordo		6. ant	12. rank, order	

ADJECTIVES

1. apertus	2. reliquus	3. timidus	4. utilis	1. open	2. remaining, rest of	3. timid	4. useful

VERBS

1. invenio	3. reporto	1. find, come upon	3. carry back, bring back
2. puto	4. spero	2. think, believe	4. hope

ADVERBS

1. satis	2. tam	3. tandem	1. enough	2. so	3. finally

PRACTICE EXERCISES

No. 178. Translate these Infinitives.

1. esse	11. duci	21. moneri
2. fuisse	12. duxisse	22. monuisse
3. inventurum esse	13. habitum esse	23. dixisse
4. inveniri	14. habere	24. dici
5. putatum esse	15. cupere	25. timeri
6. putavisse	16. cupi	26. timuisse
7. reportare	17. potuisse	27. factum esse
8. reportaturum esse	18. posse	28. facturum esse
9. speravisse	19. pugnavisse	29. videri
10. speraturum esse	20. pugnatum esse	30. visurum esse

No. 179. Translate these Participles.

1. ducens	11. sperantia	21. mittens
2. ducturus	12. speratam	22. missus
3. habentes	13. moturos	23. visuris
4. habitos	14. moventes	24. videntium
5. putata	15. venientium	25. dicturos
6. putaturis	16. ventura	26. dicens
7. invenientem	17. timenti	27. monentes
8. inventa	18. territus	28. moniti
9. reportantium	19. posituros	29. positos
10. reportaturus	20. ponentibus	30. ponens

No. 180. Translate these Ablative clauses.

1. **eis visis**	6. **puella ambulanti**	11. **urbe capta**
2. **illo capto**	7. **ducibus timidis**	12. **reliquis dicentibus**
3. **his dictis**	8. **numero parvo**	13. **verbo audito**
4. **bello facto**	9. **somno venienti**	14. **spe inventa**
5. **viris timentibus**	10. **carcere magno**	15. **generibus multis**

QUINTUS HORATIUS FLACCUS

Horace was born in 65 B.C. at Venusia, in southern Italy, the son of a freedman, and studied in Rome and Athens. He was a friend of Virgil and of Augustus, through his literary patron, Maecenas. Before his death in 8 B.C. he had gained enduring popularity from the quality and universality of his poetry and philosophy.

Integer vitae scelerisque purus
non eget Mauris iaculis neque arcu
nec venenatis gravida sagittis, Fusce, pharetra,
sive per Syrtis iter aestuosas

sive facturus per inhospitalem
Caucasum vel quae loca fabulosus lambit
Hydaspes.

Carminum Liber Primus, xxii

He who is upright of life and free from crime
needs neither Moorish javelins nor a bow
nor a quiver heavy with poisoned arrows, Fuscus,
whether he is going to journey through the hot
Quicksands
or through the inhospitable
Caucasus or the places which the storied
Hydaspes laps.

First Book of Odes, 22

CARMINA BURANA

In the early nineteenth century, a manuscript from the thirteenth century was found in the monastery of Benedictbeuren in Bavaria, from which it gets its name, **CARMINA BURANA.** These **carmina**, or songs, were mostly poems, chiefly in Latin or German, or a combination of both, composed by the goliards, or wandering students and monks, on a wide variety of topics. By the Middle Ages the classical pronunciation and meter had changed and the use of rhyme had been introduced in poetry. These poems provided both inspiration and text for the contemporary German composer Carl Orff's famous "Carmina Burana."

Omnia sol temperat	The sun, pure and clear,
purus et subtilis,	Tempers everything,
nova mundo reserat	A new world resows
facies Aprilis,	The appearance of April;
ad amorem properat	The sweetheart's spirit
animus erilis,	Hurries to love,
et iucundis imperat	And over pleasant things rules
deus puerilis.	The boyish god, Cupid.
Rerum tanta novitas	So much newness of nature
in sollemni vere	In the festive springtime
et veris auctoritas	And the power of the spring
iubet nos gaudere,	Order us to rejoice,
vias praebet solitas,	Show us the accustomed ways,
et in tuo vere	And in your own springtime

fides est et probitas	There is trust and the right
tuum retinere.	To cling to your loved one.
Ama me fideliter,	Love me faithfully,
fidem meam nota,	Mark my trust,
de corde totaliter	In my heart completely,
et ex mente tota,	And with my whole mind
sum praesentialiter	I am in your presence,
absens in remota;	Even when absent at a distance;
quisquis amat taliter,	Whoever loves in such a way,
volvitur in rota.	Is turned on a wheel of torture.
Ecce gratum	Behold, pleasing
et optatum	And longed for,
ver reducit gaudia,	The spring brings back our joys;
purpuratum	Clad in purple
floret pratum,	The meadow is in flower,
sol serenat omnia,	The sun makes all serene,
iam iam cedant tristia.	Now, now, sorrows depart,
aestas redit,	Summer returns,
nunc recedit	Now retreats
hiemis saevitia.	The severity of winter.
Iam liquescit	Now there melts
et decrescit	And disappears
grando, nix, et cetera,	All hail, snow, and such,
bruma fugit,	Winter flees,
et iam sugit	And now the spring
ver aestatis ubera;	Sucks in the richness of summer;
illi mens est misera,	His heart is wretched,
qui nec vivit,	Who neither lives,
nec lascivit	Nor plays
sub aestatis dextera.	Under the joys of summer.
Gloriantur	They glory
et laetantur	And delight
in melle dulcedinis	In the honey of sweetness
qui conantur	Who try
ut utantur	To use
praemio Cupidinis;	The favor of Cupid;
simus iussu Cypridis	Let us be, at the command of Venus,
gloriantes	Boasting
et laetantes	And rejoicing
pares esse Paridis.	To be the equals of Paris.

DICTIONARY—LATIN-ENGLISH

A

a, ab from, away from; by
accido, accidere, accidi happen
acer, acris, acre sharp, active, keen
acies, aciei, f. battle line
ad to, toward
adoro, adorare, adoravi, adoratus worship, adore
adulescens, adulescentis, m. youth
adventus, adventus, m. arrival, approach
aedificium, aedificii or **aedifici, n.** building
aedifico, aedificare, aedificavi, aedificatus build
aeger, aegra, aegrum sick, ill
aequus, aequa, aequum equal, level, fair
aestas, aestatis, f. summer
Africa, Africae, f. Africa
ager, agri, m. field
agricola, agricolae, m. farmer
ala, alae, f. wing
alius, alia, aliud other, another
alter, altera, alterum the one, the other
altus, alta, altum high, deep
ambulo, ambulare, ambulavi, ambulatus walk
amicus, amica, amicum friendly
amicus, amici, m. friend
amo, amare, amavi, amatus like, love
amor, amoris, m. love
amphitheatrum, amphitheatri, n. amphitheater
angustus, angusta, angustum narrow
animal, animalis, n. animal
animus, animi, m. mind, spirit
annus, anni, m. year
ante before, in front of
antea before
antiquus, antiqua, antiquum ancient, old
apertus, aperta, apertum open
Apollo, Apollonis, m. Apollo
appello, appellare, appellavi, appellatus address, call, name
apud among, in the presence of
aqua, aquae, f. water
arbor, arboris, f. tree
arca, arcae, f. chest, box
arena, arenae, f. sand
Ariadne, Ariadnes, f. Ariadne
arma, armorum, n. pl. arms, weapons
armo, armare, armavi, armatus arm
aro, arare, aravi, aratus plow
Atalanta, Atalantae, f. Atalanta
Athenae, Athenarum, f. pl. Athens
Atlas, Atlantis, m. Atlas
atque, ac and also, also
audacia, audaciae, f. boldness, bravery, daring
audax, audacis bold
augeo, augere, auxi, auctus increase, enlarge
aureus, aurea, aureum golden
aurum, auri, n. gold
aut or
aut . . . aut either . . . or
auxilium, auxilii or **auxili, n.** aid, help
avunculus, avunculi, m. uncle

B

Bacchus, Bacchi, m. Bacchus
barbarus, barbara, barbarum savage, uncivilized, barbarian
barbarus, barbari, m. barbarian
bellum, belli, n. war
bene well
bis twice
bonus, bona, bonum good
brevis, breve short, brief
Britannia, Britanniae, f. Britain

C

cado, cadere, cecidi, casurus fall
caedes, caedis, f. slaughter, murder
caelum, caeli, n. sky, heaven
canis, canis, m. and **f.** dog
capio, capere, cepi, captus take, seize, capture
captivus, captivi, m. captive
caput, capitis, n. head
carcer, carceris, n. prison
casa, casae, f. cottage
castra, castrorum, n. pl. camp
causa, causae, f. cause, reason
celer, celeris, celere quick, swift
celeritas, celeritatis, f. speed, swiftness
cera, cerae, f. wax
Cerberus, Cerberi, m. Cerberus
Ceres, Cereris, f. Ceres
certe certainly, surely, indeed
Charon, Charontis, m. Charon
cibus, cibi, m. food
Cincinnatus, Cincinnati, m. Cincinnatus
circum around, about
civis, civis, m. and **f.** citizen
civitas, civitatis, f. state
clamo, clamare, clamavi, clamatus shout, cry
clarus, clara, clarum clear, famous, bright
classis, classis, f. fleet
cognosco, cognoscere, cognovi, cognitus learn, recognize, know
cogo, cogere, coegi, coactus collect, drive, compel
collis, collis, m. hill
Colosseum, Colossei, n. The Colosseum
conficio, conficere, confeci, confectus finish, complete, carry out
conloco, conlocare, conlocavi, conlocatus place, station
consilium, consilii or **consili, n.** plan, advice
conspicio, conspicere, conspexi, conspectus observe
constituo, constituere, constitui, constitutus decide, establish
contendo, contendere, contendi, contentus hasten, strive, contend
contra against
convenio, convenire, conveni, conventus come together, assemble
copia, copiae, f. supply, abundance
copiae, copiarum, f. pl. troops
cornu, cornus, n. horn, wing
corpus, corporis, n. body
cras tomorrow
Creta, Cretae, f. Crete
Creusa, Creusae, f. Creusa
cum with; when, while
Cupido, Cupidinis, m. Cupid
cupio, cupere, cupivi, cupitus desire, wish, want
cur why
cura, curae, f. care
curo, curare, curavi, curatus care for, cure
curro, currere, cucurri, cursurus run
Cyclops, Cyclopis, m. Cyclops

D

Daedalus, Daedali, m. Daedalus
de about, concerning, down from
dea, deae, f. goddess
debeo, debere, debui, debitus owe, ought
decem ten
dedo, dedere, dedidi, deditus give up, surrender
deligo, deligere, delegi, delectus choose, select
demonstro, demonstrare, demonstravi, demonstratus point out, show
deus, dei, m. god
dictator, dictatoris, m. dictator
dies, diei, m. and **f.** day
difficilis, difficile difficult, hard
difficultas, difficultatis, f. difficulty
diligentia, diligentiae, f. diligence, care
discedo, discedere, discessi, discessurus withdraw, go away, leave
diu, long, for a long time
do, dare, dedi, datus give

doceo, docere, docui, doctus teach, show
doleo, dolere, dolui, doliturus grieve, be sorry
domi at home
domina, dominae, f. mistress
dominus, domini, m. master
domus, domus, f. house, home
donum, doni, n. gift, present
dormio, dormire, dormivi, dormiturus sleep
duco, ducere, duxi, ductus lead
dulcis, dulce sweet
dum while
duodecim twelve
dux, ducis, m. leader

E

e, ex from, out from
educo, educere, eduxi, eductus lead out
ego, mei I
enim for
eques, equitis, m. horseman, knight
equus, equi, m. horse
et and
et . . . et both . . . and
etiam even, also
Europa, Europae, f. Europe
Eurydice, Eurydices, f. Eurydice
Eurystheus, Eurysthei, m. Eurystheus
ex, e from, out from
excito, excitare, excitavi, excitatus arouse, stir up
exercitus, exercitus, m. army
exspecto, exspectare, exspectavi, exspectatus await, expect, wait for

F

fabula, fabulae, f. story
facilis, facile easy
facio, facere, feci, factus make, do
fama, famae, f. rumor, renown, report
femina, feminae, f. woman
filia, filiae, f. daughter
filius, filii or fili, m. son
finis, finis, m. end, border
fines, finium, m. pl. territory
finitimus, finitima, finitimum neighboring
finitimus, finitimi, m. neighbor
flumen, fluminis, n. river
fons, fontis, m. fountain, spring
formica, formicae, f. ant
fortis, forte brave, strong
fortuna, fortunae, f. fortune, fate, luck
forum, fori, n. forum, market place
fossa, fossae, f. ditch
frumentum, frumenti, n. grain
fuga, fugae, f. flight, escape
fugio, fugere, fugi, fugiturus flee, run away, escape

G

Gallia, Galliae, f. Gaul
Gallus, Galli, m. a Gaul
gaudium, gaudii or gaudi, n. joy
genus, generis, n. kind, class
Germania, Germaniae, f. Germany
Germanus, Germani, m. a German
gero, gerere, gessi, gestus carry on, wage
gladiator, gladiatoris, m. gladiator
gladius, gladii or gladi, m. sword
gloria, gloriae, f. glory
Graecia, Graeciae, f. Greece
gratus, grata, gratum pleasing
gravis, grave heavy, severe, serious

H

habeo, habere, habui, habitus have, hold
habito, habitare, habitavi, habitatus dwell, live
Hannibal, Hannibalis, m. Hannibal
Hellespontus, Hellesponti, m. The Hellespont
Hercules, Herculis, m. Hercules
Hero, Herus, f. Hero
Hesperides, Hesperidum, f. pl. the Hesperides
hic here, in this place
hic, haec, hoc this; he, she, it
hiems, hiemis, f. winter
Hippomenes, Hippominis, m. Hippomenes
Hispania, Hispaniae, f. Spain
hodie today
Homerus, Homeri, m. Homer
homo, hominis, m. man
hora, horae, f. hour
Horatius, Horati, m. Horatius
hortus, horti, m. garden
hostis, hostis, m. enemy

I

iacio, iacere, ieci, iactus throw
iam now, already
ibi there, in that place
Icarus, Icari, m. Icarus
idem, eadem, idem the same; he, she, it
idoneus, idonea, idoneum fit, suitable
ignis, ignis, m. fire
ille, illa, illud that; he, she, it
immortalis, immortale immortal
impedimentum, impedimenti, n. hindrance
impedio, impedire, impedivi, impeditus hinder
imperator, imperatoris, m. commander, general, emperor
imperium, imperii or imperi, n. command
impetus, impetus, m. attack
in in, on; into, onto
incendo, incendere, incendi, incensus set fire to, burn
incito, incitare, incitavi, incitatus arouse, stir up, incite
incola, incolae, m. or f. inhabitant
Inferi, Inferorum, m. pl. Those Below
inimicus, inimica, inimicum unfriendly
inimicus, inimici, m. personal enemy
iniuria, iniuriae, f. injury, harm
inopia, inopiae, f. want, scarcity
instruo, instruere, instruxi, instructus draw up, form, train
insula, insulae, f. island
inter among, between
interea meanwhile
interficio, interficere, interfeci, interfectus kill
invenio, invenire, inveni, inventus find, come upon
ipse, ipsa, ipsum himself, herself, itself; very
is, ea, id he, she, it; this, that
ita thus, so; yes
Italia, Italiae, f. Italy
itaque and so, therefore
iter, itineris, n. journey, march, way
iubeo, iubere, iussi, iussus order, command
Iulia, Iuliae, f. Julia
Iuno, Iunonis, f. Juno
Iuppiter, Iovis, m. Jupiter
iuvo, iuvare, iuvi, iutus help, aid

L

labor, laboris, m. work, toil, labor
laboro, laborare, laboravi, laboratus work
labyrinthus, labyrinthi, m. labyrinth
laetus, laeta, laetum happy
lana, lanae, f. wool
latinus, latina, latinum Latin
Latinus, Latini, m. Latinus
Latium, Lati, n. Latium
latus, lata, latum wide
laudo, laudare, laudavi, laudatus praise
Leander, Leandri, m. Leander
legatus, legati, m. lieutenant, legate
lex, legis, f. law
liber, libera, liberum free
liber, libri, m. book
libero, liberare, liberavi, liberatus free, set free
lingua, linguae, f. language
littera, litterae, f. letter
loco, locare, locavi, locatus place, put
locus, loci, m. place
longus, longa, longum long
ludus, ludi, m. game
luna, lunae, f. moon
lupa, lupae, f. wolf
lux, lucis, f. light

M

magis more
magnitudo, magnitudinis, f. size, great size
magnopere greatly
magnus, magna, magnum large, great
maior, maius larger
male badly
malus, mala, malum bad, evil
maneo, manere, mansi, mansus remain, stay
manus, manus, f. hand; group
Marathonius, Marathonia, Marathonium of Marathon
mare, maris, n. sea
maritus, mariti, m. husband
mater, matris, f. mother

matrimonium, matrimonii or matrimoni, n. marriage
maxime most, especially
maximus, maxima, maximum largest
medius, media, medium middle, middle of
melior, melius better
memoria, memoriae, f. memory
Mercurius, Mercuri, m. Mercury
meus, mea, meum my, mine
Midas, Midae, m. Midas
miles, militis, m. soldier
mille passus mile
milia passuum miles
minime by no means, not at all
minimus, minima, minimum smallest
minor, minus smaller
Minos, Minois, m. Minos
Minotaurus, Minotauri, m. the Minotaur
miser, misera, miserum wretched, unhappy
mitto, mittere, misi, missus send
modus, modi, m. manner, way
moneo, monere, monui, monitus warn, advise
mons, montis, m. mountain, mount
monstro, monstrare, monstravi, monstratus point out, show
mora, morae, f. delay
mors, mortis, f. death
mortalis, mortale, mortal
moveo, movere, movi, motus move
mox soon, presently
mulier, mulieris, f. woman
multitudo, multitudinis, f. great number, multitude
multo much, by much
multus, multa, multum much
murus, muri, m. wall

N

nam for
narro, narrare, narravi, narratus tell, relate
natio, nationis, f. nation
nato, natare, natavi, natatus swim
natura, naturae, f. nature
nauta, nautae, m. sailor
navigo, navigare, navigavi, navigatus sail, cruise
navis, navis, f. ship
-ne indicates a question
neco, necare, necavi, necatus kill
neque and not
neque . . . neque neither . . . nor
nihil, nil, n. nothing
noctu at night
nomen, nominis, n. name
non not
nonne indicates a question expecting the answer "yes"
nos, nostrum we
noster, nostra, nostrum our, ours
novem nine
novus, nova, novum new
nox, noctis, f. night
nullus, nulla, nullum no, none
num indicates a question expecting the answer "no"
numerus, numeri, m. number
numquam never
nunc now
nuntio, nuntiare, nuntiavi, nuntiatus announce, report
nuntius, nuntii, or nunti, m. message, messenger

O

ob on account of, because of
obtineo, obtinere, obtinui, obtentus secure, obtain
occupo, occupare, occupavi, occupatus seize, take possession of
oceanus, oceani, m. ocean
oculus, oculi, m. eye
olim formerly, once
omnis, omne all, every
onus, oneris, n. burden, weight
oppidum, oppidi, n. town
opprimo, opprimere, oppressi, oppressus overcome, crush
oppugno, oppugnare, oppugnavi, oppugnatus attack
optimus, optima, optimum best
opus, operis, n. work
oraculum, oraculi, n. oracle
ordo, ordinis, m. rank, order
Orpheus, Orphei, m. Orpheus
ovis, ovis, f. sheep

P

paene almost, nearly
paeninsula, paeninsulae, f. peninsula
paro, parare, paravi, paratus prepare, get ready
pars, partis, f. part
parum too little, not enough
parvus, parva, parvum small
passus, passus, m. pace
pater, patris, m. father
patria, patriae, f. native country
pax, pacis, f. peace
pecunia, pecuniae, f. money
pedes, peditis, m. foot soldier
peior, peius worse
per through
periculum, periculi, n. danger
Persae, Persarum, m. pl. the Persians
pervenio, pervenire, perveni, perventus arrive
pes, pedis, m. foot
pessimus, pessima, pessimum worst
peto, petere, petivi or petii, petitus seek
plurimum posse be most powerful
plurimus, plurima, plurimum most
plus, pluris more
plus posse be more powerful
Pluto, Plutonis, m. Pluto
poena, poenae, f. punishment, fine
poeta, poetae, m. poet
Polyphemus, Polyphemi, m. Polyphemus
pomum, pomi, n. apple
pono, ponere, posui, positus put, place
pons, pontis, m. bridge
populus, populi, m. people
porta, portae, f. gate, door, entrance
porto, portare, portavi, portatus carry
portus, portus, m. harbor, port
post behind, in back of
postea afterwards
posterus, postera, posterum next, following
postquam after, when
postridie on the next day
postumus, postuma, postumum next, following
praeda, praedae, f. booty, plunder
praemium, praemii or praemi, n. reward
praesidium, praesidii or praesidi, n. guard, garrison
pretium, pretii or preti, n. price
primum, primo first, at first
primus, prima, primum first
pro in front of; for, instead of; for, in behalf of
proelium, proelii or proeli, n. battle
prohibeo, prohibere, prohibui, prohibitus keep off, hinder, prohibit, prevent
propero, properare, properavi, properatus hurry, hasten
propinquus, propinqua, propinquum near
propter because of, on account of
Proserpina, Proserpinae, f. Proserpina
provincia, provinciae, f. province
proximus, proxima, proximum next, nearest
Psyche, Psyches, f. Psyche
puella, puellae, f. girl
puer, pueri, m. boy
pugna, pugnae, f. fight
pugno, pugnare, pugnavi, pugnatus fight
pulcher, pulchra, pulchrum pretty, beautiful
pulchritudo, pulchritudinis, f. beauty
puto, putare, putavi, putatus think, believe
Pythia, Pythiae, f. Pythia

Q

quam as possible; than
quam diu how long
quamquam although
-que and
qui, quae, quod who, which, that; which, what
quis, quid who, what
quod because
quoque also

R

recipio, recipere, recepi, receptus take back, receive
reduco, reducere, reduxi, reductus lead back
regina, reginae, f. queen
regio, regionis, f. region, boundary
regno, regnare, regnavi, regnatus rule
regnum, regni, n. kingdom
rego, regere, rexi, rectus rule

relinquo, relinquere, reliqui, relictus leave, leave behind
reliquus, reliqua, reliquum remaining, rest of
reperio, reperire, repperi, repertus find, discover
reporto, reportare, reportavi, reportatus carry back, bring back
res, rei, f. thing
rex, regis, m. king
ripa, ripae, f. river bank
robustus, robusta, robustum strong, robust
rogo, rogare, rogavi, rogatus ask, ask for
Roma, Romae, f. Rome
Romanus, Romana, Romanum Roman
Romanus, Romani, m. a Roman
ruri in the country

S

Sabini, Sabinorum, m. pl. the Sabines
saepe often
sagitta, sagittae, f. arrow
sagittarius, sagittarii or sagittari, m. archer
sapientia, sapientiae, f. wisdom
satis enough
saxum, saxi, n. stone, rock
scio, scire, scivi, scitus know
scribo, scribere, scripsi, scriptus write
sed but
semper always
septem seven
serpens, serpentis, f. snake, serpent
servo, servare, servavi, servatus save, preserve
servus, servi, m. slave, servant
sex six
Sibyllinus, Sibyllina, Sibyllinum Sibylline
signum, signi, n. signal, standard
Silenus, Sileni, m. Silenus
silva, silvae, f. forest, woods
similis, simile like, similar
simulo, simulare, simulavi, simulatus pretend
sine without
socius, socii or soci, m. comrade, ally
sol, solis, m. sun
solum alone, only
solus, sola, solum alone, only
somnus, somni, m. sleep
soror, sororis, f. sister
Sparta, Spartae, f. Sparta
specto, spectare, spectavi, spectatus look at, watch
spero, sperare, speravi, speratus hope
spes, spei, f. hope
stella, stellae, f. star
sto, stare, steti, status stand
studium, studii or studi, n. zeal, eagerness
sub under
sum, esse, fui, futurus be
summus, summa, summum greatest, highest, top of
superbus, superba, superbum proud, haughty
supero, superare, superavi, superatus surpass, overcome, conquer
supra over, above
suscipio, suscipere, suscepi, susceptus take up, undertake
suus, sua, suum his, her, its, their

T

tam so
tamen however, nevertheless
tandem finally
tango, tangere, tetigi, tactus touch
Tarquinius, Tarquini, m. Tarquin
telum, teli, n. weapon
tempestas, tempestatis, f. storm, bad weather
templum, templi, n. temple
tempus, temporis, n. time
teneo, tenere, tenui, tentus hold, keep, have
terra, terrae, f. land, earth
terreo, terrere, terrui, territus frighten, scare, terrify
Thermopylae, Thermopylarum, f. pl. Thermopylae
Theseus, Thesei, m. Theseus
timeo, timere, timui fear, be afraid of
timidus, timida, timidum timid
timor, timoris, m. fear, dread
totus, tota, totum all, whole
trado, tradere, tradidi, traditus give up, surrender
trans across
Troia, Troiae, f. Troy
tu you
tum then
turris, turris, f. tower
tuus, tua, tuum your, yours

U

ubi where, when
Ulixes, Ulixis, m. Ulysses
ultimus, ultima, ultimum last, farthest
umerus, umeri, m. shoulder
umquam ever
unus, una, unum one
urbs, urbis, f. city
ut as
uterque, utraque, utrumque each, every
utilis, utile useful
uxor, uxoris, f. wife

V

venio, venire, veni, ventus come
ventus, venti, m. wind
Venus, Veneris, f. Venus
verbum, verbi, n. word
vero truly, in truth
verto, vertere, verti, versus turn
vester, vestra, vestrum your, yours
via, viae, f. road, way, street
victoria, victoriae, f. victory
video, videre, vidi, visus see
vinco, vincere, vici, victus conquer
vir, viri, m. man
virtus, virtutis, f. courage, valor
vita, vitae, f. life
voco, vocare, vocavi, vocatus call
volo, volare, volavi, volatus fly
vos, vestrum you
vox, vocis, f. voice
vulnus, vulneris, n. wound

Z

Zephyrus, Zephyri, m. Zephyr, west wind

ANSWERS

Practice Exercise No. 1

1. **aquas,** the waters
2. **puellarum,** of the girls
3. **terrae,** the lands
4. **agricolis,** for the farmers
5. **stellis,** by the stars
6. **vocant,** they call
7. **laboratis,** you work
8. **portamus,** we carry
9. **laudamus,** we praise
10. **amant,** they like

Practice Exercise No. 2

1. of the farmers
2. the, a girl
3. the cottages
4. for the woman
5. by the lands
6. he, she, it is praising
7. you call
8. they are working
9. we like
10. you do carry

Practice Exercise No. 3

1. we 2. he, she, it 3. I 4. you 5. they 6. you

Practice Exercise No. 4

1. direct object 2. prepositional phrase 3. subject 4. indirect object 5. possession

Practice Exercise No. 5

1. **portamus**
2. **amat**
3. **porto**
4. **laudamus**
5. **vocant**
6. **laboratis**
7. **portat**
8. **vocas**
9. **amamus**
10. **laudatis**

Practice Exercise No. 6

1. **casam parvam**
2. **mearum filiarum**
3. **pulchras stellas**
4. **tua terra**
5. **filiae malae**
6. **casis Romanis**
7. **puellas parvas**
8. **aquam bonam**
9. **feminae parvae**
10. **casarum pulchrarum**

Practice Exercise No. 7

1. you are
2. he, she, it is; there is
3. they are; there are
4. I am
5. you are
6. we are

Practice Exercise No. 8

1. **natantne?** Do they swim?
2. **portasne?** Are you carrying?
3. **amamusne?** Do we like?
4. **laboratne?** Does he (she, it) work?
5. **vocatisne?** Are you calling?
6. **suntne?** Are they? Are there?
7. **natamusne?** Do we swim?
8. **portatne?** Is he (she, it) carrying?
9. **estisne?** Are you?
10. **laudasne?** Do you praise?
11. **laudatne?** Does he (she, it) praise?
12. **vocantne?** Are they calling?
13. **estne?** Is he (she, it) there?
14. **natasne?** Do you swim?
15. **amantne?** Do they love?

Practice Exercise No. 9

1. you love, are loving, do love
2. we praise, are praising, do praise
3. you call, do call, are calling
4. I work, am working, do work
5. they love, are loving, do love
6. you call, are calling, do call
7. he (she, it) swims, is swimming, does swim
8. we carry, are carrying, do carry
9. you work, are working, do work
10. he (she, it) praises, is praising, does praise

Practice Exercise No. 10

1. the girl's cottage
2. a supply of water
3. the farmers' land
4. the cottages of the women
5. the sailor's native country
6. the sailor's island
7. the farmer's daughter
8. the sailors' cottages
9. an abundance of stars
10. the woman's native country

Practice Exercise No. 11

1. **Feminae,** the women
2. **Puella,** the girl
3. **Agricolae,** the farmers
4. **Copiae,** the troops
5. **Nauta,** the sailor
6. **Agricola,** the farmer
7. **Filiae,** the daughters
8. **Patria,** the native country
9. **Insulae,** the islands
10. **Filia,** the daughter

Practice Exercise No. 12

1. **magna,** big
2. **pulchrae,** pretty
3. **bonae,** good
4. **mea,** mine
5. **Romanae,** Roman
6. **mala,** bad
7. **tua,** yours
8. **parvae,** small
9. **pulchra,** beautiful
10. **bona,** good

Practice Exercise No. 13

1. **agricola,** a farmer
2. **nautae,** sailors
3. **patria mea,** my native country
4. **insula,** an island
5. **casae,** cottages
6. **nauta,** a sailor
7. **feminae,** women
8. **puella,** a girl
9. **agricolae,** farmers
10. **silva,** a forest

Practice Exercise No. 14

1. toward the road
2. in the cottage
3. with the woman
4. into the woods
5. out of the cottages
6. away from the land
7. away from the cottages
8. out of the forests
9. into the islands
10. toward the streets
11. into the forests
12. with the girl
13. in or on the water
14. toward the water
15. away from the girls
16. toward the island
17. out of the land
18. with the farmer
19. in the native country
20. with the girls

Practice Exercise No. 15

1. **aquam,** water
2. **fabulam,** a story
3. **aquam,** water
4. **Nautam,** the sailor
5. **Agricolas,** the farmers
6. **fabulam,** a story
7. **viam,** the road
8. **Terram,** the land
9. **terram,** the land
10. **Insulas,** islands

Practice Exercise No. 16

1. **Feminae,** to the woman
2. **Nautae,** to the sailor
3. **Nautis,** to the sailors
4. **Puellae,** to the girl
5. **Puellis,** to the girls
6. **Feminis,** to the women
7. **Agricolis,** to the farmers
8. **Feminae,** to the woman
9. **Puellis,** to the girls
10. **Agricolae,** to the farmer

Practice Exercise No. 17

1. you walk; you are walking; you do walk
2. he, she tells; he, she is telling; he, she does tell
3. they walk, they do walk, they are walking
4. I dwell, I am dwelling, I do dwell
5. we sail, we are sailing, we do sail
6. you give, you are giving, you do give
7. he, she, it gives; he, she, it is giving; he, she, it does give
8. they call; they are calling; they do call
9. you work; you are working; you do work
10. we carry; we are carrying; we do carry
11. you praise; you are praising; you do praise
12. they love; they are loving; they do love
13. you are
14. we are
15. they swim; they are swimming; they do swim
16. you swim; you are swimming; you do swim
17. he, she, it fights; he, she, it is fighting; he, she, it does fight
18. we fight; we are fighting; we do fight
19. I attack; I am attacking; I do attack
20. they attack; they are attacking; they do attack

Practice Exercise No. 18

1. **Europam antiquam**
2. **aquae pulchrae**
3. **silvis parvis**
4. **stellas claras**
5. **insularum multarum**
6. **terra Romana**
7. **filias bonas**
8. **famam malam**
9. **puellarum pulchrarum**
10. **incolis multis**

Practice Exercise No. 19

1. **casae, f.**
2. **feminae, f.**
3. **stellae, f.**
4. **aquae, f.**
5. **fabulae, f.**
6. **insulae, f.**
7. **puellae, f.**
8. **copiae, f.**
9. **filiae, f.**
10. **nautae, m.**
11. **terrae, f.**
12. **Britanniae, f.**
13. **famae, f.**
14. **Italiae, f.**
15. **silvae, f.**
16. **patriae, f.**
17. **incolae, m. or f.**
18. **Europae, f.**
19. **agricolae, m.**
20. **viae, f.**

Practice Exercise No. 20

1. **amare**
2. **laudare**
3. **navigare**
4. **esse**
5. **vocare**
6. **oppugnare**
7. **monstrare**
8. **dare**
9. **habitare**
10. **portare**
11. **narrare**
12. **laborare**
13. **natare**
14. **pugnare**
15. **ambulare**

Practice Exercise No. 21

1. Nominative Case, Subject; Predicate Noun or Adjective
Genitive Case, Possession
Dative Case, Indirect Object
Accusative Case, Direct Object; Prepositional Phrases
Ablative Case, Prepositional Phrases

2. **insula lata,** wide island
insulae latae, of the wide island
insulae latae, to, for the wide island
insulam latam, wide island
insula lata, from, with, by, in the wide island

insulae latae, wide islands
insularum latarum, of the wide islands
insulis latis, to, for the wide islands
insulas latas, wide islands
insulis latis, from, with, by, in the wide islands

via longa, long road
viae longae, of the long road
viae longae, to, for the long road
viam longam, long road
via longa, from, with, by, in the long road

viae longae, long roads
viarum longarum, of the long roads
viis longis, to, for the long roads
vias longas, long roads
viis longis, from, with, by, in long roads

3. **laboro,** I work; I am working; I do work
laboras, you work; you do work; you are working
laborat, he, she, it works; he, she, it is working; he, she, it does work

laboramus, we work; we are working; we do work
laboratis, you work; you are working; you do work
laborant, they work; they are working; they do work

laudo, I praise; I am praising; I do praise
laudas, you praise; you are praising; you do praise
laudat, he, she, it praises; he, she, it is praising; he, she, it does praise

laudamus, we praise; we are praising; we do praise
laudatis, you praise; you are praising; you do praise
laudant, they praise; they are praising; they do praise

sum, I am	**sumus,** we are
es, you are	**estis,** you are
est, he, she, it is; there is	**sunt,** they are; there are

Practice Exercise No. 22

1. we are
2. they conquer, they are conquering, they do conquer

3. he, she, it stands; he, she, it is standing; he, she, it does stand
4. he, she, it is; there is
5. you wait for; you are waiting for; you do wait for
6. he, she, it builds; he, she, it is building; he, she, it does build
7. they are; there are
8. we swim; we are swimming; we do swim
9. he, she, it overcomes; he, she, it is overcoming; he, she, it does overcome
10. they sail; they are sailing; they do sail
11. you give; you are giving; you do give
12. you call; you are calling; you do call
13. we build; we are building; we do build
14. they walk; they are walking; they do walk
15. you stand; you are standing; you do stand

Practice Exercise No. 23

1. in Italy
2. toward Britain
3. with the women
4. toward Italy
5. in the province
6. with the troops
7. on the peninsula
8. in front of the cottages
9. behind the cottages
10. with the girl
11. in the woods
12. toward the road
13. toward the island
14. into the cottages
15. in front of the ditch

Practice Exercise No. 24

1. of the inhabitant; to, for the inhabitant; the inhabitants
2. Why do they work?
3. You help your native country.
4. He is carrying the booty.
5. He fights well.
6. They are pretty.
7. of many victories
8. a famous native country
9. a long story
10. out of the cottage
11. away from the road
12. Where is he (she, it)?
13. Here I am.
14. in front of the island
15. after the victory
16. with the troops
17. out of the provinces
18. There are troops here.
19. toward the streets
20. There is the province.
21. There are the women.
22. There is glory.
23. There are many girls.
24. Where are they?
25. Here they are.

Practice Exercise No. 25

1. to, for, from, with, by, in the field
2. to, for, from, with, by, in the wars
3. of the battles
4. of the boy; the boys
5. the ally
6. the friends
7. the camp
8. the swords
9. the help, aid
10. to, for, from, with, by, in the message, messenger
11. the dangers
12. of the weapons, arms
13. of the town
14. the man
15. the enemies

Practice Exercise No. 26

1. **amici,** the friends
2. **puerorum,** of the boys
3. **agris,** to, for, from, with, by, in the fields
4. **bellorum,** of the wars
5. **oppida,** the towns
6. **viri,** the men
7. **pericula,** dangers
8. **gladiorum,** of the swords

9. **nuntios,** messengers
10. **auxiliis,** to, for, from, with, by, in the aids
11. **nuntiis,** to, for, from, with, by, in the messages
12. **viris,** to, for, from, with, by, in the men
13. **periculis,** to, for, from, with, by, in the dangers
14. **agri,** the fields
15. **bella,** the wars

Practice Exercise No. 27

1. of
2. the, an
3. the, a
4. about
5. through
6. of
7. of
8. the
9. the
10. of

Practice Exercise No. 28

1. out of the field
2. are they arming?
3. a narrow street
4. friends
5. with the boy
6. He plows there.
7. behind the camp
8. of the friends
9. with the man
10. They fight a war.
11. They point out the towns.
12. They give arms to the man.
13. We tell stories about the war.
14. He likes dangers.
15. The camp is in the field.
16. You walk through the fields.
17. There are towns.
18. You give aid.
19. Swords kill.
20. They live in camp.

Practice Exercise No. 29

1. My friend is there.
2. toward your cottages
3. out of the deep ditches
4. in the long road
5. with famous men
6. in front of the Roman camp
7. in back of my fields
8. about good water
9. through the large forest
10. of the bad friend; the bad friends

Practice Exercise No. 30

1. **virorum mult*orum***
2. **filiae me*ae***
3. **frumento bon*o***
4. **equis tu*is***
5. **me*is* filiis**
6. **pueros aeg*ros***
7. **puellae miser*ae***
8. **soci liber*i***
9. **feminam miser*am***
10. **agris pulchr*is***

Practice Exercise No. 31

Column I	Column I	Column II	Column II
1. many **viros**	6. good **fili**	3. **multos**	6. **boni**
2. sick **pueri**	7. bad **famam**	5. **aegri**	8. **malam**
3. pretty **oppidum**	8. wretched **equis**	1. **pulchrum**	9. **miseris**
4. many **servorum**	9. Roman **terrae**	2. **multorum**	10. **Romanae**
5. happy **puellam**	10. happy **agricola**	4. **laetam**	7. **laetus**

Practice Exercise No. 32

1. **curamus**
2. **liberas**
3. **laboratis**
4. **laudant**
5. **portat**
6. **aro**
7. **necant**
8. **nuntiat**
9. **occupamus**
10. **statis**

Practice Exercise No. 33

1. They are free.
2. of the happy mistresses
3. into deep water
4. concerning great cares
5. in wide fields
6. about good masters
7. Why are you happy?
8. There are many people.
9. We are ill.
10. with good friends
11. in free lands
12. She is pretty.
13. Are they pretty?
14. He is unhappy.
15. many things

Practice Exercise No. 34

1. **nostram**
2. **tuas**
3. **sua**
4. **meis**
5. **sua**
6. **vestrae**
7. **nostram**
8. **sui**
9. **suarum**
10. **meam**

Practice Exercise No. 35

1. I fear; I am fearing; I do fear
2. he, she, it sees; he, she, it is seeing; he, she, it does see
3. you fear; you are fearing; you do fear
4. he, she, it adores; he, she, it is adoring; he, she, it does adore
5. they rule; they are ruling; they do rule
6. you see; you are seeing; you do see
7. they fear; they are fearing; they do fear
8. we have; we are having; we do have
9. we rule; we are ruling; we do rule
10. they have; they are having; they do have
11. he, she, it fears; he, she, it is fearing; he, she, it does fear
12. you see; you are seeing; you do see
13. I have; I am having; I do have
14. you rule; you are ruling; you do rule
15. you adore; you are adoring; you do adore

Practice Exercise No. 36

1. ancient gods
2. of, to, for the Roman goddess; Roman goddesses
3. of my friends
4. of your sailor; your sailors
5. your booty
6. our daughters
7. his, her, its, their master
8. his, her, their son
9. his, her, its, their wisdom; from, with, by, in his, her, its, their wisdom
10. our glory

Practice Exercise No. 37

1. Your glory is not great.
2. Why do you kill your enemy?
3. Is the messenger telling many things?
4. The men are walking across their own fields.
5. The women are in their cottages.
6. Your daughters are sick today.
7. Many people sail across the ocean.
8. They are our goddesses.
9. They are our gods.
10. The woman cares for her daughters.
11. I am standing in front of the cottages.
12. He does not have many things.
13. We are telling about the moon.
14. Your fortune is good.
15. The slaves fear their masters.
16. Why are you not afraid?
17. We see beautiful temples.
18. He has a camp there.
19. We see the boys in back of the ditch.
20. You have great wisdom.

Practice Exercise No. 38

1. aedificare	4. superare	7. regnare	10. curare	13. timere
2. nuntiare	5. videre	8. arare	11. necare	14. habere
3. exspectare	6. liberare	9. stare	12. adorare	15. occupare

Practice Exercise No. 39

1. deae, f.	8. amici, m.	15. victoriae, f.
2. proelii or proeli, n.	9. inimici, m.	16. viri, m.
3. provinciae, f.	10. reginae, f.	17. gladii or gladi, m.
4. belli, n.	11. pueri, m.	18. curae, f.
5. oceani, m.	12. agri, m.	19. praedae, f.
6. socii or soci, m.	13. castrorum, n.	20. equi, m.
7. fortunae, f.	14. periculi, n.	

Practice Exercise No. 40

1. a. Cur viris frumentum non datis?
   b. Datne incolis insularum curam bonam?

2. **sto** I stand; I am standing; I do stand
   stas you stand; you are standing; you do stand
   stat he, she, it stands; he, she, it is standing; he, she, it does stand

   stamus we stand; we are standing; we do stand
   statis you stand; you are standing; you do stand
   stant they stand; they are standing; they do stand

   timeo I fear; I am fearing; I do fear
   times you fear; you are fearing; you do fear
   timet he, she, it fears; he, she, it is fearing; he, she, it does fear

   timemus we fear; we are fearing; we do fear
   timetis you fear; you are fearing; you do fear
   timent they fear; they are fearing; they do fear

Practice Exercise No. 41

1. our farmers
2. of the happy daughters
3. high sky
4. of, to, for a free country; free countries
5. your slave
6. his, her, their sons
7. wretched people
8. narrow roads
9. your messenger; your message
10. my fortune; from, with, by, in my fortune
11. many people
12. small boy
13. of the wide fields
14. good care; from, with, by, in good care
15. of the long sword

Practice Exercise No. 42

1. You have friends, haven't you? Certainly.
2. Are they building cottages? Yes. They are building cottages.
3. You are indeed afraid, aren't you? I am indeed afraid.
4. The people are not fighting, are they? The people are not fighting.

5. The roads are not long, are they? The roads are not at all long.
6. Why are they walking toward the town?
7. Is the man staying in the building? The man is staying in the building.
8. Is the province free? The province is truly free.
9. He isn't sailing on the ocean, is he? He is not sailing on the ocean.
10. Is your queen great? My queen is certainly great.

Practice Exercise No. 43

1. e	4. a	7. e	10. a	13. a
2. a	5. e	8. e	11. a	14. a
3. e	6. a	9. e	12. e	15. a

Practice Exercise No. 44

1. **Ambulare**	3. **Necare**	5. **Vocare**	7. **Iuvare**	9. **Oppugnare**
2. **Pugnare**	4. **Superare**	6. **Natare**	8. **Laborare**	10. **Manere**

Practice Exercise No. 45

1. Why is he preparing grain there?
2. You like the Latin language, don't you?
3. Where do your buildings stand?
4. You ought not to give swords to the boys.
5. The gods also have their own weapons.
6. They tell the story about the long war of Troy.
7. Aeneas is sailing with his men to Italy.
8. The god helps the people of Greece.
9. Why do the Romans fear their allies?
10. He sees the clear moon in the sky.

Practice Exercise No. 46

1. **debebamus**	5. **timebat**	9. **locabas**	13. **laudabam**	17. **portabatis**
2. **parabam**	6. **videbas**	10. **dabatis**	14. **manebas**	18. **iuvabat**
3. **properabant**	7. **curabam**	11. **habebatis**	15. **videbamus**	19. **vocabat**
4. **manebant**	8. **adorabamus**	12. **stabat**	16. **habebas**	20. **timebamus**

Practice Exercise No. 47

1. he, she, it was pointing out; used to point out, did point out
2. I call; I am calling; I do call
3. we prepare; we are preparing; we do prepare
4. you were ruling; you used to rule; you did rule; you ruled
5. you ought
6. you fear; you are fearing; you do fear
7. he, she, it was; there was
8. you fight; you are fighting; you do fight
9. I was hurrying; I used to hurry; I did hurry; I hurried
10. they saw; they used to see; they did see; they were seeing
11. you were praising; you used to praise; you did praise; you praised
12. you carry; you are carrying; you do carry

13. you were conquering; you used to conquer; you did conquer; you conquered
14. they tell; they are telling; they do tell
15. we remain; we are remaining; we do remain
16. he, she, it was saving; used to save; did save; saved
17. I was placing; I used to place; I did place; I placed
18. you were attacking; you used to attack; you did attack; you attacked
19. you were having; you used to have; you did have; you had
20. you were

Practice Exercise No. 48

1. when he was standing
2. with the daughter
3. when we work
4. when I wait for, await
5. with friends
6. when he conquers
7. with a wolf
8. when you see
9. when he was; when there was
10. when you were fighting
11. with the girl
12. when they were; when there were
13. with my uncle
14. with the Romans
15. with many women

Practice Exercise No. 49

1. He does not have men in camp, does he?
2. We were preparing today to be there.
3. Your friend has a good reputation in our town.
4. I was preparing to stay with the girls.
5. He often kills many wolves in the forests, doesn't he?
6. The Romans ought not to fear the swords of the Sabines.
7. When they build a town, they place temples and buildings there.
8. Why do they give rewards to their slaves?
9. The farmer was in the field with his friend.
10. You are without water, aren't you?

Practice Exercise No. 50

1. he, she, it attacks
2. they were setting free
3. I shall see
4. he, she, it will remain
5. they were; there were
6. they are; there are
7. they ought; they owe
8. to love; to like
9. you will have; hold
10. you were fighting
11. they were giving
12. he, she, it will be; there will be
13. they will stir up; arouse
14. he, she, it will warn; advise
15. to carry
16. he, she, it will fear
17. you will fight
18. we shall conquer; overcome
19. we were preparing; getting ready
20. they will be; there will be
21. they will tell; relate
22. he, she, it was inciting; arousing
23. you were warning
24. we are
25. we were attacking
26. he will arouse; incite; stir up
27. they were swimming
28. you were placing
29. you will save; preserve
30. you will help; aid

Practice Exercise No. 51

1. down from a clear sky
2. neighboring to my country
3. near to the islands
4. with our friend
5. toward the high buildings
6. in the wide ditches
7. pleasing to his comrade
8. in front of the fields
9. friendly to the slaves
10. after the war
11. unfriendly to the queen
12. concerning your victory
13. through many battles
14. suitable to the man
15. without booty

Practice Exercise No. 52

1. present
2. future
3. imperfect
4. present
5. imperfect
6. imperfect
7. future
8. present
9. future
10. future
11. future
12. imperfect
13. future
14. imperfect
15. future
16. imperfect
17. future
18. imperfect
19. imperfect
20. future

Practice Exercise No. 53

1. He (she) will walk toward the narrow streets.
2. They were standing in front of the temples.
3. You were swimming out of the ocean.
4. They will fight on the water.
5. She was pleasing to the women.
6. They ought to have a free country.
7. The girls will swim.
8. He liked his neighbors.
9. You will save your uncles.
10. They will praise the queen.
11. Where ought you to be?
12. You were calling the boy.
13. He will be unfriendly to the messenger.
14. It is not near to the province.
15. We shall not fear your swords.
16. Your slaves are helping.
17. The man will remain there.
18. We were preparing a deep ditch.
19. The master will tell a story.
20. We shall plow the field.

Practice Exercise No. 54

1. walk (s.)
2. love (pl.)
3. swim (pl.)
4. fight (s.)
5. praise (pl.)
6. sail (pl.)
7. give (pl.)
8. dwell (s.)
9. fear (pl.)
10. see (s.)
11. stand (pl.)
12. have (pl.)
13. hold (s.)
14. rule (s.)
15. hold (pl.)
16. conquer (pl.)
17. stand (s.)
18. help (pl.)
19. warn (pl.)
20. stay (s.)

Practice Exercise No. 55

1. a farmer
2. sailors
3. Britain
4. a friend
5. a girl
6. our allies
7. a boy
8. enemies
9. a friend
10. boys

Practice Exercise No. 56

1. friends
2. wars
3. goddesses
4. god
5. master
6. mistress
7. son
8. glory
9. messengers
10. my slave
11. good man
12. good language
13. many friends
14. good farmer
15. our friend

Practice Exercise No. 57

1. The sick boy, your son, will stay in the town.
2. You ought to have allies in the battle, friend.
3. Arouse your men, Roman people, against war.
4. Warn the inhabitants of Gaul, messengers.
5. I shall call the Sabines, our neighbors, to the games.

6. See the temples, girls, beautiful buildings.
7. Rome, a town in Italy, will be famous.
8. Remember Gaul, my son.
9. Shall we have a big forum, friends?
10. I shall wait for my uncles, the messengers.

Practice Exercise No. 58

1. simple question
2. simple question
3. simple question
4. answer yes
5. answer no
6. answer yes
7. answer no
8. simple question
9. simple question
10. simple question

Practice Exercise No. 59

1. **debebam**
2. **locabas**
3. **incitabat**
4. **properabant**
5. **parabatis**
6. **tenebamus**
7. **servabas**
8. **tenebam**
9. **manebamus**
10. **monebat**

Practice Exercise No. 60

1. **videbo**
2. **stabunt**
3. **timebis**
4. **regnabit**
5. **necabitis**
6. **habebimus**
7. **aedificabo**
8. **superabis**
9. **curabimus**
10. **nuntiabunt**

Practice Exercise No. 61

1. **serva, servate**
2. **mone, monete**
3. **incita, incitate**
4. **mane, manete**
5. **naviga, navigate**
6. **para, parate**
7. **tene, tenete**
8. **propera, properate**
9. **neca, necate**
10. **pugna, pugnate**

Practice Exercise No. 62

1. **popule, populi**
2. **memoria, memoriae**
3. **legate, legati**
4. **amice, amici**
5. **femina, feminae**
6. **bellum, bella**
7. **avuncule, avunculi**
8. **vir, viri**
9. **puer, pueri**
10. **puella, puellae**
11. **fili, filii**
12. **agricola, agricolae**

Practice Exercise No. 63

1. you will be feared
2. I was praising
3. I am being cared for
4. they are praised
5. they will be related, told
6. I shall stand
7. he, she, it was being armed
8. you are plowing
9. he, she, it will be seized
10. you will stand
11. he was killing
12. they will be built
13. I shall overcome; conquer; surpass
14. he will sail
15. I was living in
16. I was being pointed out
17. they were walking
18. he, she, it will be given
19. you are being helped; aided
20. I shall be called

Practice Exercise No. 64

1. **exspectabar**
2. **tenentur**
3. **monebitur**
4. **videbatur**
5. **amabitur**
6. **habetur**
7. **videbamini**
8. **portabitur**
9. **movebimini**
10. **parantur**
11. **laudabuntur**
12. **locamini**
13. **properabuntur**
14. **timemur**
15. **incitor**
16. **monebaris**
17. **servaris**
18. **debebatur**
19. **videntur**
20. **monebantur**

Practice Exercise No. 65

1. with the lieutenant
2. with a sword
3. by the boys
4. with ditches
5. by friends
6. by a messenger
7. with uncles
8. by wars
9. by the masters
10. with a comrade
11. with horses
12. by arrows
13. by an archer
14. by a goddess
15. with a slave
16. with wisdom
17. by the people
18. with enemies
19. with water
20. by a man

Practice Exercise No. 66

1. Money will be given to the man and the girl because the boy is ill.
2. I was remembered when I was moving to the neighboring town.
3. They seem to grieve, but a gift will be brought.
4. On account of the dangers the men were afraid of the letters.
5. Fight well for Britain, your native country.
6. Many people were walking toward the temples of the gods.
7. Where (when) will the game be given by your friend?
8. We were living in the cottage where you see the girls.
9. The man will not be attacked by a sword, will he?
10. The people were preparing to move camp, weren't they?

Practice Exercise No. 67

1. of the long peace
2. for the soldier
3. famous soldiers
4. Roman peace
5. your heads
6. to, for their dictators
7. your head
8. by happy men
9. suitable part
10. in an ancient city
11. of our sea
12. strong soldiers
13. good men
14. long peace
15. on their heads
16. against dictators
17. with the men
18. without your soldiers
19. about pleasing peace
20. friendly man

Practice Exercise No. 68

1. of
2. of
3. the, a
4. the, a
5. in, on
6. the
7. with
8. of
9. the
10. about

Practice Exercise No. 69

1. **paces,** the peaces
2. **militibus,** from, with, by, in the soldiers
3. **capitibus,** to, for the heads
4. **partes,** parts
5. **hostibus,** to, for the enemy
6. **urbium,** of the cities
7. **caedes,** slaughters
8. **pontes,** bridges
9. **homines,** men
10. **capita,** heads
11. **militum,** of the soldiers
12. **partium,** of the parts
13. **homines,** the men
14. **pacum,** of peaces
15. **dictatores,** the dictators
16. **pontibus,** to, for the bridges
17. **marium,** of the seas
18. **pontium,** of the bridges
19. **hostes,** the enemy
20. **urbibus,** from, with, by, in the cities

Practice Exercise No. 70

1. Cincinnatus was being called from his field and was giving aid.
2. Men rule on earth, but the gods rule heaven and earth.

3. Rewards will be given to a great man by the Roman people.
4. The Latin language will always be preserved.
5. He will not plow tomorrow, but he will soon save our country.
6. He was swimming toward the river bank because the bridge was not standing.
7. Fight well, Horatius, for your country with your sword.
8. The soldiers, my sons, will be armed with swords.
9. Because of the dangers you ought to save your water.
10. The sailor loves the sea, but the farmer loves his fields.

Practice Exercise No. 71

1. gods and goddesses
2. the god and the goddess
3. we have and we give
4. he had and he gave
5. a man and women
6. of the men and of the women
7. toward the sun and moon
8. toward the sun and moon
9. from the sea and land
10. from the land and sea

Practice Exercise No. 72

1. in the middle of the roads
2. in many towns
3. in a great war
4. on the tops of the buildings
5. in a good part
6. on (in) wide oceans
7. in many lands
8. in the middle of the sky
9. on the top of the sea
10. in the middle of the ocean

Practice Exercise No. 73

1. toward the sea
2. from the cities
3. with their fathers
4. in front of the forum
5. behind the temple
6. concerning the box
7. without a plan (advice)
8. across the ocean
9. through the seas
10. because of wings
11. for your queen
12. against the people
13. among the enemy
14. by (away from) the men
15. away from the towns
16. in front of the camp
17. through the dangers
18. toward the master
19. across the field
20. concerning peace

Practice Exercise No. 74

1. he, she, it will be; there will be
2. he, she, it will be frightened
3. he, she, it was flying
4. he, she, it will swim
5. they are grieving
6. we are being carried
7. he, she, it was being held
8. we shall be loved; liked
9. I shall move
10. they were being praised
11. he, she, it was fighting
12. you will place
13. I shall be called
14. we were being warned
15. they will work
16. they are being stirred up; aroused
17. he, she, it will owe; ought
18. they are preparing
19. they were being cared for
20. you will be freed

Practice Exercise No. 75

1. The man, my uncle
2. Good friends
3. Good son
4. Of the nations, Italy and Germany
5. Because of the money, the reward
6. Of the women, queens
7. Famous man
8. The boy, a slave
9. To, for the girls, my daughters
10. Our father

Practice Exercise No. 76

1. **vocare,** to call
2. **debere,** to owe
3. **ambulare,** to walk
4. **stare,** to stand
5. **esse,** to be
6. **monere,** to warn
7. **timere,** to fear
8. **narrare,** to tell
9. **curare,** to take care of
10. **dolere,** to grieve
11. **nuntiare,** to announce
12. **volare,** to fly
13. **terrere,** to frighten
14. **adorare,** to worship
15. **movere,** to move
16. **parare,** to prepare
17. **servare,** to preserve, save
18. **laudare,** to praise
19. **dare,** to give
20. **videre,** to see

Practice Exercise No. 77

1. **paravi,** I have prepared
2. **incitavi,** I have aroused
3. **aravi,** I have plowed
4. **debui,** I have owed
5. **liberavi,** I have freed
6. **locavi,** I have placed
7. **terrui,** I have frightened
8. **aedificavi,** I have built
9. **habitavi,** I have lived in
10. **monui,** I have warned
11. **properavi,** I have hurried
12. **habui,** I have had, held
13. **dedi,** I have given
14. **tenui,** I have held, kept
15. **servavi,** I have preserved, saved
16. **monstravi,** I have shown, pointed out
17. **timui,** I have feared
18. **natavi,** I have swum
19. **movi,** I have moved
20. **mansi,** I have remained, stayed

Practice Exercise No. 78

1. **amatus,** having been loved
2. **habitus,** having been had
3. **liberatus,** having been freed
4. **necatus,** having been killed
5. **monitus,** having been warned
6. **exspectatus,** having been waited for
7. **narratus,** having been told
8. **territus,** having been frightened
9. **occupatus,** having been seized
10. **portatus,** having been carried
11. **datus,** having been given
12. **monitus,** having been warned
13. **servatus,** having been saved
14. **iutus,** having been helped
15. **visus,** having been seen; seemed
16. **adoratus,** having been worshipped
17. **motus,** having been moved
18. **spectatus,** having been seen
19. **obtentus,** having been obtained
20. **locatus,** having been placed, put

Practice Exercise No. 79

1. Both your mother and your father were giving advice about courage.
2. In the middle of the town there were many buildings.
3. The report about my nation will be carried by the messengers.
4. The girl and the boy are swimming under the water.
5. We ought to walk around the city and see many things.
6. You remember many bad things, don't you?
7. The sun seemed to be on the top of the water.
8. The nations of Europe will not always fight.
9. Sailors sail on seas and oceans.
10. Roman soldiers have great courage.

Practice Exercise No. 80

1. dolere
2. terrere
3. movere
4. vocare
5. obtinere
6. dare
7. spectare
8. volare
9. laudare
10. manere
11. debere
12. timere
13. habere
14. videre
15. necare
16. parare
17. occupare
18. stare
19. iuvare
20. monere

Practice Exercise No. 81

1. spectavi
2. curare
3. moneo
4. dedi
5. motus
6. paravi
7. servatus
8. territus
9. habito
10. laudare

Practice Exercise No. 82

1. of the animals and men
2. by the father
3. by the mothers
4. the sea and star
5. fathers and mothers
6. of speed and size
7. by Mercury
8. by the soldiers
9. by Pluto
10. war and peace

Practice Exercise No. 83

1. he, she, it was being praised
2. they will grieve
3. we were being warned
4. they are being killed
5. you are being called
6. we shall obtain, secure
7. you are being seen; you seem
8. you were helping
9. I shall have, hold
10. you will be moved
11. they are being occupied, seized
12. they were being feared
13. he, she, it will be prepared
14. you will give
15. you are being saved
16. we were being prepared
17. it will be owed
18. you were being cared for
19. we were being watched, looked at
20. they will frighten, terrify

Practice Exercise No. 84

1. ambulavi
2. laudavi
3. monui
4. debui
5. portavi
6. servavi
7. vocavi
8. movi
9. dedi
10. rogavi

Practice Exercise No. 85

1. he, she, it has asked
2. they have watched
3. we have warned, advised
4. I have helped, aided
5. you have been
6. you have killed
7. you have told, related
8. I have lived in, dwelt
9. I have seen
10. they have feared
11. you have grieved
12. you have had, held
13. we have owed, ought
14. they have worked
15. you have overcome, conquered
16. he, she, it has pointed out, shown
17. they have told, related
18. you have occupied, seized
19. we have prepared
20. he, she, it has flown

Practice Exercise No. 86

1. I had walked
2. they had adored
3. he, she, it had plowed
4. they had moved
5. we had remained, stayed
6. you had seen
7. you had prepared
8. you had given
9. you had held, kept
10. I had stood
11. he, she, it had prepared
12. they had placed
13. you had stirred up, aroused
14. you had cared for
15. I had swum
16. we had grieved
17. he, she, it had asked
18. they had watched, looked at
19. he, she, it had seen
20. you had called

Practice Exercise No. 87

1. you will have loved
2. he, she, it will have cared for
3. I shall have praised
4. we shall have placed
5. they will have had
6. he, she, it will have frightened
7. he, she, it will have moved
8. they will have given
9. you will have stood
10. he, she, it will have held
11. we shall have called
12. I shall have saved
13. he, she, it will have carried
14. they will have prepared
15. you will have announced
16. we shall have told, related
17. you will have had
18. he, she, it will have owed
19. they will have worshipped
20. you will have walked

Practice Exercise No. 88

1. they have been
2. he, she has walked
3. he has been carried
4. they have been loved
5. you have been cared for
6. they have been praised
7. I have been warned
8. we have owed, ought to have
9. you have stood
10. it has been related, told
11. we have been called
12. I have swum
13. you have been saved
14. it has been announced
15. they have been moved
16. you have feared
17. he has been prepared
18. they have been placed
19. they have praised
20. you have moved

Practice Exercise No. 89

1. they had given
2. he, she, it had moved
3. he had been frightened
4. you had remained, stayed
5. you had held
6. he, she, it had fought
7. I had been praised
8. they had been cared for
9. you had been loved
10. you had been aroused, incited
11. they had been prepared
12. you had occupied, seized
13. you had been freed
14. he had been killed
15. we had been saved
16. he had warned, advised
17. you had had
18. you had held, kept
19. we had been helped
20. they had worshipped

Practice Exercise No. 90

1. I shall have warned, advised
2. he, she, it will have been
3. it will have been carried
4. they will have been warned
5. they will have had
6. you will have frightened
7. we shall have moved
8. you will have been seen
9. he, she, it will have feared
10. she will have been moved
11. we shall have given
12. they will have stood
13. we shall have been
14. you will have been killed

15. we shall have been praised
16. you will have been armed
17. they will have been cared for
18. it will have been placed
19. they will have been; there will have been
20. she will have been saved

Practice Exercise No. 91

1. it had been had
2. I shall have seen
3. they will have been attacked
4. you will have been praised
5. you had been carried
6. it will have been owed
7. they had owed
8. you have waited for
9. you have seen
10. it has been pointed out, shown
11. they have been warned, advised
12. we have been asked
13. they have looked at, watched
14. we have been moved
15. we had prepared
16. he has been warned, advised
17. he, she, it had stood
18. they had been given
19. they have told, related
20. I shall have held, kept

Practice Exercise No. 92

1. for many years
2. in the next year
3. for many hours
4. in the next hour
5. for seven hours
6. in the middle of the year
7. in six hours
8. for long years
9. in an hour
10. for twelve hours

Practice Exercise No. 93

1. to the cities
2. from the towns
3. from Rome
4. to Rome
5. into the camp
6. in front of the forum
7. in back of the garden
8. in the field
9. into the fields
10. down from the hills
11. out of the cottage
12. in the country
13. at home
14. away from the river
15. under the seas
16. under the walls
17. into the ditch
18. away from the temple
19. out of the roads
20. about, down from the sun

Practice Exercise No. 94

1. I shall see
2. he, she, it had fought
3. you were standing
4. we shall work
5. he, she, it had been; there had been
6. they will obtain
7. we were swimming
8. he, she, it will be; there will be
9. we see
10. it has been looked at
11. he, she, it will be moved
12. they had been built
13. you have been
14. we were being attacked
15. they have remained, stayed

Practice Exercise No. 95

1. Next year we shall move to Rome.
2. For six hours they remained in the city.
3. They had been attacked half way up the hill.
4. I stayed in Italy for many hours.
5. He (she) will be there for an hour.
6. They will work for many years, won't they?
7. He walked toward the town for many long hours.
8. He has not been freed by the king.
9. Are they in the garden with the boys?
10. I moved seven miles from the city.

Practice Exercise No. 96

1. they are sending
2. I have been shown, taught
3. we are being sought
4. he, she, it ought; owes
5. you had been warned
6. they will have been prepared
7. he, she, it has led
8. you have freed
9. I was worshipping
10. he, she, it will have sent
11. he, she, it will order
12. we were being watched, looked at
13. you are showing
14. they will ask
15. you were leading
16. he, she, it will send
17. I have saved, preserved
18. you had feared
19. you had sought
20. they have remained, stayed

Practice Exercise No. 97

1. on account of the injury
2. from the battles
3. for six hours
4. on the road, march, journey
5. out of the territory
6. toward Gaul
7. away from the hill
8. in the letter
9. by the men; away from the men
10. into the river bank

Practice Exercise No. 98

1. I seek them.
2. of these, those books
3. his, her garden
4. I gave these, those things to them.
5. He was fighting.
6. You have seen him.
7. in these, those places
8. to, for his (her) father
9. They are being sent by him.
10. You sent them.
11. this, that hour; in this, that hour
12. her, his, their own signals
13. out of these, those cities
14. this, that woman
15. We are being led by them.
16. their apples
17. his, her, their own kings
18. with them
19. this, that road, journey
20. this, that cause

Practice Exercise No. 99

1. **ducitur**
2. **ductus sum**
3. **ducebam**
4. **duxerunt**
5. **ducar**
6. **missus es**
7. **mittebant**
8. **mittetis**
9. **misisti**
10. **missus erat**
11. **petiti sunt**
12. **petiverimus**
13. **petetur**
14. **petit**
15. **petebas**
16. **currentur**
17. **cursus est**
18. **currit**
19. **currebantur**
20. **cucurrerat**

Practice Exercise No. 100

1. in, on the feet
2. away from the hill
3. toward the rivers
4. out of the fields
5. into the fire
6. in, on the walls
7. about the body
8. in the country
9. from Rome
10. to Rome
11. at home
12. out of the night

Practice Exercise No. 101

1. he, she, it had been; there had been
2. we have ruled
3. he has been asked
4. you will have carried
5. they have given
6. they have placed

7. they have been given
8. you have sent
9. it will have been sought
10. it had been increased
11. we have moved
12. we have been
13. they had been aroused
14. you had hurried
15. they will have been; there will have been
16. I have been asked
17. he, she, it stood
18. you have called
19. we shall have been praised
20. he had had

Practice Exercise No. 102

1. in the next year
2. for seven hours
3. in the next hours
4. late in the year
5. for six years
6. on this, that night
7. for these, those nights
8. for these, those years
9. in this, that year
10. in this, that hour

Practice Exercise No. 103

1. his, hers, its
2. them
3. they
4. to, for him, her, it; they
5. it
6. them
7. she; they; them; from, with, by, in her
8. their
9. to, for, from, with, by, in them
10. him
11. they
12. from, with, by, in him, it

Practice Exercise No. 104

1. this, that love
2. of this, that boldness
3. these, those names
4. these, those causes
5. to, for, from, with, by, in these, those territories
6. of these, those journeys
7. these, those apples
8. to, for this, that woman
9. this, that body
10. of this, that place
11. to, for this, that king
12. this, that night
13. these, those laws
14. from, with, by, in this, that mountain
15. of this, that signal

Practice Exercise No. 105

1. because of the delay
2. because of my care
3. because of the dangers
4. because of fear
5. because of death
6. because of diligence
7. because of speed
8. because of boldness
9. because of the delays
10. because of the time

Practice Exercise No. 106

1. with zeal, eagerness
2. with great care
3. with great diligence, care
4. with great fear
5. with speed
6. with much zeal, eagerness
7. with great zeal, eagerness
8. with delay
9. with great speed
10. with great delay

Practice Exercise No. 107

1. **posui**
2. **superare**
3. **dedi**
4. **capere**
5. **servatus**
6. **facio**
7. **verti**
8. **terrui**
9. **duco**
10. **paratus**

Practice Exercise No. 108

1. he, she, it has ordered
2. you have led
3. they have shown
4. I was asking
5. we have made, done
6. he, she, it is being shown
7. you are being sent; will be sent
8. you are being taken, seized
9. he, she, it will look at, watch
10. we shall increase
11. they will seek
12. they were flying
13. you were obtaining, getting
14. he, she, it was being turned
15. he, she, it had terrified
16. you had sought
17. they had taken, seized
18. they will have been moved
19. we had been led
20. he, she, it was taking, seizing

Practice Exercise No. 109

1. because of the hour
2. because of the weapon
3. in front of the camp
4. from fear
5. down from the tree; about the tree
6. by the king; away from the king
7. out of the trees
8. into this, that place
9. with the father
10. with care
11. in, on the water
12. under the ocean
13. around the walls
14. against him
15. between, among the towns
16. through the field
17. in back of the camp
18. without them
19. across the sea
20. about, concerning the men

Practice Exercise No. 110

1. this wall
2. that city
3. in that place
4. these leaders
5. to, for those soldiers
6. to, for that lieutenant
7. these commanders
8. those plans
9. of that ocean
10. of these men
11. in that garden
12. that goddess
13. of that foot soldier
14. about this master
15. out of that tree
16. this hindrance
17. to, for these fathers
18. these ships
19. that book
20. to that girl
21. these weapons
22. of these parts
23. about that peace
24. of those sands
25. in these years
26. for that hour
27. that sign, standard
28. of this horse
29. toward these women
30. those messengers

Practice Exercise No. 111

1. his, her, its
2. he
3. to, for him, her, it; they
4. them
5. to, for, from, with, by, in them
6. of them, their
7. it; from, with, by, in him, it
8. to, for him, her, it
9. she; from, with, by, in her; them; they
10. they
11. she; them; they
12. her
13. them
14. him
15. them

Practice Exercise No. 112

1. the goddess herself, the very goddess
2. out of the temples themselves, out of the very temples
3. the same city
4. the men themselves, the very men
5. by the same youth
6. the same name, the very name
7. of the same nation
8. with the same horsemen
9. the same roads, ways
10. to, for, from, with, by, in the same men
11. out of the field itself, out of the very field
12. in the years themselves, in the very years
13. the boys themselves, the very boys
14. of the lieutenant himself, of the very lieutenant
15. the same hour; in the same hour
16. the law itself, the very law
17. the mountain itself, the very mountain
18. the girls themselves, the very girls
19. the same journey, road, way
20. by the women themselves, by the very women
21. at the same time
22. of the same generals
23. the same towns
24. in the cities themselves, in the very cities
25. of the same people
26. the same men
27. out of the same places
28. in the same years
29. on the very night, in the night itself
30. peace itself, the very peace

Practice Exercise No. 113

1. to, for him (himself), her (herself), it (itself); they (themselves)
2. of (the same) him, her, it
3. (the same) it
4. she (herself); they (themselves); them (themselves)
5. them (themselves)
6. (the same) she; they; them; from, with, by, in her
7. (the same) him
8. of (the same) them
9. out of (the same) them
10. of him (himself), her (herself), it (itself)

Practice Exercise No. 114

1. they were able to lead
2. you can stay
3. he, she was not able to worship
4. he, she, it will be able to free
5. they can care for
6. we were not able to kill

7. I had been able to order
8. you can show, point out
9. we were able to ask
10. I was not able to increase
11. we shall be able to help
12. you will be able to fight
13. they have not been able to call
14. I can not work
15. you have been able to stay

Practice Exercise No. 115

1. in one year
2. no care
3. of which gift
4. to, for any ship
5. for all the years
6. with the father alone
7. of no deaths
8. to neither nation
9. in the other road
10. with, by another name
11. to which river
12. of any hill
13. to, for one book
14. for no reasons
15. by neither man

Practice Exercise No. 116

1. they had feared
2. you have been
3. they will send
4. he, she, it took
5. he, she, it will fear
6. they were looking at
7. they will be held
8. I shall be sent
9. they have been praised
10. it had been done, made
11. you were sailing
12. they were being given
13. he, she, it carries on, bears
14. they had been; there had been
15. they have had

Practice Exercise No. 117

1. one is a boy, the other is not
2. at no time
3. of any war
4. toward which camp
5. the women themselves alone
6. of neither youth
7. other cities
8. one part
9. about neither girl
10. another road, journey, way

Practice Exercise No. 118

1. in a short hour
2. of a bold slave
3. swift horse
4. in, on a swift river
5. by bold men
6. for all times; all times
7. by a keen lieutenant
8. short life
9. at all hours
10. in a swift ship
11. bold work
12. in a short time
13. active troops
14. of a swift horse
15. active women
16. swift death, quick death
17. short journeys, roads
18. to a bold man
19. for a short year
20. in every, each place

Practice Exercise No. 119

1. of the golden sun
2. out of neither place
3. on the top of the mountain
4. of an easy journey
5. any hours
6. grave punishments
7. of the nearest nations
8. bold citizen
9. strong body
10. of swift rivers
11. Latin books
12. other men
13. your ship
14. of many fathers
15. of each king

Practice Exercise No. 120

1. Who are you?
2. To whom did he give those things?
3. Whom shall I see?
4. whose eyes?
5. What things does he know?
6. With whom does he (she) walk?

7. By whom has he been captured?
8. Who is shouting?
9. Who is fighting?
10. whose weapons?
11. What do you have?
12. Whom has he killed?
13. To whom shall I give it?
14. What has been asked?
15. To whom have you sent the gift?
16. Whom do you like?
17. Who is fleeing?
18. What is easy?
19. Whose is it?
20. with whom?
21. Whom will he send?
22. What is he doing?
23. Who are struggling?
24. By whom has it been carried on?
25. Who is calling?

Practice Exercise No. 121

1. pugnare **2. mittere** **3. regere** **4. dare** **5. laudare** **6. rogare** **7. scribere** **8. videre** **9. cognoscere** **10. necare** **11. capere** **12. timere** **13. habere** **14. movere** **15. parare** **16. ducere** **17. augere** **18. servare** **19. vincere** **20. terrere**

Practice Exercise No. 122

1. demonstrari **2. duci** **3. moveri** **4. iuberi** **5. verti** **6. armari** **7. amari** **8. faci** **9. doceri** **10. occupari** **11. mitti** **12. geri** **13. accipi** **14. timeri** **15. vocari** **16. interfici** **17. iuvari** **18. teneri** **19. cognosci** **20. simulari**

Practice Exercise No. 123

1. they take, seize
2. it had been learned
3. they have been conquered
4. they will turn
5. we were killing
6. they have done, made
7. you had taken, seized
8. he, she, it was fleeing
9. he, she, it will be put
10. they will have carried on, waged
11. he, she, it writes
12. you throw
13. they will hurry
14. they have been put
15. it has been carried on, waged

Practice Exercise No. 124

1. because of death
2. because of injury
3. with great diligence
4. because of the general
5. because of food
6. because of the fleets
7. with a small punishment, fine
8. with great zeal, eagerness
9. because of the hindrance
10. because of the sand

Practice Exercise No. 125

1. him
2. his, hers, its
3. them
4. that
5. he
6. their
7. the same things; she
8. his, hers, its
9. he
10. their
11. whom
12. what
13. whose
14. to, for whom
15. with whom

Practice Exercise No. 126

1. he, she was able to shout
2. they were able to take
3. you can do, make
4. we can put, place
5. you have been able to conquer
6. he, she will be able to hurry
7. they have been able to write
8. we were able to recognize, learn
9. you are able to turn
10. they are able to carry on, wage

Practice Exercise No. 127

1. of one work
2. of all the citizens
3. another hindrance
4. new weapons
5. in a short time
6. to, for the whole stone
7. of no fear
8. any injury
9. bold horsemen, knights
10. swift punishment

Practice Exercise No. 128

1. **pulchre,** beautifully
2. **longe,** far, distant
3. **magnopere,** greatly
4. **nove,** recently, newly
5. **acriter,** keenly
6. **graviter,** seriously
7. **breviter,** briefly
8. **alte,** high, on high
9. **grate,** with pleasure
10. **audacter,** boldly
11. **misere,** wretchedly
12. **proxime,** next, most recently
13. **fortiter,** bravely
14. **celeriter,** swiftly
15. **libere,** freely

Practice Exercise No. 129

1. you carry, do carry
2. I have, hold
3. they lead, are leading
4. he throws, is throwing
5. you have heard
6. he has been freed
7. they had been seen; had seemed
8. they have been heard
9. you have been received, accepted
10. I had been heard
11. they were hearing
12. he will have been prepared
13. he, she, it will hear
14. they have sought
15. they hear, do hear
16. you were being helped
17. we were being heard
18. we were turning
19. they will be taken, seized
20. you will be heard
21. you are being heard
22. he, she, it has done, made
23. they will ask
24. we have heard
25. they had been heard

Practice Exercise No. 130

1. they are fighting bravely
2. we saw very recently
3. he, she, it carried on with difficulty
4. they will be widely accepted
5. we are being taught well
6. he, she walks far
7. they stand well
8. he easily recognized
9. he, she liked greatly
10. not keenly enough

Practice Exercise No. 131

1. The place will be defended easily.
2. At first nothing was able to be prepared.
3. Because of fear you did not fight bravely.

4. Which door do you like?
5. The land by nature has been defended with difficulty.
6. Not only the king but also the queen heard it.
7. About whom has he (she) written boldly?
8. In that year we were preparing many things.
9. Eurydice lived unhappily under the earth.
10. He led them far from this place.

Practice Exercise No. 132

1. 1. who are making the journey with their forces
   2. The men, who are making the journey with their forces, are brave.
2. 1. which he built
   2. The tower, which he built, was keeping the barbarians from the town.
3. 1. with whom I was walking
   2. The woman, with whom I was walking, is my mother.
4. 1. whose name we can not see
   2. The ship, whose name we can not see, is sailing toward Italy.
5. 1. to whom I gave the letter
   2. The boy, to whom I gave the letter, will come quickly.
6. 1. which you will have
   2. The fear, which you will have, soon will not be remembered.
7. 1. to which they were fleeing
   2. The river, to which they were fleeing, was deep and wide.
8. 1. about which he wrote
   2. The place, about which he wrote, is far from the city.
9. 1. which he had
   2. Everything, which he had, now is mine.
10. 1. whose boys you see
    2. The men, whose boys you see, are friends.

Practice Exercise No. 133

1. in what places?
2. which man?
3. what town?
4. what booty?
5. which men?
6. with what speed?
7. in what year?
8. of what name?
9. at what hour?
10. at what time?
11. with what soldiers?
12. of what citizens?
13. what baggage?, what hindrances?
14. of what size?
15. with what plan?

Practice Exercise No. 134

1. they make, do
2. he, she, it will order
3. you have found, learned
4. he, she, it will arrive
5. to be had
6. he, she, it was running
7. he, she, it had been
8. he, she, it took, seized
9. they have looked at
10. it was happening
11. you hear
12. you have arrived
13. he, she, it was fighting, hurrying
14. they had given
15. to be seen; to seem
16. they have prohibited
17. they will be; there will be
18. I shall be seen; I shall seem
19. to be asked
20. I shall have

Practice Exercise No. 135

1. he, she, it has not been able
2. of that place
3. your sons
4. others come; some come
5. he, she wishes to come
6. brave people
7. because of the storm
8. with great zeal
9. he, she remained at home
10. of this (that) nation
11. in the next year
12. my friend
13. all men
14. he, she fears nothing
15. not only your mother

Practice Exercise No. 136

1. for many paces
2. your group; your hand
3. long attack
4. because of his arrival
5. each wing
6. of our armies
7. on your wing
8. out of the army
9. into the house
10. for six miles
11. against the armies
12. because of your arrival
13. the attack (attacks) of the enemy
14. group (groups) of soldiers
15. by the army

Practice Exercise No. 137

1. their battle lines
2. late in the day
3. on the next day
4. because of these things
5. of any hope
6. the whole thing
7. for one day
8. of what things
9. our battle lines
10. what things
11. in what battle line
12. of each day
13. because of this (that) thing
14. in these battle lines
15. much hope

Practice Exercise No. 138

1. he, she has walked
2. we are seen; we seem
3. they were; there were
4. he, she, it had done, made
5. he, she was fleeing
6. he, she, it finds
7. it had been given
8. he, she, it can, is able
9. it has been drawn up
10. to be seen; to seem
11. they have been left behind
12. they will fight
13. he, she, it has drawn up
14. he, she makes a journey
15. they will be heard

Practice Exercise No. 139

1. All things seem to be easy.
2. After six days neither soldier had any hope.
3. The captives whom you led back came out of their army.
4. Who hindered the strong attack greatly?
5. In one hour the men will come home.
6. For what reason was he drawing up his battle line on the hill?
7. Among these things which we have is a small supply of water.
8. The soldiers in that wing are turning their horses toward the field.
9. Neither the wing nor the battle line saw hope.
10. Who among these peoples hold the royal power?

Practice Exercise No. 140

1. you
2. we; us
3. by you
4. their; of them
5. she; they; them; from, with her
6. to, for her, him, it; they
7. you; from, with, by, in you
8. I
9. him
10. to, for me

11. with us
12. you
13. to, for you; from, with you
14. them
15. that; it
16. to him, her, it
17. his, her, its
18. with you
19. their; of them
20. toward you
21. to you
22. your; of you
23. our; of us
24. about me
25. to, for them; from, with, by them
26. about them
27. she; from, with, by her; they; them
28. with her
29. their; of them
30. them

Practice Exercise No. 141

1. to, for himself, herself, itself; to, for themselves
2. yourself; from, with, by, in yourself
3. by myself
4. yourselves
5. himself, herself, itself; themselves; from, with, by, in himself, herself, itself, themselves
6. to, for yourselves; from, with, by, in yourselves
7. to, for myself
8. to, for ourselves; from, with, by, in ourselves
9. myself; from, with, by, in myself
10. ourselves

Practice Exercise No. 142

1. The man himself knows us.
2. I sent help to you.
3. We found you in this place.
4. Will you come with me?
5. You give books to us.
6. You do not hear him.
7. They were fleeing toward us.
8. He sent these things to me.
9. He (She) will not be able to walk home with you.
10. This is our native country.
11. You will tell this (that) to them.
12. We shall lead her home.
13. They were seeking peace from them.
14. I was being terrified by you and your sword.
15. We had saved ourselves at that time.
16. You can help us, can't you?
17. He saw their city.
18. We ourselves shall order them to come.
19. You will point out these things to us.
20. His spirit did not frighten me long.

Practice Exercise No. 143

1. **late**, widely
2. **acriter**, keenly
3. **difficile**, with difficulty
4. **misere**, wretchedly
5. **longe**, far
6. **magnopere**, greatly
7. **laete**, happily
8. **libere**, freely
9. **parum**, too little, not enough
10. **anguste**, narrowly

Practice Exercise No. 144

1. I shall come
2. he, she knew
3. he has been heard
4. we were arriving
5. they will be hindered
6. they find, discover
7. you were being heard
8. it had been known
9. they have wished
10. you will be heard

Practice Exercise No. 145

1. whose
2. whom
3. who, which, that
4. who
5. with whom
6. we; us; ourselves
7. to, for me, myself
8. me; myself; from, with, by, in me, myself
9. of you
10. to, for you, yourself
11. with you, yourself
12. his, her, its
13. their, of them
14. him
15. her

Practice Exercise No. 146

1. to, for the army
2. the thing; things
3. of the horn, wing
4. the battle line
5. hope
6. of the hands, bands
7. on, from, with, by the day
8. to, for, from, with, by, in the attacks
9. the arrival
10. home; the house
11. to, for, from, with, by, in the things
12. horns, wings
13. of the armies
14. to, for the hand, group
15. to, for hope

Practice Exercise No. 147

1. fifteen
2. nine
3. twenty
4. five
5. sixteen
6. ten
7. three
8. seventeen
9. four
10. eleven
11. one hundred
12. fourteen
13. eight
14. nineteen
15. two
16. thirteen
17. seven
18. one
19. eighteen
20. one thousand
21. twelve
22. six

Practice Exercise No. 148

1. fourth
2. eighth
3. tenth
4. third
5. seventh
6. second
7. fifth
8. ninth
9. first
10. sixth

Practice Exercise No. 149

1. a thousand ships
2. three men
3. of thousands of soldiers
4. for fourteen days
5. of one man
6. twenty miles
7. a hundred boys
8. for five years
9. six of the soldiers
10. in seven hours
11. in a hundred years
12. eight of the boys
13. for two days
14. of ten laws; ten of the laws
15. three places
16. two of the provinces
17. in twelve days
18. of six animals
19. eighteen of the kings
20. in three years

Practice Exercise No. 150

1. to, for, of the tenth girl
2. on the eighth day
3. in the sixth hour; the sixth hour
4. the seventh ship
5. in the fifth summer
6. for the third day
7. in the tenth winter
8. the seventh attack
9. to, for, of the ninth hour; ninth hours
10. in the first year

Practice Exercise No. 151

1. a difficult way, road
2. a wretched home
3. of the free men
4. keen fears
5. similar armies
6. a long day, for a long day
7. on a high mountain
8. swift rivers
9. wide streets
10. of pretty girls

Practice Exercise No. 152

1. narrower streets
2. a taller boy
3. of happier girls
4. a friendlier people
5. a longer road, way
6. in more pleasing places
7. of more famous sisters
8. a longer winter, for a longer winter
9. wider rivers
10. bolder man

Practice Exercise No. 153

1. of a very sweet spring
2. out of very pretty gardens
3. a very narrow temple
4. because of very wretched memories
5. very famous oracles
6. a very happy citizen
7. out of a very wide field
8. with very pretty mothers
9. on a very new ship
10. very short names

Practice Exercise No. 154

1. This is a very wretched place.
2. The bravest men arrived at the island.
3. The very keen horses were among the first.
4. What is an easier way to Greece?
5. The people of Italy are very free.
6. This is the narrower part of the water.
7. These things are also very similar.
8. We saw a very deep and rather wide river.
9. Our men chose a shorter way to the city.
10. You can see a high building from this place.

Practice Exercise No. 155

1. These towers are higher than those.
2. You are taller than your father.
3. Those roads are not easier than others.
4. You are more like your father than your mother.
5. Men are much stronger than women.
6. His house in the country is newer than that in the city.
7. The boy is happier than his sister.
8. The barbarians are much bolder than their neighbors.
9. He will be friendlier to you than to me.
10. Is the hand quicker than the eye?

Practice Exercise No. 156

1. they will be; there will be
2. it has been shown
3. he, she, it decided
4. he, she, it will be prepared
5. they were leading
6. he has been left behind
7. he, she, it will be sent
8. you are being carried
9. we were seeing
10. he, she has walked

Practice Exercise No. 157

1. more things
2. better
3. of the worst
4. of a bigger
5. of smaller
6. of very many
7. to, for, from, with, by, in more
8. the next
9. more suitable; of more suitable
10. most suitable

Practice Exercise No. 158

1. in very many cities
2. out of smaller springs
3. the greatest courage
4. best voice
5. down from higher walls
6. more water
7. more suitable time
8. of the worst thing; to, for the worst thing
9. toward a better part
10. with a bigger army
11. on a longer day
12. very many states
13. worse end
14. best years
15. smallest sister
16. of very many difficulties
17. better way
18. of the worst summer
19. very many gifts
20. of a smaller ship

Practice Exercise No. 159

1. wide
2. widely
3. wider
4. more widely
5. very wide
6. very widely
7. free
8. freely
9. freer
10. very free
11. more freely
12. very freely
13. pretty
14. more pretty
15. very pretty
16. prettily
17. more prettily
18. very prettily
19. swift
20. swiftly
21. swifter
22. more swiftly
23. very swift
24. very swiftly
25. keen
26. keenly
27. keener
28. more keenly
29. keenest
30. most keenly

Practice Exercise No. 160

1. They were being attacked most severely.
2. He fights more bravely.
3. They have been burned quickly.
4. They will speak much more briefly.
5. He will be warned very boldly.
6. They drew up the battle line with difficulty.
7. He waged war more keenly.
8. They walk proudly.
9. He gave more pleasingly.
10. He is praised very highly.
11. They have been sent more widely.
12. He gave very freely.
13. He sails very far.
14. He moves more wretchedly.
15. They were seen recently.
16. They move more beautifully.
17. He will fear very keenly.
18. They have been taken boldly.
19. He was speaking very briefly.
20. They fight bravely.

Practice Exercise No. 161

1. well
2. greatly
3. badly
4. much
5. little
6. long
7. often
8. longer
9. more
10. more
11. better
12. worse
13. less
14. more often
15. most
16. most
17. longest
18. most often
19. best
20. worst
21. least

Practice Exercise No. 162

1. They arrive more often.
2. He fought as long as possible.
3. He has been aroused more.
4. He was being hindered more.
5. You have been loved best.
6. It has been heard most often.
7. He walks with less difficulty.
8. They are very powerful among us.
9. He flies more swiftly.
10. He will stay much longer.

Practice Exercise No. 163

1. one of the sisters
2. three rivers
3. two years; for two years
4. a thousand years
5. two wives
6. a hundred words
7. of one voice
8. twenty springs, fountains
9. the fourth hour; in the fourth hour
10. on the fifth day
11. in the second year
12. the seventh word
13. the first oracle
14. in the fourth harbor, port
15. out of the sixth gate, door

Practice Exercise No. 164

1. the longer winter; for the longer winter
2. the very pretty summer
3. of the longest years
4. the sweeter word
5. a very similar burden
6. of an immortal voice
7. easier way, journey
8. clearer lights
9. of a very keen difficulty
10. of stronger husbands

Practice Exercise No. 165

1. sweet, sweeter, sweetest
2. keen, keener, keenest
3. long, longer, longest
4. similar, more similar, most similar
5. high, higher, highest
6. free, freer, freest
7. swift, swifter, swiftest
8. wide, wider, widest
9. clear, clearer, clearest
10. bold, bolder, boldest

Practice Exercise No. 166

1. big, bigger, biggest
2. small, smaller, smallest
3. good, better, best
4. bad, worse, worst
5. much, more, most
6. many, more, very many
7. suitable, more suitable, most suitable

Practice Exercise No. 167

1. he was walking farther
2. he has been oppressed miserably
3. he sleeps little
4. it will burn for a very long time

5. they have been more keenly aroused
6. they were touching more
7. they have surrendered more easily
8. they are very powerful
9. it, he, she will be more powerful
10. they will be forced less easily

Practice Exercise No. 168

1. to warn
2. to have increased
3. to be thrown
4. to be about to place
5. to have fled
6. to hinder
7. to have swum
8. to be about to frighten
9. to have remained
10. to be about to hear
11. to have written
12. to be about to fight
13. to be about to praise
14. to be aroused
15. to have been sought
16. to send
17. to be touched
18. to have been attacked
19. to be known
20. to be about to carry on
21. to be received
22. to have been conquered
23. to be said
24. to be about to walk
25. to have feared

Practice Exercise No. 169

1. **petere,** to seek
2. **cepisse,** to have taken
3. **habere,** to have
4. **rexisse,** to have ruled
5. **portare,** to carry
6. **vocavisse,** to have called
7. **facere,** to do, make
8. **dedisse,** to have given
9. **instruere,** to draw up
10. **vertere,** to turn

Practice Exercise No. 170

1. **narrari,** to be told
2. **defensum esse,** to have been defended
3. **videri,** to be seen; to seem
4. **iuvari,** to be helped
5. **pugnatum esse,** to have been fought
6. **motum esse,** to have been moved
7. **vocari,** to be called
8. **inveniri,** to be found
9. **necatum esse,** to have been killed
10. **relinqui,** to be left

Practice Exercise No. 171

1. **futurum esse,** to be about to be
2. **iussurum esse,** to be about to order
3. **facturum esse,** to be about to make
4. **defensurum esse,** to be about to defend
5. **oppugnaturum esse,** to be about to attack
6. **properaturum esse,** to be about to hurry
7. **capturum esse,** to be about to take
8. **inventurum esse,** to be about to find
9. **daturum esse,** to be about to give
10. **positurum esse,** to be about to place

Practice Exercise No. 172

1. Those soldiers said the men would carry aid.
2. Do you think your work has been done?
3. We were hoping the enemy would come as quickly as possible.
4. The girls seem to be happy.
5. This king wished to rule well.
6. He will not want to be called.
7. To defend our town is best.
8. To have had hope was better than to have retreated.
9. He announced that the speed could be increased.
10. He ordered us to find a better place.

Practice Exercise No. 173

1. calling
2. having been moved
3. about to send
4. receiving
5. about to come
6. having been watched
7. arriving
8. about to take
9. placing, putting
10. having been announced
11. having been warned
12. fearing
13. about to say
14. having been aroused
15. seeing

Practice Exercise No. 174

1. the ships, sailing
2. the leader, about to order
3. they, having been attacked
4. the men, about to arrive
5. seeking peace
6. the dog, running
7. the cities, having been captured
8. the temples, having been built
9. the harbors, having been found
10. the rivers, running

Practice Exercise No. 175

1. The people of the cities, which had been captured, were as brave as possible.
2. The men, who were about to arrive, were making the trip as quickly as possible.
3. The king, who is now ruling your country, seems to be timid.
4. The woman will give aid, when (if) she sees your difficulty.
5. The storm will not be very fierce, if it does not increase.
6. The father had great joy, because he was about to see his sons.
7. They were running as fast as possible, because they fear our men.
8. The men, who (because they) had been defeated, were especially frightened.
9. When she arrived in the town, she told her story.
10. They, who are defending the gate, were not friends.

Practice Exercise No. 176

1. bravely
2. as quickly as possible
3. least, not at all
4. for a very long time
5. more keenly
6. with difficulty
7. very easily
8. better
9. badly
10. greatly
11. more often
12. very unhappily

Practice Exercise No. 177

1. When the oracle had been heard, many people decided to come to our land.
2. When the signal had been given, they made an attack onto the field.
3. The men, although their weapons were not many, nevertheless fought bravely.
4. Because many soldiers had been killed, they sought peace.
5. The men, because the booty is large, will be received at home with great joy.
6. When this thing has been done, the boys will come home.
7. If he is the leader, we shall do it without difficulty.
8. When these things had been reported to me, I wanted to make the trip from the city.
9. If these have been killed, the people will be ruled better.
10. When the day had been set, they prepared everything as quickly as possible.
11. Because the door was open, he was able to come into the cottage.
12. He had no hope, because the city had been captured.
13. When these things had been done, the king was more powerful.
14. If the rest have been seen, we shall run toward the forest.

15. When his father is the leader, they do everything boldly.
16. When peace has been made, he will sail away from the island.
17. If many are timid, they will not be able to find the rivers.
18. Because the time is now short, no help will arrive.
19. Because the place is suitable, you wish to stay here longer.
20. Because help was given, there was great joy.

Practice Exercise No. 178

1. to be
2. to have been
3. to be about to find out
4. to be found out
5. to have been thought
6. to have thought
7. to carry back, report
8. to be about to carry back, report
9. to have hoped
10. to be going to hope
11. to be led
12. to have led
13. to have been had
14. to have
15. to wish, want
16. to be wished, wanted
17. to have been able
18. to be able
19. to have fought
20. to have been fought
21. to be warned
22. to have warned
23. to have said
24. to be said
25. to be feared
26. to have feared
27. to have been made, done
28. to be about to make, do
29. to be seen; to seem
30. to be going to see, seem

Practice Exercise No. 179

1. leading
2. about to lead
3. having, holding
4. having been had
5. having been thought
6. about to think
7. finding out
8. having been found out
9. carrying back, reporting
10. about to carry back, report
11. hoping
12. having been hoped
13. about to move
14. moving
15. coming
16. about to come
17. fearing
18. having been frightened
19. about to place, put
20. putting, placing
21. sending
22. having been sent
23. about to see
24. seeing
25. about to say
26. saying
27. warning
28. having been warned
29. having been placed, put
30. placing, putting

Practice Exercise No. 180

1. they having been seen
2. he, it having been captured
3. these having been said
4. the war having been made
5. the men fearing
6. the girl walking
7. the leaders being afraid
8. the number being small
9. sleep coming
10. the prison being big
11. the city having been captured
12. the remaining speaking
13. the word having been heard
14. hope having been found
15. the kinds being many